AMERICAN SOCIETY

AMERICAN SOCIETY
Public and Private
Responsibilities

edited by

WINTHROP KNOWLTON

and

RICHARD ZECKHAUSER

Center for Business and Government
at the
John F. Kennedy School of Government
Harvard University

BALLINGER PUBLISHING COMPANY
Cambridge, Massachusetts
A Subsidiary of Harper & Row, Publishers, Inc.

International Standard Book Number: 0-88730-129-0

Library of Congress Catalog Card Number: 86-17481

Printed in the United States of America

Library of Congress Cataloging-in-Publication Data

American society.

   Includes index.
   1. United States—Social policy—Congresses.
   2. United States—Economic policy—Congresses.
   I. Knowlton, Winthrop. II. Zeckhauser, Richard.
   HN53.A64 1986   361'.973   86-17481
   ISBN 0-88730-129-0

Contents

Acknowledgment

The editors and the Center for Business and Government gratefully acknowledge the generous financial support of Frank Weil, which has made this celebratory volume possible on the occasion of Harvard University's 350th and the John F. Kennedy School of Government's 50th anniversaries. The papers that make up this book were originally presented and discussed during a symposium held at the Center on March 14–15, 1986. In his opening remarks to that gathering, Mr. Weil offered his vision of the central concerns of the undertaking:

"The sometimes conflicting, sometimes complementary roles of government and the private sector have been a subject of increasing interest and debate in recent years. From the Massachusetts Bay Colony until the time of Teddy Roosevelt and Justice Brandeis, the private sector in U.S. society had a far greater effect on the lives of most Americans than did the public sector. Thereafter, the public sector grew in size and importance through Franklin Roosevelt's alphabet soup New Deal and Lyndon Johnson's exuberant Great Society, until it influenced the lives of every American, more deeply than ever before.

"In the disheartened era following Vietnam, Watergate, and OPEC, and with the decline of American competitiveness, citizens lost confidence in the competence of either the public or private sector to meet modern challenges. At the same time, the intersections between public and private worlds became both more numerous and more subtle. Our current concern about appropriate public and private roles reflects both the enormous growth of the two sectors, in size and complexity, and their apparent inability to solve society's most pressing problems.

"This concern will endure as long as our free society. Unless we go the way of other nations where there is no real private sector as we know it, we must forever struggle to understand and shape the interplay between the public and private elements in the United States.

"The purpose of this symposium and of these papers is to identify key intersections and roles as a first step toward better and wider understanding of the true underpinnings of the issue. With that understanding we can perhaps move away from faddish or ideological views that one sector, or the other, holds the key to solving America's problems."

PART I

INTRODUCTION

CHAPTER 1

Overview

Winthrop Knowlton and Richard Zeckhauser

The United States recently celebrated its bicentennial. Harvard now passes its 350th anniversary. Despite a revolution, a civil war, depressions great and small, and technological marvels beyond imagination, our economic system remains much as it was in its earliest days. We retain a capitalist system, but the government plays a major role. In colonial times it was an alien government that ruled, and its rule proved sufficiently intrusive to provoke an eventual battle for independence. In recent years, our homegrown government in its turn has been widely damned as intrusive; our last two presidents, representing both parties, have run campaigns against government itself.

Just who is hostile to government action depends on the action at issue. Those who endorse greater public efforts to fight poverty, for example, are less likely to favor devoting government resources to battle communism in Latin America than are those who prefer to let the market work its miracles for the poor. And just who opposes government action on the abortion issue may depend on the locale and the year. State policies on the issue differ, and the federal government has moved, in quick succession, from prohibiting abortions to subsidizing them, and now to curbing financial support.

This volume addresses America's situation as we near the end of the twentieth century. It engages perennial concerns, at the risk of neglecting the topical. There is no analysis here of nuclear plant safety or South Africa. Though economic performance claims much of our attention, there is little discussion of Japan, except for a brief final note in the chapter on history. Our contributors were encouraged to take the long view, and so they have. Thus we have an appraisal of the corporate income tax but not of Gramm-Rudman; the virtues of corporate mergers are addressed but not those of Carl Icahn.

Our theme is public and private responsibilities for the effective performance of American society. In Part I, this introductory overview chapter is complemented by a historical assessment that reveals how the nation's past has shaped its present institutions and options. The two chapters of Part II delineate economic and philosophical justifications for alternative allocations of responsibilities among different sectors of our society. The remaining ten chapters take up particular policy areas, asking which roles are performed by which sectors, how effectively, and how responsibilities might be reassigned to improve performance. These analyses are grouped in two sections: III, The Mind and the Spirit, and IV, The Corporation and the Economy. More poetic titling might have labeled these sections The Soul and The Sustenance.

This volume could cover only a limited range of topics, in limited detail. Though we believe the subjects are of utmost importance, we include no discussion here· of religion, defense, labor, foreign policy, and many other topics our readers might savor. Our analyses may encourage experts in other areas to define their own typologies of responsibility and prescriptions for shaping our nation's future course. Our aim is not to be comprehensive and encyclopedic but rather to distill major themes from disparate debates. This overview outlines some of those themes, and subsequent chapters flesh out the outline. We identify three major themes: a chronic oversimplification of the public-private debate; the problem of agency; and the importance of specific institutions.

OVERSIMPLIFICATION OF THE PUBLIC-PRIVATE DEBATE

Listening to the rhetoric of our major political parties, one might think that the United States was cycling through eras of nationalization and denationalization of industry, that a large expanse of the government's traditional domain was about to be turned over to the private sector, or that our expenditures on social programs were now vastly lower than a few years ago. Reality is much less dramatic. However inflamed the rhetoric, actual change is usually limited. The battles themselves—as distinct from the rhetoric that animates them—tend to be fought along rather narrow spectrums that do not engage the deepest values of the participants.

We use the term *responsibilities* in this volume, not jurisdictions or territories, for we believe that it reflects America as we find it. In most important areas the public and private sectors have multiple and overlapping responsibilities, as might a mother and a teacher jointly nurturing a child. Under such circumstances, claims for credit and blame are difficult to establish. And it is difficult to formulate prescriptions for dramatic improvements in conditions.

"Public" and "private" hardly capture the richness of the institutions that have evolved in America to produce and allocate our resources, much less those that aim to serve our souls. Michael Walzer presents an eloquent argument for greater reliance on the private nonprofit sector to meet many of society's more delicate needs, though he observes that public financial support may be required. His theme is reinforced by our chapters on the arts, on education, and on science. Many of our nonprofit institutions, including the one whose birthday we celebrate, Harvard University, receive a thorough admixture of public and private support. Richard Zeckhauser sees the public-private mixture as a much more pervasive condition, stretching from health care to income redistribution, and argues that the resulting muddle of responsibilities is often unfortunate. But Thomas Schelling and Glenn Loury, looking at smoking behavior and poverty respectively, suggest that the preferred strategy may be a multipronged attack, with public, private, nonprofit, and personal or family initiatives reinforcing one another. And Thomas McCraw concludes his historical review with misgivings about the level of hostility to public action in the United States, for he fears that collective endeavors, beyond the market's capacity to mediate, may be required to restore American productivity. The area of longest continuing debate about the public role in American society is the management of the macroeconomy, the subject of our closing chapters by Paul Samuelson and Lawrence Summers. Scholars at Harvard, including a number at the Littauer School—the immediate forebear of the Kennedy School, whose 50th anniversary this volume celebrates too—were early and important contributors to this debate, as Samuelson's deft intellectual history of macroeconomics reveals.

THE PROBLEM OF AGENCY

Each of these chapters asks, from its own perspective and in its own terms, what forms of organization can best carry out specific tasks. Robert Clark inquires whether a corporation's ownership should be determined solely through the decisions of its directors and the votes of its shareholders. Alvin Warren asks whether corporations—those fictitious persons—are appropriate subjects of taxation. When Diane Ravitch takes up education, or Glenn Loury poverty, the issue is one of responsibility and accountability—public versus private, of course, but also collective versus personal or familial. Decisions about responsibility summon the question of agency: How can we best ensure that the institution assigned to perform a given task will have the capacity, motivation, and information needed to deliver the goods? For each task, what kind of agent will best serve our interests as the principals—for example, as customers, patients, voters, patrons, taxpayers, and citizens?

The public–private debate in the United States is often debased by too-broad assertions about alternative forms of agency. "If hospitals are profit-seeking, they will cut corners in providing health care." "Keep the government out of the energy business; it will only impose a wasteful bureaucracy." The assiduous reader may ferret out an occasional remark of that nature here, but in general the authors ask more careful, more specific questions about the relative competence, in particular areas, of public and private, of for-profit and nonprofit.

Two themes related to agency arise in several of these essays. The first is ambiguity about principals (which frequently induces ambiguity about principles.) Both Diane Ravitch and Robert Clark show us agents torn by multiple mandates. Should educators take their cues from parents, seek to serve students directly, attend to agendas set by Congress in the name of various interests, or try to meet industry's needs for skilled workers? Should corporate boards base decisions on tender offers on shareholder interests only, or should they also worry about managers, workers, communities, and other claimants? Some observers, harking back to an age-old philosophical debate, would challenge this individualistic approach and posit a "social good," distinguishable from the sum of individual interests, that should guide institutions' actions.

The second theme concerns the question: To whom can the future be entrusted? How can we ensure that our agents—public or private—do not attend to more immediate, more readily observable benefits at the cost of disproportionate sacrifices in less visible, future benefits? Public officials' time horizons too often extend no further than the next election, or even the next opinion poll. Business executives are tempted to pump up quarterly earnings by neglecting research or maintenance. Several authors cite issues where the consequences of decisions far outlast the decisionmaker's tenure. The lopsided calculus of credit and blame can impose incentives to shortchange the future. Gerald Edelman quotes Mark Kac's dictum that "universities should be that part of our society dedicated to fifty years hence" and charges that the universities, pressed to prove their practicality, are abandoning that task. Richard Zeckhauser worries that a "short-term orientation seems endemic to American institutions." Winthrop Knowlton fears that as public and private patrons rush to join the latest trend, nobody is worrying about the cultivation and preservation of the best of our artistic heritage.

THE ROLE OF INDIVIDUAL INSTITUTIONS

Casual observers often assume that the dimension of public versus private suffices to explain what an institution seeks to do and how well it does it. But as noted earlier, this dichotomy is far too simple; there are complex gradations of publicness and privateness. Many articles cite institutions, moreover, that escape explanation by any metric of inherent characteristics, however subtle. Which particular institution delivers a good or service may be more important than whether it qualifies for charitable contributions or files a tax return. It could be that the quality of public or private is analogous to an individual's genotype, the genetic code that guides (but only generally) his or her development and limits (but only broadly) his or her potential. The institution's social context and its specific history, like the individual's environment and upbringing, determine which of its myriad possibilities become its reality.

Zeckhauser argues that the styles of public and private production may reflect their particular endeavor, their scale, and their history, more than their ownership. Harvard University is more like Berkeley—a large, first-class research institution, albeit public and

Californian—than a next-door private institution that concentrates on training teachers. The chapters by Ravitch, Knowlton, and Edelman address important cultural sectors of society—education, the arts, and science—and highlight the roles of particular institutions in fostering excellence. Perhaps the key lesson is that, especially in areas of endeavor where the products are subtle and hard to measure, where the value of achievement can be weighed only over time, we must find ways to identify and nurture those institutions capable of durable distinction. Within any area a few institutions—public or private—are outstanding, while many are mediocre.

This brings us to the question of the corporation. What is its role? What is its identity? Is it something beyond the collection of resources it comprises? In the two chapters on the corporation, Robert Clark directs his attention to changes in ownership and control, and Alvin Warren asks whether and to what ends the corporation itself (as separate from its owners) should be subject to taxation. In America, as debates on issues ranging from environmental quality to plant closings make clear, corporations have become objects of public policy. It takes the piercing eyes of the theorist (or is it his blinders?) to perceive the corporation as no more than a device for organizing ownership and to see restraints and impositions placed on it as no more than levies on its shareholders. The corporation, a human creation, has taken on a troubled life of its own.

Our contributors express deep concerns about the health and performance of institutions. Are they simply assessing the organizational means of individual ends, the pipelines through which welfare flows? Or should we worry about the well-being of Harvard University (or San Francisco General Hospital, or Monsanto, Inc.) independent of its performance on behalf of the individuals it serves?

A TOUR OF THE BOOK*

In the chapter that follows, Thomas McCraw reviews historical influences on modern American attitudes about the proper place and function of public authority. The nation was formed in an outburst of anti-authoritarianism. Its isolation, its richness in resources, and

*We thank John Donahue, whose written account of the symposium served as a map for this tour.

especially the ever-beckoning frontier inspired in the eighteenth and most of the nineteenth centuries an obsession with the "release of energy" while most other nations—more circumscribed economically and geographically—were preoccupied with managing conflict. Inevitably the New World cultivated a sharply different view of government from that of the Old World. Government's role was limited, and—at least as important—power was dispersed, shared, and in many contexts fundamentally ambiguous. This heritage of America's revolutionary and frontier past endures today; the consequences constitute many of the subjects of this book.

The second section of this volume, The Allocation of Responsibility, presents two chapters—one more descriptive, the other more prescriptive—on the division of responsibility between the public and private sectors in America. Richard Zeckhauser surveys the intricate intertwining of functions and authority in the United States. The classic concept of a mixed economy suggests that functions are assigned by sensible criteria to the public or the private realm, or appropriately shared where, say, the public sector should finance while the private produces. But in fact, Zeckhauser writes, many assignments are governed by historical accident and the peculiarities of politics, and accord with no theoretical model of relative competence. The result is costly, inefficient, and resistant to reform.

Michael Walzer, raising a challenge that echoes through the volume, questions the dichotomous distinction between "public" and "private" and proposes instead four categories of institutional arrangements: the family, the state, profit-seeking firms, and a final category he terms the "social sector." The social sector is the realm of voluntary organizations; it is distinguished from the state by the absence of coercion and from the market by dedication to ends beyond individual gain. Walzer prescribes a substantial assumption of responsibilities by the social sector, responsibilities transferred from both the state and the market and supported by governmental revenues.

The third section, The Mind and the Spirit, examines aspects of our society that contribute subtly to our well-being in a manner likely to be overlooked in GNP statistics. Michael O'Hare asks what makes for a successful physical environment and then explores the forces—often invisible, certainly not limited to laws and the profit motive—that have led to the creation of so many successful environments in the United States. Winthrop Knowlton asks parallel questions for the arts: How can we arrange our institutions and support mechanisms to produce enduring works of value? Thomas Schelling examines smoking, a metaphor for a wide range of bad behaviors, from dropping out of school to becoming obese, that represent a failing of the mind or the spirit. The assignment of Glenn Loury's chapter on poverty to this section, rather than to the Economy section, reflects the author's distinctive approach to his subject, which attends principally to the behavior and personal opportunities of the poor within America. Diane Ravitch and Gerald Edelman consider education and science respectively, both sectors designed, as the economists would drily record, to augment the stock of human capital and technological capability. But to the educator or the scientist, the charge is to enrich the mind, to ennoble the spirit, to challenge the unknown. That the economy benefits is a happy coincidence.

O'Hare's chapter reappraises both the intentions and the instruments of environmental policies. The common conception that the "natural" is the measure of environmental quality, he argues, is at once too restrictive and too vague. He identifies five qualities that "favor positive interaction between an environment and a person. They are coherence, complexity, honesty, evidence of a process, and significance." Given that the purpose of many public and private actions is to create a favorable environment for human beings, it is not surprising that O'Hare's qualities are taken up repeatedly as our authors discuss the arts, education, science, and the economy. Though the terminology may vary, the creative tension between fostering policies sufficiently *coherent* to provide direction and convey understanding, yet sufficiently *complex* to be of interest and to meet the diverse needs of our variegated society, ripples throughout this volume. O'Hare argues that in activities as mundane as painting one's home, or as prolonged and discontinuous as those that have created Harvard University's physical environment, a vast range of influences—both public and private, some unseen, some barely recognized—impinge on the choices that produce our environments. He calls for a public approach that emphasizes guiding and encouraging, rather than simply circumscribing, private creativity in shaping our physical surroundings.

Knowlton examines public policies in support of the arts and finds them overly ambitious and anachronistic. Governments, he argues, are ill equipped to identify individual artists with both the talent and the character to produce and persevere. He suggests the need for a subtle stitching together of public and private support with more sensitivity paid to the life cycles of individual artists and arts institutions. In his scheme of things the individual private patron commits first. The public sector's role is one of recognition rather than of discovery. It works through institutions (predominantly denizens of Walzer's "social sector") to conserve the best of what we already have. If institutions thus become a necessary means of preservation, is the end art itself or its impact on the human beings who view it? And what, Knowlton asks, is *their* responsibility, in turn, to the art in question?

Following Knowlton's disquisition on ways to promote the aesthetic and uplifting, Schelling considers how to suppress the unattractive and self-destructive. His chapter explores the allocation of responsibility within society for defining and controlling undesirable behavior. Cigarette smoking is his proxy for a range of activities in which society must decide how much discretion an individual should have for making choices—even unwise ones, even ones that may harm other people. He also asks how the portfolio of available actors—family, friends, employer, church, and government—should be organized to influence personal behavior.

Loury appraises alternative views of the causes of and remedies for poverty in America. He first looks to causes: To what extent is poverty a *private* problem, a reflection of pathological individual behavior, and to what extent a public failure of which the poor themselves are blameless victims? And who should bear responsibility if the family is to blame? Loury shows that conclusions about causation are essential to any intelligent approach to his second question: What is to be done about poverty? He posits a precarious balance between helping the stricken and discouraging the behavior that causes their plight, and he discusses the judgments and facts that should govern where that balance is struck.

Ravitch explores the history, status, and prospects of American education. Reiterating a theme raised by McCraw, she shows that the allocation of responsibility—and indeed the distribution of competence and achievement—results more from historical accident, conscious political judgments, and the idiosyncratic development of specific institutions than from any inherent characteristics of public or private schools, much less from a well-weighed decision on how best to educate our young.

Edelman's chapter examines responsibilities for supporting scientific research, what he calls "imagination in support of verifiable truth." Science underlies our material prosperity and is ultimately the wellspring of profit. But basic research—with its uncertainty, its long time horizon, its nebulous links to practical purposes, and its indiscriminate dispersion of benefits to society at large—will be underfunded in a society composed solely of rational entrepreneurs. Thus, basic science becomes a responsibility of the public or the public spirited. Edelman finds, however, that government programs, inherently short-sighted and limited in scope, are badly designed to bridge the gap between profits and prophecy. His elegant overview of post-Mendelian breakthroughs in genetics and immunology documents his argument that an unhurried approach to the gathering of fundamental knowledge is a critical ingredient of scientific progress. Pursued in this manner, research on the biological bases of the brain's activity could, Edelman asserts in a "millennial prophecy," bring about a revolution as significant as those provoked by Copernicus, Darwin, and Einstein.

The book's fourth section deals more directly with choices about the economy and its principal engine of production, the corporation. Robert Clark speculates on the mix of motives underlying hostile corporate mergers and discusses public approaches to the regulation of the private transactions that determine how major economic institutions will be governed. Alvin Warren looks at the corporate income tax, a topic closely allied to this book's theme both because corporate taxes fund a significant (though shrinking) part of government spending, and because the tax code powerfully affects corporate investment decisions.

Paul Samuelson and Lawrence Summers—a wise old man and a wise young man of macroeconomics—stake out contrasting positions on a central debate about the government's economic role. Has macroeconomic policy, guided by fifty years' progress in economic theory beginning with the publication of Keynes' *General Theory of Employment, Interest, and Money*, improved the way the economy works? Samuelson emphatically affirms that it has, although he slings some arrows at the prominent non-Keynesian approaches to macroeconomics. During the second third of the century, Samuelson asserts, the economy was demonstrably more stable than in earlier eras, in good part because of soundly conceived and intelligently applied fiscal and monetary policies. The stagflation that has bedeviled industrialized economies since the early 1970s, he says, reflects basic properties of the humane mixed economy, challenging economic theory to devise policies ameliorating their side effects.

Summers dissents. He challenges some of Samuelson's claims about the greater stability of post-Keynesian economies. But his major objection is that stability itself is not the Holy Grail; the main goals should be productivity and growth. By his lights, the macroeconomic ideas that informed policy in the early postwar era are of limited use for explaining or correcting the persistent downturn in growth that now appears to plague the West.

Embedded in these chapters is a set of shared concerns. One is the need for a perspective that stretches backward and forward along the ribbon of time. Most of our contributors—for example, educator Ravitch, economist Samuelson, and scientist Edelman, as well as historian McCraw—incorporate a historical element in their studies, turning to the past for lessons to illuminate the present. This historical consciousness tends to introduce considerations of stewardship for the future. Will American institutions and leaders, public and private, have the patience and stamina to husband what we value and transmit it to posterity? We live in the midst of clamorous demands for immediate benefits. Calls for new international monetary accords follow each bubble in exchange or interest rates. Swiftly executed takeovers of long-established firms dominate the business headlines. Who, if anyone, is assuming responsibility for the future is not always evident.

A second concern relates to the tangled networks of claims, mandates, and imperatives that hobble our collective efforts. Part of the "muddle" to which Zeckhauser refers has to do with the overloaded agendas of our institutions. Arts policies are charged with encouraging innovation, ensuring conservation, widening access and participation, and fostering diversity. Tax policies are written not just to raise revenues and redistribute income but to stimulate and channel investment, conserve energy, encourage giving to worthy causes, and promote low-income housing. School curricula include courses on basic social skills and recreational activities, as well as on mathematics and English literature. Even our universities are caught up in the transactional snarl of serving a bewildering array of constituencies—advocates of various international causes, media in need of "expertise," public grantors and private donors questing after quid pro quos. From optimism, ambition, impatience, forgetfulness, and (sometimes) greed, we inflict on ourselves a splintering proliferation of goals. Instead of the felicitous combination of complexity and coherence that O'Hare perceives in successful environments, we find our collective endeavors are more complicated than they need be to serve our principal objectives, and less coherent than they must be if we are to hold our stewards to account. The result is a clashing of our institutional gears that makes it hard for our agents, public or private, to deliver the goods we expect of them, especially for those—the poor, the sick, the unconnected—most urgently dependent on well-performing institutions.

No bold prescriptions, no stirring manifestoes emerge from these pages. *Judiciousness* may be the word that best characterizes the temper of these chapters, a judiciousness forged from a lively awareness of a past in need of preservation, of mistakes made, of issues and roles oversimplified, of agents imperfectly guided and imperfectly faithful, of the pain of choice—and a clear recognition that the future is being shaped by the decisions made today. Our contributors recognize that the problems that beset us are woven into the fabric of America, deeply entangled with the national strengths we celebrate, the protections we cherish. They renounce the temptation to prescribe simple sweeping reforms and acknowledge that our system is, paradoxically, both delicately balanced and resistant to dramatic change.

It remains for our readers to decide whether this judiciousness is a substitute for boldness or the necessary rockbed upon which sound future initiatives must be built. They must decide as well whether the prevailing spirit of these papers is in tune with the times we celebrate: the 350th anniversary of a great university, the 50th birthday of an ambitious school of government, and a year in our lives but fourteen shy of the end of both century and millennium.

CHAPTER 2

The Historical Background

Thomas K. McCraw

T he past is not dead," William Faulkner once wrote, "it is not even past." We cannot begin to understand present-day issues of public and private responsibilities in America without careful reference to our own history: to our 200-year experience as a nation, plus our prior and almost equally long experience as a diverse collection of thirteen British colonies. Nor should we try to consider these same issues without reference to a comparative international framework. As the historian Macaulay remarked in the nineteenth century, "He knows not England who only England knows"; the same point holds for twentieth-century Americans. With those premises in mind, this chapter will first measure the American experience historically, against its own past; then cross-nationally, against other countries during the present time.

SOVEREIGNTY AND ANTI-AUTHORITARIANISM

The English settlers of the North American continent brought with them certain assumptions about the nature of sovereignty and the relationship between public and private affairs. Today it is a little difficult for us to recapture these ideas, let alone put ourselves in tune with some of them. Yet the early settlers' conceptions about the nature of government and of private enterprise became extremely important for the future course of American politics. Even now some of those early conceptions distinguish the overall relationship between business and government in America from that characteristic of other democratic market economies.

As an initial approach to the roots of public-private thinking in the United States, let us first consider the question of sovereignty. During much of the colonial period, from the late seventeenth century down to the eve of the American Revolution, sovereignty was seldom a subject of serious discussion within the colonies. Like the existence of God and the certainty of life in the hereafter, it was taken as given. The locus of sovereignty remained clear: King-in-Parliament, that distinctive system of constitutional monarchy worked out through centuries of British experience. Within this system, British citizens regarded themselves, quite accurately, as the possessors of more individual freedom than was enjoyed by any other people on earth. Even beyond that, the American colonists knew, both by intuition and from explicit reports by British visitors to America and colonial visitors to England, that they themselves enjoyed more freedom than did Englishmen living in the home country.

Within the English system of government, even "the poorest he" (a memorable phrase coined in Cromwell's time) was entitled to "the rights of Englishmen." These entitlements, many of which were codified into English law in the Bill of Rights of 1688–89, included trial by jury, limited manhood suffrage, and the right to petition the sovereign.[1] In practice, they were not always observed to the letter, and it would be a great mistake to imagine that either the English people or the colonists in America lived in a democratic society. In fact, the very concept of democracy, in our modern use of that term, was unknown to most people of the time. To some of those who did give it thought, it remained abhorrent as a system of mob rule. Both Britain and its colonies retained clear hierarchies, informed by a sure sense of class and an ingrained habit of deference to one's "betters."[2] Yet the hand of government lay lightly, at least in comparison with that of the absolutist monarchies prevalent elsewhere. The concept of the rights of Englishmen included a deeply felt sense that thus it should be and remain.

The causes of the American Revolution, in fact, can be traced more to a violation of this implied contract, as perceived by some of the colonists, than to any other single source. I say *some* colonists because, among the thirty-three British colonies in the Western Hemisphere, only thirteen actually rebelled; and, even within those thirteen, quite as many citizens wanted to remain within the Empire as to separate.[3] The essence of the Revolution, as it relates to questions about the public and private spheres, came down to this.

For about 150 years, the hand of British rule had passed lightly over the North American colonies, each of which had gradually become accustomed to a good deal of self-government. Given the absence of a system of rapid communication in the days before the steamship and telegraph, it could hardly have been otherwise. From time to time, Whitehall and Westminster might experiment with a more centralized administration of the colonial system. Yet even on those occasions, most of Britain's attention focused not on New England and the northern colonies; instead, the focus remained on the southern plantations, including the prized sugar islands of the Caribbean, which also served as convenient naval bases in Britain's ongoing wars with the French and Spanish.[4]

The Seven Years War, which ended in 1763 with Britain's victory and the acquisition of additional colonies, forced Whitehall to begin a systematic centralization of the entire imperial system. The war had proven inordinately expensive, and the British government, among its other problems, now faced the task of extracting more revenue from the colonies. In consequence, new bureaucracies were created in England, and an enlarged corps of customs collectors and other agents was sent out to administer the collection of revenue.[5]

This new situation raised for the first time, on a wide scale, the question of the *political* relationship of the colonies to the mother country. Until now the issue of sovereignty had simply been taken for granted: King-in-Parliament, supplemented by a degree of home rule within the colonies, all oriented toward protection of the rights of Englishmen. The degree of home rule had grown over the years, almost imperceptibly, as a natural consequence of time and distance. Then, in the late 1760s, when Britain's enlarged group of customs inspectors, vice admiralty judges, and other representatives of the new administrative apparatus landed in North America, the question of just who was in charge of what—that is, the question of sovereignty—suddenly became inescapable.[6]

Step by step, as British administrators applied more and more pressure, what had been unthinkable to the colonists even in the late 1760s—actual political separation from the mother country—became a reality in 1776. From the colonists' point of view, the fundamental issue at stake was aptly put in that passage of the Declaration of Independence complaining of the King's infringement of the rights of colonial Englishmen: "When a long Train of Abuses and Usurpations, pursuing invariably the same Object, evinces a Design to reduce them under absolute Despotism, it is their Right, it is their Duty, to throw off such Government, and to provide new Guards for their future Security."[7]

Thus, the American nation was *born in an outburst of anti-authoritarianism.* It is extremely important, however, that the American Revolution did not represent any violent throwing off of an ancient yoke, as was the case in subsequent revolutions such as the French and the Russian, but rather a deeply felt resistance to a new assertion of authority on the part of a people long grown accustomed to its absence. In fact, the anti-authoritarianism manifested by the American colonists is all the more striking precisely in light of the mildness of the authority actually being imposed, even under the new colonial regimes of the 1770s.

Following the defeat of the British in the Revolutionary War, however, where was the new locus of national sovereignty? If King-in-Parliament were no longer relevant and the British Constitution no longer applicable, then where did sovereignty lie? In the individual states? Partly; each of the former thirteen colonies propounded a written constitution. In the federal government, with its own landmark Constitution of 1787? Partly there also, and perhaps a little more clearly. Yet the U.S. Constitution itself vests sovereignty in separate branches of government, each of which possesses clear power to check the others, in addition to checking the rulings of state governments. Thus, the Constitution, a document regarded in 1787 by a substantial opposition to its adoption as an instrument of *undue* centralization, manifests the deep-seated aversion to authority, the passion against centralized power, in which the American nation was born.[8] As Charles Evans Hughes once remarked, the founding fathers had constructed a government that "is the most successful contrivance the world has ever known for preventing things from being done."[9] The underlying principle for their determination to circumscribe the sphere of government action was the powerful anti-authoritarianism born of the colonial and Revolutionary experiences.

Thus, in searching for the grail of sovereignty, we encounter an issue that, more than 200 years after the Revolution, has yet to be resolved. It is a question that bears directly on the issue of the public and private responsibilities in America and on their relationship with each other. Stated simply, the issue is this: If authority itself remains suspect, and if the locus of sovereignty cannot be clearly specified, then exactly where is the dividing line between the public sector and the private? In a setting where "the People rule," what, precisely, *is* the public sector, and what the private? If the distinction remains inherently blurred, then how can the relationship between the two be defined?

AMBIGUITY AS A VIRTUE IN THE SETTLEMENT OF THE CONTINENT

During the two generations after the departure of the British (and Britain's failure at reconquest in the War of 1812), the locus of sovereignty in America did not seem an unduly pressing issue. Too many other things were going on. Chief among them were the systematic expansion of the nation and the steady rise of economic opportunity (at least for white men). These two developments themselves were tightly linked in ways that shed much light on the historical legacy of the question of the public and private spheres and the overall business-government relationship.

As the United States grew steadily, through the acquisition and settlement of the Old Northwest (the present Middle West), the Louisiana Purchase, the Florida Cession, the annexation of Texas, the Mexican Cession, the Gadsden Purchase, the Oregon settlement, and the purchase of Alaska from Russia, tens of thousands of individual Americans became wealthy through land speculation. During the late eighteenth century and for most of the nineteenth, this sort of speculation was not confined to sharp operators but was engaged in by some of the most hallowed figures in American history—Washington, Franklin, Jackson, Houston, and many others.

For any study of business-government relations in American history, and particularly for a focus on the public and private spheres, the entire subject of public land development provides a rich lode of insights. The overall point in this history is that the physical growth of the United States, a public issue involving delicate diplomacy with other nations, became tightly intertwined with the increase of individual fortunes, a private affair. In the early years of the American nation, little scandal arose from behavior that today would be regarded as clear conflicts of interest: the spectacle of men holding public office simultaneously engaged in private endeavors that benefited in turn from their official acts.[10]

To put it another way, no clear separation of the public and private spheres seemed possible, or even desirable. America represented, literally, a new country—a vast, open, and richly endowed area simply waiting for development by the most energetic and resourceful elements in the society. In fact, from the beginning of the colonial period, given the scarcity of land in the Old World, the opportunity for the acquisition of land had seemed to European settlers an almost unbelievable chance to achieve wealth. In the first half of the nineteenth century, that same ethos now emerged as one of the defining elements of the American situation and the American character. The gaining of new fortunes through land speculation represented *the* get-rich-quick method of the period, and nothing seemed necessarily wrong with it.

The urge toward growth and personal enrichment that stemmed from private motives was systematically buttressed by government policy. As much as any other single thing, the ideology of Manifest Destiny effectively barred any clear distinction between the public and private spheres. Consider, for example, the rationalizations put forward in Congress and other public forums for the official American annexation of all territory from the Atlantic to the Pacific. These claims, which overrode the prior claims of other peoples or other countries, stand as a striking reminder of the determination of American settlers to use any and all means, however audacious, and any and all arguments, however specious, to achieve their aims.[11]

One of the first reasons adduced was that of "natural right." This hallowed principle, a foundation stone of the Republic, was invoked during Jefferson's administration as a basis for acquiring New Orleans and, ultimately, all of the vast Louisiana Territory. Free navigation of the Mississippi River, as a "natural right" of western white settlers, required the right of deposit in the port of New Orleans and, if that right were resisted, then possession of the port itself. Setting out to purchase New Orleans, Jefferson ended with a territory that doubled the size of the existing United States.

In the acquisition of Florida, a doctrine amounting to geographical predestination was brought forward as justification for seizure from the Spaniards. This rounding out of America's southern coastline seemed ordained by divine providence. A good deal of argument urged the acquisition of Cuba as well, under the doctrine that it constituted a natural appendage to Florida. Even for the Oregon territory, some 3,000 miles from Florida, the same sort of geographical predestination required that the natural barrier of the Rockies be overleaped and the doctrine of contiguity to existing American possessions be applied. Whereas in Europe rivers and mountains had usually defined national boundaries, in America they represented not barriers but challenges, both to the pioneer spirit and to the rationalizations of politicians.

One of the most powerful of Manifest Destiny's many sub-ideologies was the notion of "extending the area of freedom." Under this rationale, expansionists not only dispossessed the Spaniards from Florida, but also the Mexicans from Texas, New Mexico, Arizona, Nevada, Colorado, Utah, Wyoming, and California. In the case of Texas, which was among the most hotly contested of all acquisitions, antiexpansionists pointed out that because Texas would undoubtedly become a slave state, then extending the area of freedom did not appear an altogether appropriate reason for undermining Mexican rule, the more so in view of Mexico's having already outlawed slavery. Thus, an accompanying doctrine of "regeneration" came to the fore, in which Indo-Mexican papists would be shown the true path of Protestant Christianity. They would be Anglicized, imbued with the Puritan ethic, and transformed into loyal American citizens.

One could go on with this litany, persisting into the twentieth century with the "liberation" of the Philippines from Spanish tyranny, followed by a bloody guerilla war in which the American army subdued a Philippine independence movement; with Theodore Roosevelt's taking of Panama from Colombia so that a canal could be constructed; with the acquisition of the Danish (and now American) Virgin Islands as a measure of self-defense lest the Germans acquire them; and so on. The purpose of reviewing the history of Manifest Destiny, however, has not been to cast aspersions on the spread of the American nation from sea to shining sea. Rather, it has been to show the extraordinary force of the urge to acquire more and more land. That force stemmed chiefly from private sources—that is, from settlers and speculators out to make their fortunes. But it was supported, encouraged, and carried out by American public policymakers throughout the nineteenth century.

The broad point here is that public and private undertakings, in this often overlooked aspect of American history, were so intertwined as to be inseparable. The public and private spheres were one and the same, with no lively sense of conflict of interest. The overriding concern with expansion made such distinctions almost irrelevant. Whenever conflict did develop, it was usually with elements that were perceived as *external*, and these included American Indians as well as foreign nations. So long as the frontier beckoned, the domestic interests of whites served powerfully to unite the public and private sectors. Indeed, the concept of internal conflict of interest developed only gradually during the nineteenth century, for reasons to be discussed later in this chapter. For now, it is sufficient to remark that conflict of interest laws are almost all products of twentieth-century legislatures. This simple fact should tell us a great deal about the freewheeling mixture of public and private interests during the nineteenth-century age of expansion, and especially about the urge to acquire land as the American frontier moved ever westward. On that frontier, the locus of sovereignty was often simply the barrel of a gun.

PUBLIC PURPOSE, PRIVATE GAIN: LAW AND ECONOMIC GROWTH

Meanwhile, a series of parallel developments was also defining a peculiarly American relationship between public and private undertakings. Chief among these was the distinctive evolution of American law, particularly the ways in which it began to diverge very quickly from some of the patterns characteristic of its English parent. Once again, a series of ambiguous distinctions may be perceived, all tending to promote the transcendent goal of economic growth.

For example, in our own time we have become accustomed to thinking of the nineteenth century as an age of laissez-faire, in which American government, constrained by the anti-authoritarian legacy of the Revolution, let business enterprise alone. The best government governed least; the heavy hand of bureaucracy was kept off the backs of American entrepreneurs; and so forth. The historical reality, however, was not so clear cut. It is true that the size of the American civil government was tiny in comparison with its European counterparts and that state-owned enterprise remained virtually unknown. Yet within the accumulated records of American courts, as well as those of state and federal legislatures, lies a hidden history of active engagement in business affairs.[12]

American courts early took a tough line on the enforcement of contracts. They acted on the principle that in a new country populated by people unfamiliar with each other and engaged in distant dealings; written contracts must replace informal handshakes. Even during the colonial period, the consequently high need for lawyers had been a noticeable attribute of the new American society. (It is useful to recall that the leadership of the American Revolution, alone of the world's great revolutions, was dominated by lawyers: Hamilton, Madison, Jay, Jefferson, Adams, Otis, and Henry.)

In a second contrast to the practice of European courts, American ones often showed a pronounced preference for venture capital over static—a prejudice in favor of the entrepreneur over the rentier. Sometimes this preference even triumphed over the sanctity of contracts. A series of decisions by state and federal courts could be cited here, but one vivid example will suffice: the Charles River Bridge case of 1837. In this controversy, the proprietors of the Charles River Bridge, a toll bridge connecting Boston with Charlestown and incorporated by special act of the Massachusetts legislature in 1785, challenged a subsequent Massachusetts statute that permitted a competing bridge (the Warren bridge) to be constructed nearby. This later law, passed in 1828, long before the original Charles River Bridge charter was scheduled to expire, seemed to the original proprietors a de facto taking of their property since the new bridge would become free within six years and would then attract most of the traffic crossing the Charles. Thus, the proprietors sued to invalidate the 1828 charter as unconstitutional on the grounds that it impaired the value of their 1785 charter. Under existing law, the proprietors appeared to be in a powerful legal position; but in fact the U.S. Supreme Court upheld the 1828 grant on the grounds that corporate charters must be construed not solely in favor of existing property owners but often in the interest of entrepreneurs and "the community," which, in the oft-quoted words of Chief Justice Taney in his decision, "also have rights."[13]

A similar prejudice in favor of entrepreneurship appears in the evolution of American bankruptcy law. In European practice, and during the colonial period in America, bankruptcy law was generally designed to assist creditors in the collection of at least some portion of the money owed them. It was of a piece with such other practices as imprisonment for debt. After the United States became independent, imprisonment for debt was quickly abolished and bankruptcy law began to be construed in a new way, not as a method to protect creditors but rather as a means of encouraging debtors and entrepreneurs to try again even though they had previously failed in business. Indeed, the idea of a new start became an essential part of the American Dream. Perhaps the best known individual case was that of R. H. Macy, who failed again and again, in many different places, in efforts to make a go of the dry goods business. Undaunted by these setbacks, Macy kept setting up new ventures until finally he succeeded in the grandest possible style in New York City, where his department store became the largest and most famous in the world.[14]

In capital-scarce America, public law encouraged a variety of ingenious ways to create money. One of these was the permissive attitude of state legislatures toward wildcat banking, and the refusal of the U.S. government to charter a genuine central bank that might exercise discipline over loose banking practices but that might also, in the process, retard the commercial development of the young nation. Thus, the 1791 charter of Alexander Hamilton's First Bank of the United States was not renewed in 1811. Nor, in a much more dramatic controversy, was Nicholas Biddle's Second Bank of the United States, chartered in 1816, permitted to survive beyond its initial twenty-year life. Instead, Andrew Jackson's famous veto of the recharter bill defined an official hard money position but also a permissiveness toward wildcat banking that facilitated the creation of wealth in the West.[15]

Toward much the same end, the substitution of plentiful land for scarce capital marked the overall American economic way of doing things from the early colonial period onward. First appearing in the seventeenth century in the form of land grants by the English sovereign to court favorites (or to specially chartered corporations such as the London Virginia Company and the Massachusetts Bay Company), the creation of money from land reached its zenith in the nineteenth century. For many years, the public treasury's greatest single source of revenue was the systematic sale of land, a policy that lightened the tax burden borne by Americans even as it facilitated the opening up of the West. Equally important, American public policy used land as a substitute for money through the simple device of making grants of acreage and rights-of-way, first to canal companies, then, on a larger scale, to railroad corporations. Almost all of these grants went to enterprises incorporated through special charters by state legislatures.[16]

Historically, in both Britain and America, such charters had been reserved for those few enterprises regarded as serving a specific public purpose: towns, universities, banks, bridges, canals, turnpikes, and now railroads. By the late nineteenth century, however, most states had abandoned the public purpose distinction altogether and had passed laws of general incorporation. Under such laws, almost any legitimate enterprise could be incorporated for any purpose. This single step represented the U.S. government's most important stimulus to economic activity. With the stroke of a pen, it permitted the aggregation of capital and the limited liability so useful in entrepreneurial activity.[17] Incidentally, laws of general incorporation also provided individual states with unexpected sources of revenue in the form of corporate registration fees. Some states—first New Jersey and Delaware, later Maine and South Dakota—vied with each other in the realm of permissiveness. Through this competitive process, corporate exploitation of such devices as trusts and holding companies became much more commonplace in America than in other countries.

In general, the entire legal order in nineteenth-century America was preoccupied with economic growth. In the memorable phrase of the great legal historian Willard Hurst, the law seemed designed specifically to facilitate the maximum "release of energy." Given that goal, too fine a distinction between public and private interests simply could not be drawn. Any attempt to do so would have interfered with that very release of energy that so animated nineteenth-century entrepreneurs. In this sense, there was no need for a substantial public sector of the European variety.

An example will illustrate the point. Insofar as there existed a federal public sector in the nineteenth century, it was dominated by the Post Office. In 1871, when the United States had reached a population of about 41 million, only 14,324 civilians worked for the national government, apart from postal employees. (By way of comparison with our own time, this number comes to a ratio of one federal employee per 2,858 people in 1871, compared with one per 102 people in 1980—approximately twenty-seven times the 1871 figure.) In the same year, a far larger number—nearly 37,000—worked for the Post Office.[18] Many in this total were local postmasters in small and medium-sized towns all over the United States. Yet most of the officials in such towns were not exclusively federal employees. Often operating out of Post Office space, they also practiced law, sold real estate, ran stores, and performed other services in their own private interest—all in addition to being the local postmaster. Again, the point is that no strict separation of public and private functions troubled the consciences of the postmasters themselves, the legislatures, or most of the general public—at least until relatively late in the nineteenth century.[19]

THE RISE OF BIG BUSINESS AND
THE PUBLIC-PRIVATE SPLIT

Thus far I have suggested that the split between public and private interests did not seem a burning political issue before the late nineteenth century. The remainder of the chapter will be devoted to a comparison framed against two additional reference points: the American experience over the century following 1871 and the American situation today as it compares with other major market economies in Europe and Japan.

Before the 1870s neither government nor business posed much of a threat to the individual liberties of American citizens. The anti-authoritarian ethos in which the nation had been born stood intact, hardly touched by the hand of either public or private power. On those rare occasions when private power did tend to become threatening, decisive countermeasures were taken. For example, when Nicholas Biddle's Second Bank of the United States began to gather what many Americans regarded as excessive authority, President Andrew Jackson responded. Speaking privately in 1832 to the man who would become his successor, Jackson said, "The Bank, Mr. Van Buren, is trying to kill me, *but I will kill it.*" And he did, by vetoing its recharter.[20] Power itself was the problem in America, whether public or private. On the private side, few enterprises were capable, no matter how willing, of injuring the economic or political interests of large numbers of Americans. This was a very fortunate political situation. But it was also a temporary one.

Beginning in the 1850s with the railroads, and maturing in the 1880s with the rise of giant corporations, private interests suddenly acquired the power to disrupt the lives not only of individuals but of entire communities. Railroads could pronounce a death sentence on small communities by the simple device of by-passing them and building tracks through neighboring towns instead. More than this, railroads required colossal amounts of money just to go into business: the purchase of land for rights-of-way, the building of locomotives and rolling stock, the organization of a hierarchical system of management. All of these activities proved to be unprecedented business problems (and, inevitably, political ones as well), simply because of their scale and concentration of control. By 1890 several railroad corporations employed more than 100,000 people each, and the revenues of American railroads as a whole far surpassed the national budget.[21] It all added up to an abrupt end to the atomistic, yeoman-dominated commonwealth of the founding fathers and the beginning of an entirely new industrial world.

As soon as railroads became important (in a few states during the 1850s, and throughout the country by the late 1860s), the relationship between business and government inevitably changed. Now, private interests directly threatened the public welfare in many different ways. In the first place, trains turned out to be remarkably unsafe contrivances, introduced as they were into a society accustomed to the speed of the mule and the mass of the wagonload and unacquainted with portable high-pressure furnaces. Secondly, the vast revenues now concentrated in the hands of a few giant railroad corporations—a cash flow unmatched in the history of the world—opened up on a much broader scale the possibility that business might systematically corrupt politics: that the private sector might poison the public.

Because of this situation, it was natural that several new American traditions and institutions aimed at counterbalancing such private powers were born almost simultaneously.

1. *A deep concern with conflict of interest.* The most noteworthy early example of conflict of interest and the systematic suborning of public officials occurred in the state of New York, and was perpetrated by the proprietors of the Erie Railroad: Messrs. Daniel Drew, Jim Fisk, and Jay Gould. These executives, who made their fortunes primarily by manipulating the prices of Erie stock and other securities, spent some of their earnings in purchasing the votes of legislators and even the decisions of judges.[22]

2. *The systematic public reporting of such activities.* Not surprisingly, there then arose the tradition of investigative journalism, by a

corps of writers who later acquired the wonderfully expressive name of "muckrakers." In the case of the Erie Railroad, the pioneer was Charles Francis Adams, Jr., the grandson of one American president and the great-grandson of another. Adams was one of the first analysts to point out that the rise of the railroads represented a trap for the American political system. That system, he argued, had been carefully designed with certain ends in mind—notably the restraint of public power—that now made it extremely difficult to deal with this new situation of tremendous private power. When it was proposed to Adams that the solution might be public ownership of the railroads, so as to finesse the issue of public *versus* private, he responded that the public sector was simply not equipped to handle complex industrial problems. Not only that, but politics itself had sunk to a low state. So even though public ownership of railroads had been tried with much success in Europe, Adams dismissed it as a solution for America: "Imagine," he wrote in 1867, "the Erie and Tammany rings rolled into one and turned loose on the field of politics, and the result of State ownership would be realized."[23]

3. *The labor union.* The first important such organization, by no coincidence, was the Brotherhood of Locomotive Engineers. Over the next three generations, all the way until the 1970s, railway labor unions remained among the most powerful organizations in America, measured by the benefits they were able to bring to their members.

4. *The regulatory commission.* Charles Francis Adams, Jr., himself became the first important regulatory commissioner in the United States. His comments quoted above, in fact, represented part of his own concerted effort to persuade the legislature of Massachusetts to create a commission that might bring "order and science" to the now perplexing relationship between public and private affairs in railroading. The state legislature responded favorably in 1869; many other states followed suit (a few had even preceded Massachusetts); and by 1887 the first such federal agency, the Interstate Commerce Commission, had been created by Congress for the specific purpose of dealing with "the railroad problem."[24]

As time would prove, however, the real problem was not one of railroads alone. By the 1880s John D. Rockefeller's Standard Oil Company had achieved such cost-cutting innovations in oil refining and distribution that, through severe price competition, it had driven out of business dozens of competitors. In 1890 James B. Duke's American Tobacco Company had accomplished the same object through superior efficiency, in this case with a new cigarette-making machine that could supply a substantial portion of the entire world market. Duke's company, capitalized at $25 million in 1890, grew to a capitalization of $500 million in 1904. This sum would simply have been unimaginable to the America of Duke's own boyhood. The economic power that came from such technological efficiencies was equally unprecedented.[25]

These changes occurred so rapidly that public perceptions of what was happening could not possibly keep up. Nor could the law. Nor could political power in general. The pace of technological change, the rise of scale economies, and the building of vast manufacturing enterprises developed so quickly that literally nobody fully understood the ramifications. In such a setting, not only did muckraking flourish but so did such other literary genres as utopian novels. Perhaps the best example here was Edward Bellamy's *Looking Backward* (1888), which, projecting present tendencies a century into the future, somehow managed to arrive at a happy ending to it all. There, in fact, lay the rub. Because of the rise of big business, America was growing very much richer. To kill Standard Oil, the Pennsylvania Railroad, and American Tobacco would plainly be to kill American prosperity. Yet, how could this new situation possibly fail to affect the old, comfortable relationship—indeed, the *absence* of any formal relationship at all—between the public and private sectors?

The new industrial setting, therefore, went beyond any simple dichotomy between the public and private sectors in America. As noted earlier, the United States represented literally a new nation. It came into existence almost totally unencumbered with the trappings of a feudal past. It had no royal family, no hereditary aristocracy of any kind. It possessed no standing army, nor any established church that might exert powerful influence over business behavior. No mandarin class existed in America, no tradition of elite government bureaucracies on the Prussian, French, or British model. Government in America had been deliberately designed to remain weak, so as not to infringe the individual freedoms of an anti-authoritarian people. The locus of sovereignty continued to be fragmented and ambiguous.[26]

At the same time, the central preoccupations of Americans tended to be economic ones. The American Dream itself was at bottom a dream of upward economic mobility, of becoming prosperous through individual effort and will, with faith that "luck and pluck" together (Horatio Alger's phrase) would lead to rising economic status.

Thus, when big business came to America, it came with a rush, growing bigger and faster here than in any other country. The reasons why are many and are not easily summarized. But one primary reason was simply the absence of any other force sufficiently strong to challenge big business. With a weak government, no aristocracy, no standing army, no established church—not even a guild tradition, which might have protected small artisans—a vacuum of power existed. Within this vacuum, market forces could work without encumbrance. Hence the extraordinarily rapid rise of gigantic corporations in America, notably between the years 1880 and 1920. Within a few years after 1880, the United States had emerged as both the leading agricultural and the leading industrial nation of the world. And by 1920 it represented the first full-blown consumer society in human history.

All of this happened so rapidly, and to a population of such mixed ethnicity (by 1900, after two decades of heavy immigration, fewer than one American in two was both white and the child of two native-born parents[27]), that it proved decidedly difficult to understand. Some observers, such as Thorstein Veblen, condemned the new habits of conspicuous consumption and derided America's business civilization as barbaric—an anthropological curiosity with little staying power. Others, such as the German philosopher Hugo Munsterberg, probed deeper and with more penetrating insights. For a time, Munsterberg taught psychology at Harvard, where he associated with such eminent personages as William James and Josiah Royce. In 1904 he brought out a book entitled *The Americans* in which he attempted to explain for a European audience the essence of the American character and its relationship to the pursuit of wealth:

> The colossal industrial successes, along with the great evils and dangers which have come with them, must be understood from the make-up of the American character. Just as we have traced the political life of America back to a powerful instinct for free self-determination, the free self-guidance of the undivided, so we shall here find that it is the instinct for free self-initiative which has set in motion this tremendous economic fly-wheel. . . .
>
> The average European, permeated as he is with Old World culture, is, in fact, convinced that this intense economic activity is the simple result of unbounded greed. The search for gold and the pursuit of the dollar, we often

hear, have destroyed in the American soul every finer ambition; and since the American has no higher desire for culture, he is free to chase his Mammon with undisguised and shameless greed. . . .

[Yet] a German observes immediately that the American does not prize his possessions much unless he has worked for them himself; of this there are innumerable proofs, [such as] the absence of a bridal dower. . . . Even when the parents of the bride are prosperous, it is unusual for a young couple to live beyond the means of the husband. . . .

The profession of living from the income of investments is virtually unknown among men, and the young men who take up no money-making profession because they "don't need to" are able to retain the social respect of their fellows only by undertaking some sort of work for the commonwealth. A man who does not work at anything, no matter how rich he is, can neither get nor keep a social status. . . .

It is, therefore, fundamentally false to stigmatize the American as a materialist, and to deny his idealism. . . . The economic life means to the American a realizing of efforts which are in themselves precious. It is not the means to an end, but is its own end. If two blades of grass grow where one grew before, or two railroad tracks where there was but one; if production, exchange, and commerce increase and undertaking thrives, then life is created, and this is, in itself, a precious thing. [By contrast,] the European of the Continent esteems the industrial life as honest, but not as noble.[28]

Yet, however noble the pursuit of economic progress may have been in America, it also brought, as Munsterberg noted in his first line above, "great evils and dangers." To meet these, it was becoming clear to more and more Americans that a powerful public sector must be erected to counterbalance the rise of big business.

The year 1904, when Munsterberg published his analysis, happened also to be a year in which several events symbolized the emergence of more decisive governmental regulation of economic behavior. One such occurrence was the Justice Department's victory in the most important antitrust prosecution yet brought: the Northern Securities case, involving a railroad conglomerate put together by J. P. Morgan, Edward H. Harriman, and other leading financiers. This victory signaled that the days of unchallenged business autonomy were numbered. An even more important event of 1904 was the election of Theodore Roosevelt to the presidency in his own right. Roosevelt — such a young, dashing, and energetic counterpoint to his stodgy predecessors Garfield, Arthur, Cleveland, Harrison, and McKinley — had inherited the mantle of the assassinated McKinley in 1901. He had then proceeded to become the nation's first celebrity

president: a manipulator of public opinion, an official whom reporters followed around as a matter of course.[29] His landslide election in
1904 symbolized the nation's acceptance of the need for greater
activism in government.

Roosevelt himself, unlike many of his predecessors, and in vivid
contrast to the anti-authoritarian strain of American culture in general, had little fear of power in the abstract. He had none whatever
of wielding it personally. Thus, his presidency represents a clear
dividing line in the overall role of national government in American
life from a negative, passive, and small affair to a positive, active, and
substantial force designed to countervail both corporate power at
home and imperial designs by other nations overseas. Hence his de-
nunciation of "malefactors of great wealth" at home; and hence,
abroad, the taking of Panama, the Roosevelt Corollary to the Monroe
Doctrine, and other bold (and occasionally ill-advised) adventures in
foreign policy.

When Roosevelt became president in 1901, the federal government
had already begun to grow toward a larger and more independent
role in American life. As noted earlier, in 1871, on the eve of the
great industrialization marked by the rise of big business, only 1 non-
postal federal employee per 2,858 American citizens held office. In
succeeding years, the trend changed rapidly (see table below). These
numbers provide only one index of the growth of the public sector
in America, of course, and they provide perspective only on the
change within the United States from one period to another.

Growth in Federal Employment, 1871 to 1980.

Year	Population per Federal Employee (Non-Postal)
1871	2,858
1901	751
1925	431
1940	184
1950	103
1970	91
1980	102

Source: *Historical Statistics of the United States: Colonial Times to 1970*, pp. 8, 1102-
1103; *Statistical Abstract of the United States, 1982–83*, pp. 6, 264, 266-67.

THE UNITED STATES IN
CROSS-NATIONAL PERSPECTIVE

Measured by international criteria, the size and influence of government in America throughout the twentieth century has remained small, even relative to other democratic market economies. Today, for example, practically no public ownership of business enterprise exists in the United States, compared with very substantial public enterprises in Europe, not to mention developing nations and socialist economies. Then, too, the total tax take of all governments (federal, state, and local) in America is around one-third of gross national product, compared with an average closer to one-half in the nations of the European Common Market.

Compared with these other countries and with economically strong Asian nations such as Japan, the United States acquired an important public sector very late in the game. Even during World War I, the United States deliberately avoided the creation of a munitions ministry. Instead, the U.S. government called on "dollar-a-year men" from the private sector. Executives such as Bernard Baruch and Herbert Hoover managed the mobilization process through agencies such as the War Industries Board and the Food Administration, both staffed largely with civilians on leave from positions in American industry. Although Baruch, Hoover, and other war managers sometimes wielded authoritarian powers, in fact, they vigorously maintained the rhetoric of weak government and strong private enterprise. They insisted that whatever encroachments on individual rights were necessitated by mobilization would prove transitory. In this they were correct, and many of the devices for industrial coordination set up in 1917–18 were dismantled during the 1920s.[30]

Thus, before the New Deal the American government remained tiny and almost bereft of any elite civil service. The New Deal agencies proved more durable, however, and the entire Depression experience brought the public sector into private affairs as nothing else in American history had done before. The proliferation of public functions during the New Deal, some of them given a further lease on life by World War II, represented a fundamentally new phenomenon in American history. On the macroeconomic side, the expanded role of government was exemplified by two measures passed during the 1940s: broader income tax laws, including the unprecedented practice of withholding taxes from employees' paychecks, and Congress's passage in 1946 of the Employment Act. This latter law represented a Keynesian measure calculated to smooth out the ups and downs of the private economy through countercyclical taxing and spending by a much enlarged public sector.

Yet in other important respects, the anti-authoritarian, anti-statist tradition so characteristic of American history survived even the Depression and World War II. Demobilization from the second war proceeded almost as rapidly as it had for the first. In fact, had it not been for the rise of the Soviet threat, the success of the Maoist revolution in China, and the Korean War the American military might conceivably have shrunk once more to its traditionally minuscule size and role in American life. As it turned out, even the emergence of the national security state, with its intermingling of public and private affairs through the maze of defense contractors and Pentagon bureaucracies, represented an anomaly—at least in the years since the rise of big business had encouraged a strict separation of the public and the private spheres.

Even today, the pattern of public service in the United States remains fundamentally different from that of most of its trading partners and economic competitors. In economic policymaking, for example, most of the important decisions are made not by career bureaucrats but instead by "in-and-outers"—talented people summoned to Washington as Cabinet or subcabinet members, on temporary leave from the private worlds of academia, law, or business. Compared with long-standing traditions of elite civil services in Britain, France, Germany, and Japan, the United States has only a feeble tradition, centered primarily in the State Department. Subcabinet officers such as assistant secretaries average about twenty-six months in office. A career in government service does exist, fed by a few institutions such as Princeton's Woodrow Wilson School and Harvard's Kennedy School of Government. Yet most graduates of such schools do not become career civil servants but instead attach themselves to promising politicians; they ascend the ladder of power by political appointment, not by career meritocracy.[31] In all, such American schools exercise no such pervasive influence as do Oxford and Cambridge in Britain, the grandes écoles in France, or Tokyo University in Japan. Tokyo University, in fact, was originally organized for the specific purpose of training bureaucrats to manage the Japanese economy.

Since Japan itself in recent years has been taken as a model of successful merging of the public and private spheres, perhaps a brief comparison with the United States will be enlightening here. In Japan the higher civil service has long represented the most prestigious career the society has to offer. Only a few hundred new recruits are allowed to join the economic ministries each year, and these bright young people are selected solely on the basis of merit, as defined by academic performance and scores on standardized examinations. The term *bureaucrat*, so loathesome in America, connotes higher honor and status in Japan.[32] Bureaucrats there enter the public service at about age twenty-three, expecting to remain for their entire careers. Year in and year out, elite agencies such as the Ministry of Finance and the Ministry of International Trade and Industry attract the kind of talent that in America gravitates instead toward law, medicine, and private consulting. In both government and business, Japanese managers advance by seniority as much as by merit. Little leapfrogging of seniors by brilliant whiz kids occurs. In the public sector, the position held in America during the Reagan administration by so youthful a person as David Stockman would be unthinkable. And in the private, a career such as that of Mary Cunningham at Bendix Corporation would seem ludicrous—literally incredible. In these respects, America differs not only from Japan but also from other industrialized nations.

Perhaps most significantly for comparative purposes, the principle of separation of powers among different branches of government is not taken nearly so seriously elsewhere as it is in the United States. Nor is the deep-seated American belief—born of the unfettered rise of big business in the United States—that the public and private spheres must be kept rigorously insulated from each other. Most countries do not have anything remotely resembling the detailed conflict of interest laws characteristic of American government, with their cumbersome requirements for financial disclosure. In Germany, Japan, France, Italy, and similar industrial countries, relationships among the national legislature, the ruling party, the economic ministries, and the community of large businesses are characterized by almost constant intimate contact—a pattern that would not only appear unseemly in America but would often simply be illegal. As a result, for good or ill, far more public-private interaction occurs in these other nations than in the United States, and the overall pattern of government-business relationships remains different.

Lawyers, for example, have much smaller roles in other countries than they do in America. In Europe difficult social problems are often relegated not to courts, with the resultant years of vacillation as each appellate level has its say, but rather to blue-ribbon panels of private citizens. In Britain these groups go by the acronym *quangoes* — quasi-autonomous nongovernmental organizations. Throughout European countries, local quangoes, though often criticized, are still accorded a degree of respect and legitimacy that would seem strange indeed to American eyes.[33]

Furthermore, the tradition of "in-and-outers" does not operate abroad at all the way it does in America. In Japan practically no movement at all occurs from the private sector into the public at any stage of an individual's career. On the other hand, shifts from the public sector into the private are routine in Japan and, like quangoes in Europe, are viewed as legitimate and effective means of facilitating public-private relationships. Japanese bureaucrats, when they retire from government service (usually no later than age fifty-five), generally assume high-ranking positions with large companies or trade associations. Many retired bureaucrats also run for seats in the Diet. In fact, most of Japan's prime ministers over the last three decades have been former bureaucrats.[34]

What makes the Japanese pattern of public-private interpenetration relevant to the American situation today is less any abstract appeal it might have than the extraordinary performance of the Japanese economy. Whether this achievement has more to do with Japanese management techniques or the nation's business-government relationship is a question beyond the province of this chapter. Indeed, even if it could be shown that Japanese public policies were *the* most important ingredient in the country's economic success, it would also be appropriate to point out that in many respects Japan is not a model for emulation. While it is true that in comparison with other Asian polities, Japan has achieved remarkable gains in moving toward genuine democracy, it is equally true that, compared to the United States, Japan remains a relatively ethnocentric, sexist, and illiberal society.

Within the context of this chapter, the superior performance of the Japanese economy over the American does help to place certain very recent economic developments in historical perspective. Two brief examples will demonstrate how profoundly the pattern of our present economic performance differs from what went before. First, for each year between 1893 and 1971, the United States ran a trade surplus. That is, in this best single test of international competitiveness, the United States consistently came out ahead. Since 1971, however, it has run persistent deficits and in each of the last five years has set a new international record for the size of such deficits. Second, in a similar and related trend, for every year between 1914 and 1985, the United States was a net creditor nation: Capital obligations by foreigners to Americans exceeded those by Americans to foreigners. This situation too has now turned around, and with almost amazing speed. By 1993, if present trends continue, American debtors (principally the U.S. government) will owe about twice as much to foreign creditors (principally Japan) as all the beleaguered Latin American governments combined owed in 1986.[35]

Other chapters in this book will examine U.S. economic performance in greater detail. At the close of this primarily historical chapter, I raise these present-day concerns because of the discontinuities they represent with earlier American history and the contrasts they exhibit with our principal economic competitors of the present and future. But I want to emphasize that certain continuities also remain. First, the measure of individual success in America is still upward economic mobility, just as has been the case since the colonial period; second, a powerful streak of anti-authoritarianism still lies deep within the American psyche; third, and partly as a consequence of the first two, public authority remains suspect and inherently weak in almost any context except a nationally perceived crisis of the dimensions of World War II.

Given the interdependent world economy of the late twentieth century, the potential costs of these conditions threaten to become ever more serious. For example, persistent bureaucrat-bashing by the American electorate and by prominent politicians has inevitably diminished the ability of both the public *and* private sectors to respond effectively to economic challenges from abroad. Jimmy Carter in 1976 and Ronald Reagan in 1980 and 1984 each mounted successful campaigns for the White House premised on the doctrinaire proposition that government itself represented the problem, not the solution. Partly as a consequence, both the morale and, in some vital areas, even the size of the American civil government have shrunk dramatically in recent years. This has meant, among other things, that bureaucrats from the United States often cannot deal on equal terms with their foreign counterparts. American trade negotiators, for example, however talented, have been consistently outmaneuvered by more numerous and experienced negotiators from abroad. As two former State Department experts on Japan recently wrote,

In all, the Japanese now enjoy a 13 to 1 personnel advantage in almost every area of ties with the United States. . . . Japan has an elite bureaucracy, an exceptionally weak parliament, and a Confucian legal tradition. The United States has no formal senior civil service, a powerful Congress, and a legal system based on English common law. Executive agencies and departments have difficulty relating to their Japanese counterparts [such as the Ministry of International Trade and Industry] because few exist.[36]

The salient characteristics of American civil government today are its fragmentation, small size, and low overall morale. Because of the reality of intense international competition and the necessity for wise long-term economic policies, the peculiar situation has now arisen in which two treasured elements of our national ideology have come into direct conflict; that is, our conviction that government should remain weak and fragmented now threatens to limit or even thwart the pursuit of upward individual economic mobility. Without wise public policy, which can come only through talented public servants, the American private sector has little hope of recapturing lost markets for many of its products, including substantial portions of the domestic market itself.

I end this chapter, therefore, not with clear answers about the future of American business-government relations, but rather with a question. Given our traditions and our ideology, how will we as a nation be able to perform up to the standard now being set in the international marketplace by our powerful economic competitors? It is true, of course, that each of these countries has its own set of problems. But most of them do not, as Americans do, live under an institutionalized uncertainty about the locus of national sovereignty. Nor do they labor under our abiding and sometimes debilitating conviction that the public sector must remain weak and must be kept strictly separate from the private. Consequently, they do not habitually regard public-private cooperation as illegitimate on its face, irrespective of the long-run damage to the national economic interest.

NOTES

1. The English Bill of Rights culminated a long series of steps that began with the Magna Charta and intensified in the seventeenth century during the Civil War, the Restoration, and the Glorious Revolution. A convenient sourcebook of original documents on this evolution and its relation to the development of American ideology, is *The People Shall Judge*, ed. by the staff, Social Sciences 1, the College of the University of Chicago (Chicago: University of Chicago Press, 1949), Vol. I.

2. Even for a generation after the Revolution, the habit of deference remained conspicuous in America. See, for example, David Hackett Fischer, *The Revolution in American Conservatism: The Federalist Party in the Era of Jeffersonian Democracy* (New York: Harper & Row, 1965).

3. A good overview of the events leading to the Revolution, cast in the broad perspective of the British colonial system as a whole, is Charles M. Andrews, *The Colonial Background of the American Revolution* (New Haven: Yale University Press, 1924).

4. I do not mean to exaggerate here. As Stanley Nider Katz has argued, the problem of administering northern and southern colonies alike had become integral to British politics by the middle of the eighteenth century. See Katz, *Newcastle's New York: Anglo-American Politics, 1732-1753* (Cambridge, Mass.: Belknap Press of Harvard University Press, 1968).

5. The fullest account of these events and their repercussions on British colonial policy remains the magisterial four-volume work of Charles M. Andrews, *The Colonial Period of American History* (New Haven: Yale University Press, 1934-38). See also Oliver M. Dickerson, *The Navigation Acts and the American Revolution* (Philadelphia: University of Pennsylvania Press, 1951); and the brief but insightful overview by Carl Ubbelohde, *The American Colonies and the British Empire, 1607-1763* (New York: Crowell, 1968).

6. The seminal works of Bernard Bailyn and Gordon S. Wood are relevant here. See Bailyn, *Ideological Origins of the American Revolution* (Cambridge, Mass.: Harvard University Press, 1967); and Wood, *The Creation of the American Republic, 1776-1787* (Chapel Hill: University of North Carolina Press, 1969).

7. Ibid. (both sources). The quotation from the Declaration of Independence comes early in that document, in the middle of the long paragraph beginning "We hold these Truths to be self-evident," and just before the long list of crimes ascribed to George III.

8. Cecelia M. Kenyon, "Republicanism and Radicalism in the American Revolution: An Old-Fashioned Interpretation," *William and Mary Quarterly*, 19 (April 1962): 153-82.

9. Quoted by Morton Keller, "The Pluralist State: American Economic Regulation in Comparative Perspective, 1900-1930," in *Regulation in Perspective*, ed., Thomas K. McCraw (Boston: Harvard University Graduate School of Business Administration, 1981), p. 56.

10. On land speculation by the founding fathers, see Merrill Jensen, *The Articles of Confederation: An Interpretation of the Social-Constitutional History of the American Revolution, 1774-1781* (Madison: University of Wisconsin Press, 1940).

11. The following analysis of Manifest Destiny is derived principally from Albert K. Weinberg's flawed but painstaking volume, *Manifest Destiny: A*

Study of Nationalist Expansionism in American History (Baltimore: Johns Hopkins Press, 1935, Quadrangle Paperback edition 1963).

12. This discussion of the evolution of American law owes much to the pioneering work of James Willard Hurst. See, in particular, the following books by Hurst: *The Growth of American Law: The Law Makers* (Boston: Little, Brown, 1950); *Law and the Conditions of Freedom in the Nineteenth-Century United States* (Madison: University of Wisconsin Press, 1956); *Law and Social Process in United States History* (Ann Arbor: University of Michigan Law School, 1960); and *Law and Economic Growth: The Legal History of the Lumber Industry in Wisconsin, 1836–1915* (Cambridge, Mass.: Belknap Press of Harvard University Press, 1964).

   An excellent overall perspective is provided by Lawrence M. Friedman, *A History of American Law* (New York: Simon & Schuster, 1973).

13. See Stanley I. Kutler's monograph on the Charles River Bridge case, *Privilege and Creative Destruction* (Philadelphia: Lippincott, 1971).

14. Ralph M. Hower, *History of Macy's of New York: Chapters in the Evolution of the Department Store* (Cambridge, Mass.: Harvard University Press, 1943).

15. Arthur M. Schlesinger, Jr., *The Age of Jackson* (Boston: Little, Brown, 1945), chs. 4 and 7–10.

16. Carter Goodrich, *Government Promotion of American Canals and Railroads, 1800–1890* (New York: Columbia University Press, 1960); Oscar and Mary F. Handlin, *Commonwealth: A Study of the Role of Government in the American Economy, Massachusetts, 1774–1861*, 2nd ed. (New York: New York University Press, 1974); Louis Hartz, *Economic Policy and Democratic Thought: Pennsylvania, 1776–1860* (Cambridge, Mass.: Harvard University Press, 1948); Milton Sydney Heath, *Constructive Liberalism: The Role of the State in Economic Development in Georgia to 1860* (Cambridge, Mass.: Harvard University Press, 1955); and Harry N. Scheiber, *Ohio Canal Era: A Case Study of Government and the Economy, 1820–1861* (Athens: Ohio University Press, 1969).

17. Oscar and Mary F. Handlin, "Origins of the American Business Corporation," *Journal of Economic History* 5 (May 1945); see also the books on legal history by Hurst and Friedman cited in note 12 above; and James Willard Hurst, *The Legitimacy of the Business Corporation in the Laws of the United States 1780–1970* (Charlottesville: The University Press of Virginia, 1970).

18. U.S. Department of Commerce, *Historical Statistics of the United States: Colonial Times to 1970* (Washington, D.C.: Government Printing Office, 1975), pp. 8, 1102–103; *Statistical Abstract of the United States, 1982–83* (Washington, D.C.: Government Printing Office, 1982), pp. 6, 264, 266–67.

19. I am indebted to Richard John for this information; see John's forthcoming Harvard Ph.D. dissertation on the nineteenth-century Post Office.

20. Schlesinger, *The Age of Jackson*, ch. 8.
21. See Alfred D. Chandler, Jr., ed., *The Railroads: The Nation's First Big Business* (New York: Harcourt, Brace & World, 1965).
22. Charles Francis Adams, Jr., "A Chapter of Erie," *North American Review* 109 (July 1869): 30-106.
23. Charles Francis Adams, Jr., "The Railroad System," *North American Review* 105 (April 1867): 476-511; Charles Francis Adams, Jr., "Railroad Inflation," *North American Review* 108 (January 1869): 130-64.
24. Thomas K. McCraw, *Prophets of Regulation* (Cambridge, Mass.: Belknap Press of Harvard University Press, 1984), chs. 1-2.
25. Alfred D. Chandler, Jr., *The Visible Hand* (Cambridge, Mass.: Belknap Press of Harvard University Press, 1977), pts. 2-4; John Moody, *The Truth About The Trusts* (New York: Moody, 1904).
26. The argument for American exceptionalism is made most forcefully in Louis Hartz, *The Liberal Tradition in America* (New York: Harcourt, Brace, 1955); see also Morton Keller, "The Pluralist State," in McCraw, ed., *Regulation in Perspective.*
27. Calculated from the United States Census of 1900.
28. Quoted in Henry Steele Commager, ed., *America In Perspective: The United States Through Foreign Eyes* (New York: Random House, 1947; Mentor paperback edition, 1948), pp. 232-38.
29. Lewis L. Gould, "The Price of Fame: Theodore Roosevelt as a Celebrity, 1909-1919," *Lamar Journal of the Humanities* 10 (Fall 1984): 7-18.
30. Robert D. Cuff, *The War Industries Board* (Baltimore: Johns Hopkins University Press, 1973); Robert F. Himmelberg, *The Origins of the National Recovery Administration: Business, Government, and the Trade Association Issue, 1921-1933* (New York: Fordham University Press, 1976).
31. On American "in-and-outers," see Carl Brauer, "Tenure, Turnover, and Post-Government Employment Trends of Presidential Appointees," Research in Progress Paper #4 (1985), John F. Kennedy School of Government, Harvard University, Cambridge, Mass.
32. The best existing longitudinal study of a Japanese bureaucracy is Chalmers Johnson's *MITI and the Japanese Miracle: The Growth of Industrial Policy, 1925-1975* (Stanford, Calif.: Stanford University Press, 1982).
33. On quangoes and related issues in Japan, Britain, France, Germany, and the United States, see Joseph L. Badaracco, Jr., *Loading the Dice: A Five-Country Study of Vinyl Chloride Regulation* (Boston: Harvard Business School Press, 1985).
34. On the recruitment of bureaucrats in Japan, see Akira Kubota, *Higher Civil Servants in Postwar Japan: Their Social Origins, Educational Backgrounds, and Career Patterns* (Princeton, N.J.: Princeton University Press, 1969). On the Japanese bureaucratic system in general, see Ardath W. Burks, *The Government of Japan*, 2nd ed. (New York: Crowell, 1963), ch 7

35. The themes discussed at the end of this chapter are elaborated at length in Thomas K. McCraw, ed., *America Versus Japan* (Boston: Harvard Business School Press, 1986), which is a comparative analysis of the two countries across nine areas of business-government relations. The estimate of $1 trillion in foreign obligations comes from research conducted by the Industrial Bank of Japan and published in "Coping with the Trade Friction Crisis," *Japanese Finance and Industry* (November 1985): 25.

36. Ronald A. Morse and Edward A. Olsen, "Japan's Bureaucratic Edge," *Foreign Policy* 52 (Fall 1983): 168, 176, and *passim*. Morse and Olsen add that the bureaucratic mismatches include the presence of the Pentagon in the United States and the absence of any counterpart in Japan. Thus, in their 13 to 1 illustration, they are not arguing about overall levels of government staffing, but rather about agencies that directly affect U.S.-Japanese relations principally along economic dimensions.

PART II

THE ALLOCATION OF RESPONSIBILITY

CHAPTER 3

The Muddled Responsibilities of Public and Private America

Richard Zeckhauser

W hen the citizen takes his new car for a spin in the neighborhood, he will probably travel on roads maintained by municipal workers but constructed by a private firm at public expense. The
vehicle, if American, is strictly a product of a private corporation,
though if a Chrysler, it owes its existence to an active government
financial rescue, which at one time included warrants to purchase
one-fifth of the company. If a crash sends the driver to the hospital,
it is probably a private nonprofit institution, though it could be municipal or even proprietary. His physician's education has been heavily subsidized by the federal government, in large part indirectly
through its support of biomedical research. The medical school itself
may have been public or private but was almost certainly nonprofit
(unless the physician attended one of the overseas institutions cater-
ing to Americans, schools that are most often proprietary). And depending on the citizen's income and age, the government may help
pay his bill for treatment directly; whatever his age, he will benefit
from tax breaks on medical payments or insurance.

Research for this chapter was supported by the Business and Government Research Center of Harvard University. Edward Banfield, John Donahue, Howard Frant, William Hogan,
Nancy Jackson, Steven Kelman, Herman Leonard, Mancur Olson, David Riesman, Irwin
Stelzer, Edith Stokey, and Mark Thompson provided helpful comments. Further work on
the commitment problem is being undertaken with John Donahue and Stephen Johnson.

The institutions that manufacture automobiles, build highways, and provide medical care can be seen as agents working on behalf of the citizen. Would he rather they were public or private? Under what circumstances is one sector preferred over the other? When the framers of the U.S. Constitution defined the roles of government, they could not have imagined its present melange of activities. Government may pay for and maintain but not build; bail out but not invest directly or produce; monopolize or produce in competition; subsidize factors of production, organizations, or purchases. These undertakings do not sound much like what the founding fathers had in mind when they pledged themselves to "establish Justice, insure domestic Tranquility, provide for the common defence, promote the general Welfare, and secure the Blessings of Liberty to ourselves and our Posterity. . . . " The Constitution specified no role for government in assuring the prosperity of the economy or redistributing citizens' income.[1]

Today, however, government activity is inextricably interwoven with that of the private sector in carrying out these two roles. Labeling ours a "mixed" economy recognizes the participation of both sectors but ignores the extent to which their distinctive identities have been eroded. Instead of a jar that contains a mixture of blue and yellow marbles, we have a lumpy soup of varying shades of green. Ours is a mongrel economy. It presents a muddle of public and private responsibilities.

Economic science offers substantial guidance as to where government participation is likely to prove beneficial or desirable. The latest edition of the premier economics text indicates the appropriate roles and limits for government. It "sets the economic framework—laws, constitutions, and rules of the economic game; [handles] macroeconomic stabilization policy . . . ; allocates resources to collective goods by taxing, spending, and regulation when market failure becomes important; redistributes resources by social welfare transfers."[2]

In much of its activity, government has strayed outside the bounds of this prescription. When government builds the city streets, the deadweight costs of tolls and their collection are avoided. Government research on Alzheimer's Disease assures that all will share the costs of providing this valuable information. Environmental regulation helps to cope with market failure. But these justifications do not apply to many established functions of government, such as the vast subsidies and direct payments for health care and education or the regulation of safety in the workplace. Except for the rather substantial military budget, only a small portion of government activities can be justified primarily on the basis that they provide public goods or remedy market failures such as monopoly power and externalities.

Nor have we heeded the lessons of economics in defining the government's distributional role. Redistribution in kind (e.g., subsidized housing) swamps redistribution in cash (social welfare transfers), and the manipulation of private sector activity to promote distributional goals is rampant. Moreover, the incidence of most redistribution is substantially unrelated to the recipients' economic status. (Indeed, so are many of the arguments made for redistributional measures.)

We have strayed from the expectations of our founding fathers and the prescriptions of our economists—not because we have found alternative justifications for a government role but as a result of the inevitable tug-of-war of politics. A dramatic rearrangement of the relative responsibilities of our public and private sectors now seems unlikely. Few outside the academy are concerned with what our founding fathers wrote on this issue, much less with what contemporary economists prescribe. Moreover, as with significant tax reform, there would be no practical way to compensate those who suffered from such a rearrangement. Thus, even though wholesale reallocation of responsibilities might offer substantial net benefits, it would probably be politically infeasible.

Much of the intellectual argument for and against more public or private activity comes from people primarily interested in the overall level of government activity rather than in the nature of its components. In this chapter I am primarily concerned with the composition issue. The parallel for tax reform would be to look only at revenue-neutral reforms. I shall try to be realistic, identifying areas where various arrangements are likely to arise independent of their merits. And, to be frank about my pessimism at the start, I find no evidence of a powerful invisible hand that ensures a desirable division of responsibilities in society.

I shall look at the private (for profit) and public sectors and the understudied nonprofit sector, first as producers of various goods and services, and second as agents for their equitable distribution. Politics rules the government's participation in these processes. Unfortunately, politics is motivated more by economic interests than by economic performance. For both production and distribution, the political process has produced a muddled division of responsibilities in our society. Though the powerful forces that fostered this situation are not to be denied, it may be possible to channel them more effectively. I shall offer some suggestions, principally related to improved accountability, as to what might be done. But on a subject as broad as public and private responsibilities, the selection of both topics and illustrations must be arbitrary. Readers should test my argument, summarized at the chapter's end, against their areas of personal expertise.

FINANCE AND PRODUCTION: PUBLIC, PRIVATE, AND NONPROFIT

Private production is the supposed norm in our society, barring market failure. Because of competition, it produces goods and services at the lowest resource cost. And it meets a market test. Only if citizens are willing to pay that cost is something produced. Once produced, goods and services are allocated to those who will pay the most for them.

Given its coercive powers, the government can produce almost anything it wishes, but the political process constrains it.[3] In the United States, where the belief that public production is less efficient is widespread, government has largely restricted its direct productive activities to areas where competitive private activity is difficult to organize (military and police, patent office, massive research endeavors), contracting for private services would be too costly, or public production will be superior. Contracting is most likely to be unsatisfactory where outputs are hard to measure or where goals and the tradeoffs among them are hard to define. Whatever measurable outputs were used as the basis for payments to a privatized public health facility, it would have a financial incentive to ignore some conditions. Even if payment were made on the basis of lost work and school days and mortality, for example, it would be profitable to overlook childhood lead poisoning, which affects mental functioning more than physical functioning. And it seems preposterous even to speculate on turning over our State Department and foreign policy to a for-profit entity—that might be paid one billion dollars, say, per departing dictator.

Even though government is less efficient in converting inputs to outputs, it may have a productive advantage in some situations because it is trusted. Thus those who are concerned about exploitation of customers who cannot shop around or make informed judgments might wish to see government supply such goods as nursing home services. And those interested in the inculcation of certain values and ensured uniform quality might put the government in charge of primary education. Private operation of the patent office seems out of the question, for whoever awards patents has the power to grant or deny massive wealth on the basis of sometimes ambiguous claims. And when government, following textbook prescriptions, provides information as a public good, it wields a weighty stamp of authority. Economic interests or ideologies may be threatened. Witness the fierce debates over the Surgeon General's warning on cigarettes or the Secretary of Education's recently issued report on "What Works" for primary and secondary education.

Types of Government Intervention

Where the government is directly involved in the economy, the manner of its participation is a central question. In health care, for example, the federal government has supported the training of doctors, has been the major source of financing for hospital construction and biomedical research, and pays for Medicaid and Medicare directly. The federal government runs the vast Veterans Administration hospital system, and local governments run hospitals of their own alongside the private nonprofit and for-profit sectors. Even if we agree that the health field merits government support, it is not obvious how subsidies should be administered. Once we have Medicaid, do we also need municipal hospitals? If not, does this imply that we should introduce vouchers for primary and secondary education?

Financing or Providing as Well. Once government becomes involved, the central choice is usually between merely financing or providing as well. Should government make or buy? Most arguments for government participation call only for financing. The argument for privatization is strongest, it would seem, where competition could still operate, for competition offers substantial advantages over monopoly, the norm with government production. Even if financing rather than production is clearly the right form for any government participation—as in the arts—the appropriate focus of intervention is unclear. Should it support the museums, their purchases or particular shows, arts education, established artists, or struggling apprentices?

Providing without Financing. Of the four possibilities—public or private finance, public or private provision—this might seem the odd case. Nevertheless, suppose the government has an advantage in production. That does not mean it must pay for the activity. State universities and city bus services, for example, could in many cases be made to pay their own way. Rarely does this happen, however. Indeed, if some public objective can be identified—the university fosters research that will boost the state's agricultural production, for example—a generalized subsidy is likely. But that choice may be more a matter of shrewd politics than good economics.

Government as Monopoly. Many of the problems associated with government provision derive from its monopoly position with respect to most of the goods and services it provides. When government is the monopolist, the pricing mechanism is sometimes removed, and competitors can often be legislated away, as with the conduct of lotteries or (partially) the Post Office.

Beyond their power to impose excessive prices, the major problem of private monopolies (or concentrated industries with considerable market power) is an organizational slack that tolerates inefficient production and overpriced inputs. Before the onslaughts of foreign competition, our auto and steel industries built cumbersome bureaucracies and were coerced into paying above-market wages to blue-collar workers, who could thus pick off some of the monopoly profits. Regulation used to provide the protection from competition in the airline industry. Pilots, flight attendants, and other organized workers happily claimed a share of the surplus, which the deregulated industry no longer affords.

Government provision suffers these same inefficiencies, whether in the police force, with its two-officer patrol car, or the Defense Department, with its procurements at inflated prices. Interestingly, where the government competes directly with the private sector, as in higher education, its production technology substantially reflects that of the industry as a whole. The University of California at Berkeley much more closely resembles Harvard, a geographically distant private competitor, than any nearby public junior college, which would serve different markets. Performance seems to depend substantially on industry structure as well as on the choice between public and private production.

Nonprofit Production. Public production may be justified when an activity is too important or too subject to abuse to be left to the avarice of the private sector. Health care and education debates frequently revolve around this assertion. The nonprofit sector is a further alternative with many advantages. Our society relies heavily on nonprofit organizations in the arts, education, health care, the provision of social services, frequently alongside profit-seeking and/or government providers. In contrast to government providers, nonprofits may be insulated from some political pressures. A further advantage, from the standpoint of society, is that nonprofits cannot insulate themselves from competition by imposing a monopoly. Michael Walzer outlines the philosophical and performance justifications for directing resources through nonprofit organizations, which compose what he calls the social sector, in Chapter 4. Chapter 6 on the arts and Chapter 10 on science show that nonprofit institutions have an important role to play as repositories of and nurturers of values, culture, and learning.

Regulation. Through regulation the government sets permissible terms of business operations, specifying the amount of pollution that can flow from the factory, for example, or the price that can be charged for electricity.[4] The intervention is justified on the basis of market failure. An economist would say that pollution creates a "negative externality," that is, one party's behavior hurts another. Economies of scale in electricity production make that industry a natural and efficient habitat for monopoly; the price-disciplining role of competition is lost.[5]

Regulatory activities now go much further. The government specifies how many shoes may enter the country, the configuration of machines in the workplace and plumbing in the home, and, quite important, floor or ceiling prices for labor or apartments. Such regulatory activities are primarily designed to redistribute resources either directly or indirectly and have tremendous capability to do so. This use of regulation will be discussed further under the equity and distribution section of this chapter.

What the Government Counts. The government frequently gets into the business of production because it takes into account more considerations, more parties, than would any private profit-seeking or nonprofit producer. Given the government's pervasive role in our society, it is often in a position to receive a fiscal benefit external to the program but internal to the overall government budget, what might be called a flowback. Given the existence of income and other transfer programs, even a mean-spirited administration may find activities financially worthwhile that could not be financially viable in the private sector. If unemployment insurance or welfare payments are saved through a jobs program, the government reaps the benefit; a private training agency would not. The government's self-interest is well served if the new job holder's wage minus his foregone transfers and increased tax payments is less than his product. Thus, there may be a gain in efficiency when we build the Hoover (Boulder) Dam during the Depression or put potential welfare recipients to work beautifying the city. Frequently, the gains are reaped across time periods. Supporters of threatened teenage pregnancy counseling programs have proclaimed that each $1 reduction in their current budgets will increase future government expenditures by $3 per year.

Sometimes a flowback effect is explicitly noted—for example, the future tax benefits of a construction project—but often it is ignored (or at least not publicly mentioned). For example, it is seldom pointed out that government-supported scholarships that enable students to increase their future earning capacity may pay for themselves through higher tax revenues. Perhaps the supporters of scholarships think it better not to mention their income-enhancing role.

The flowback possibility raises an interesting consideration for federalism: If government decisionmakers are to have appropriate incentives, they must pay for activities in proportion to the benefits they or their constituents receive. From this perspective, the federal government should support tuition subsidies at state universities (because increased taxes will flow from the increased earnings the education produces) but not the construction of hospitals.[6] Unfortunately, substantial flowbacks are widespread. If government(s) intervene in response, there is no logical stopping point to such activities. This implies that in whatever muddle of responsibilities we find ourselves, a *qualitative* justification will almost always be available for present government endeavors.

Industry Structure. Industry structure helps us understand which services will be public, which private. Except in instances of corruption, government production offers no opportunities for financial gain. The returns then come from power (in administering a vast organization), from patronage, and from the security of tenure. The pressures for expansion of the public sector come disproportionately from the people whose jobs will be protected. One could predict that government will engage in labor-intensive production. The city is likely to use more workers to take down the tree at your curb than would the private contractor who removes the tree on your lawn. Computer-aided instruction is more widely employed for training in industry than for teaching in high school.

The most likely offerings for privatization are government ventures that must meet some sort of bottom-line constraint and are losing a lot of money. Amtrak is an example. If the losses are steady or accelerating, the pressures may be great, even independent of service quality. The institution is a drain and embarrassment. (Witness Japan, now considering privatizing its fabled national railways, which lose $7 billion a year, or the many nations actively considering privatizing their national airlines.) Few port authorities, by contrast, are likely to be turned private. Getting their principal resources for free, they are high-profit monopolies whose abundant revenues make them fun to run.

If a government provider is already pricing at market, perhaps because there are private firms in its industry, there will be a natural lid on prices. Pressures from present customers against privatization will be diminished, for they have less to lose. Thus, a fully privatized rail system has better political prospects than a privatized Bonneville Power Authority. Western state citizens will fight fiercely to keep their present below-market electricity rates.

The demand side of privatization is crucial. Private interests will not wish to take over a government operation on which they cannot expect to make money. England thus could sell 51 percent of its telephone system last year, but no one wishes to own and operate all of British Leyland, a major loser. And there are a number of bids for Conrail, now highly profitable. If only a few firms will be able to handle some government resource or operation, they will be able to capitalize on their scarce capabilities to earn excess profits, what economists label *rents*. With rents to be earned, the pressures for putting a public activity or resource into private hands may be great. Thus the oil companies, knowing competition would be limited, strongly encouraged leasing offshore lands, ranchers maintained effective pressure for below-market-price grazing privileges on federal lands, the major hospital chains fought fiercely to take over the ownership or operation of municipal and nonprofit hospitals, and new ventures such as the Corrections Corporation of America incur substantial organization and start-up costs to occupy the market niche of running prisons.

The process, of course, does not completely neglect efficiency. The less efficiently the prisons are run, the more margin there is for a private takeover, for the state could be offered substantially reduced costs or improved performance for the same cost. But efficiency alone might not lead to action without the inducement of an abnormal profit to be reaped. For example, imagine a day care movement initially organized by local municipalities and heavily subsidized. Such operations would probably not be switched to a private activity, for day care is basically a competitive industry in which no one could secure excess returns. Moreover, if the operation were made private, its subsidies would be clearer and more vulnerable. The parents, the customers for the services, would in self-interest object to privatization. The production workers, the municipal day care employees, would also be opposed. The major potential beneficiaries of privatization—people whose earnings as day care workers or proprietors would exceed their present wage—would be working in supermarkets, factories, or homes and would not be organized in any way. Finally, there would be a heartstring argument for public provision. Can we leave the care of our most precious asset to the profitmaking machinations of the private sector, particularly when monitoring is so difficult?

In any industry with competition, we have the comforting belief that natural forces will organize resources in an efficient manner. But the struggle over the division of responsibilities between public and private sector pushes toward efficiency only on a crude basis: Where government operation is most inefficient, the private sector will have the strongest incentive to enter. However, in the most competitive arenas, where the private sector will be at its most efficient, with no rents to be reaped, those pressures will be small.

One Thing Leads to Another: Pyramiding Intervention. Most government interventions, say subsidies or regulatory edicts, create distortions, which may inspire further corrective policies. The price of milk is supported. We get too much of it and compensate by paying dairy farmers to kill their cows. With apartments' rents controlled, landlords, as expected, let their buildings deteriorate. Building codes must be enforced. But then as profits are squeezed, condominium conversion becomes attractive. It must be outlawed. Under such conditions, no one will build rental housing. It must be subsidized. And so government action itself, in addition to the flowback possibilities considered above, encourages the cycle of intervention to continue. Complexity increases; price signals become ever less meaningful indicators of resource cost. And public and private responsibilities become increasingly jumbled together.

Contract and Commitment

Private Actions. When the market turned up its nose at the IBM PC-Jr. keyboard, Big Blue provided a superior model free of charge to those who had already purchased. This was a standout performance among American manufacturers, who have been increasingly accused of producing shoddy consumer products. Replacing the keyboards was not inexpensive, nor do IBM executives possess superior morality. Rather, the explanation of IBM's admirable behavior relates to maintenance of reputation. Because of the extraordinary respect it currently commands, IBM would sacrifice a great deal if it did not remain above reproach.

Even if everyone understands that IBM is "being ultraresponsible" only for self-serving reasons, the system still works. A hard-earned reputation will not be sacrificed, just as a highly profitable factory will not be closed. Many Americans believe that our premier manufacturers have lost their commitment to product quality and to their employees. Once reputations are tarnished, such commitments may be hard to keep. In such an atmosphere, it is no surprise that the government has often stepped in, whether through plant-closing legislation, consumer product regulation, occupational safety protection, or a federally run pension-guarantee corporation. Such measures tend to homogenize the market, deterring the worst or poorest performers but also diminishing incentives for others to rise above the government standard. It becomes too difficult to distinguish oneself. What meets government approval becomes the norm.

Anyone concerned about the performance of the American economy or American social institutions must wonder why reputation is becoming less effective as a device of assurance.[7] Conceivably, the long-term trend toward divorcing ownership and control may be a contributing factor. It is easier to lay off Ford employees when no Ford is in a decisionmaking capacity. To capitalize on the assurance that is brought through personal reputation, both public and private organizations often bring in a Mr. Clean to clear up a messy situation—witness Donald Rumsfeld at Searle or William Ruckelshaus at EPA.

A firm's reputation can serve as a self-denying ordinance that binds it to good behavior. Because employees sink roots and become tied to their employer or customers make purchases that commit them to a manufacturer's service or supplies, a firm will always have an incentive to exploit. But if new employees are being hired or new products brought to market, the bad reputation earned through such exploitation hurts the firm in a wider area. As the growth rate of the U.S. economy, and particularly of its larger firms, has slowed, the benefits of maintaining reputation have undoubtedly declined. Keeping commitments is a bit like depreciation drag—a salient expense only with slow growth. And perhaps even the fabled reliability of large Japanese firms for employment security and product quality will falter with a slowing of that nation's economy and sales growth.

Government Actions. Some functions seem to belong to government because of its unique contracting capabilities. Only the government can mandate participation in a program like Social Security or bank deposit insurance. It is hard to see how the armed forces could be privatized, given society's restrictions on forced employment, particularly where danger is involved. The members of a private-sector army might quit when it came time to risk their lives. But when government runs the military, desertion can be severely punished.

The government is uniquely able to change contracts in midstream in response to unforeseen conditions, though passions and politics constrain its action. The recent adventures of Social Security reflect both the changes and the constraints: A deficit looms and cost-of-living adjustments are reduced, but both 1984 presidential candidates forswear any further reductions. No insurance company would have nearly as much flexibility in restructuring a retirement program.

The problem of the government in committing itself to the future often parallels that of the private sector. In both cases it may be attributable to a short time frame. An administration holds power for only a few years. If the problems of deferred maintenance will not show up for decades, who will choose to spend tax dollars now? But the central problem may be commitment. Rarely is the government able to tie its hands for the future. If a state, for example, wishes to promote business investment, it may have no way to assure that it will not dramatically raise business taxes at some later time. Similarly, utility executives will be concerned that future price regulation may be tilted against them.

The government suffers two major disadvantages in its ability to make commitments. First, it is an elected body and thus does not control its own destiny. There is no mechanism for the electorate to commit itself to vote a certain way in the future. Second, for many important functions, governments cannot—without incurring prohibitive political costs—contract with private parties over long periods of time, say to protect them against changes in regulation or tax laws.[8]

The ability of the government to change terms of contracts after the fact is generally a substantial disadvantage, for it represents an *inability* to commit itself to future action. Firms that invest physical capital in a community are at risk for increased taxes, or, in the Third World, expropriation. The builder of rental housing is worried about rent control. The speculator who invests in a commodity that may unexpectedly become scarce must calculate the likelihood that windfall taxes will be imposed. These are resource takings. The government also cannot commit against noncontractual beneficence—leaving an exploitable opening for heinous criminals who become model prisoners or model defense contractors who encounter heinous overruns.

This problem has long been recognized, and governments have some means of commitment at their disposal. Securing commitment is a primary role of constitutions, which place substantial barriers in the way of change in order to make it less likely that the rules will alter as the game goes along. On a less fundamental level, the need for commitment underlies reliance on precedent in the law. And most deliberative bodies, including our legislatures, rely considerably on precedent, even when they are not required to do so. To the extent that a government can make each decision dependent on many others, the mantle of precedent is spread. For example, concern for the general business climate, which is promoted by most businessmen and many political leaders, makes an isolated action against a single industry an implied threat to others, hence more costly and less likely.

Trust. There is little quick reward for the habitual liar who tries to reform. But those with pure reputations have a strong incentive to continue telling the truth. A parallel argument carries over for corporations and governments, whether the issue is providing full information about their products or adhering to high quality standards. Here monopolies may have an advantage over less concentrated industries. When an American appliance manufacturer makes an unreliable washer, part of the consumer's wrath sweeps off onto the American appliance industry as a whole. An economist might label this a reputational externality. Any such averaging of reputations across a group (i.e., stereotyping), even if done on a careful statistical basis, provides the wrong incentives for those in the group.

There are some ways around this problem. Fewer people would litter if more of us returned their droppings personally. The Japanese, I have observed, internalize their nation's reputation to such an extent that they routinely apologize for the poor behavior or performance of a countryman. We all benefit because *Consumer Reports* publishes frequency-of-repair records. But we would all be still better off if more people read them.

Monopolies help protect us against the reputational externality problem. In the old days, we all knew who was doing a bad job when telephone service was poor. And more than once, the New York Stock Exchange has bailed out a member firm and protected the public. But as financial exchanges proliferate, the collapse of an individual firm may not hurt any identifiable body in the industry enough to prompt rescue efforts. Immediately identifiable entities play the role of monopolies. Celebrities are paid to endorse products for the assurance as well as the glamor they provide. And Tylenol capsules were taken off the market after a second well-publicized incident of poisoning, whereas lesser known products might have been merely temporarily recalled.

The federal government, in this respect a monopoly, sheds reputational externalities mostly to itself, a pattern that enhances responsibility. If Social Security is cut, NASA actions misrepresented, or military strength distorted, we all know who has reneged on a commitment or shaded a statistic. There may be reputational externalities from government actions to future administrations and, for state and local governments, to others at the same level. (If Albany dismisses police when budgets get tight, patrolmen will have less confidence in Buffalo.)

Trust has been identified as a major factor in the great debate over which functions of society should be assigned to the public sector, which to the private. The evidence often consists of catalogues of failures. One side cites the insecurity of Social Security funding; the other highlights pension failures. Equivalent charges are made about words. Have we been honestly informed about military procurement or the safety of the Dalkon Shield? And do mixed systems, such as those that protect our bank deposits, investments in stock offerings, or food supplies, win and merit our trust?[9] Beyond attempting to assign responsibilities to the more trustworthy sector, our nation must seek improved accountability and commitment to promote trust.

EQUITY AND DISTRIBUTION

Discussions of political economy are likely to start by identifying two major objectives for government, promoting efficiency and fostering equity.[10] To economists, equity questions focus almost entirely on the distribution of income. To noneconomists—be they politicians, taxpayers, or welfare recipients, of liberal or conservative persuasion—the income distribution is just one, relatively minor component of equity questions. Thus it is not surprising that when the government becomes an equity promoter, when it pays particular attention to distributional consequences, the redistribution of money from rich to poor is only a minor part of its activity. Today Medicaid payments swamp welfare expenditures in most jurisdictions, and many of the big-ticket redistributions are not squarely aimed at the poor. High-paid jobs in the U.S. auto industry have been protected by American-encouraged Japanese voluntary export quotas, at a total cost to American consumers of $27 billion to-date, or $300,000 a year for each job saved.[11] We now pay $24 billion annually to stabilize the income of farmers, mostly by supporting prices.

With the significant exception of defense spending, most government programs make distributional claims. That is, they are justified in part on the grounds that they provide a good or a service to a deserving constituency. That constituency may be midwesterners or dialysis patients or those who make shoes. Objective disadvantage of the type measured by money may be the alleged source of this entitlement. But quite frequently some other criterion is invoked.

The Claims of the Status Quo

In general, groups that argue they have lost something they once had can make a strong case; their claims are particularly compelling if some government policy has contributed to the unfortunate circumstance. Though economists bemoan such distributional efforts, theorists of public choice suggest that they will inevitably triumph because they are supported by organized constituency groups who benefit at the expense of a diffuse citizenry. In fact, most citizens seem to think that loss-restoration strategies are desirable.[12]

Over the past few decades Americans have come to believe that the status quo carries a substantial property right. Those of us who think redistribution should go to the needy must count ourselves lucky when we can simply buy off the losers, forestalling vastly wasteful protectionist programs to prevent the dreaded change from coming about. But the law or social mores may perceive such payments as bribes, hence forbidden. Even if payments are permissible, the "loser" groups recognize that their power will diminish rapidly once the contended change goes through and that accepting any payment will diminish the legitimacy of their initial, value-laden claims, thus beginning the dissolution of their political group. That is why straight cash buyouts are rarely permitted. If farmers are going under, we shore up the institutions providing them credit. We do not pay premium prices for their farms. Price supports, subsidized loans, and voluntary quotas are the norms, cash assistance the exception.

Distribution to the Poor

A sense of obligation to the poor may not be as old as civilization itself, but it has deep roots. The great religions and many distinguished philosophers have attempted to define that obligation. In recent years, the rise of the welfare state has dramatically diminished the relative role of private charity to the poor. Have we done well through this public assumption of functions formerly performed by individuals or nongovernmental bodies such as churches?

The central economic argument supporting government's conduct of compassionate redistribution is that income distribution is a public good. Even if all nonpoor citizens are altruistic, private charity will result in substantially too little giving, since no individual can hope to achieve a noticeable reduction in the poverty problem through his own contributions. Hence all will attempt to ride free, and no ride will be forthcoming.

Private Philanthropy. Private philanthropy survives in a number of realms, providing evidence that the public-goods argument for redistribution is at best overstated. Harvard University and street musicians have great success soliciting gifts, though few individual donations are large enough to make a real difference. Generosity, it appears, must spring from something other than a calculation of the direct benefit one provides in relation to the dollars one spends. At least three additional forces appear to be at play.

First, individuals may get some direct benefit from giving. It is no surprise when a local charity names an automobile dealer as Man of the Year, or the socially aspiring newcomer knocks herself out raising money—including disproportionately her own—for the children's shelter. Opera and symphony programs list contributors in classes defined by the size of their gift. A number of Jewish charities require public announcements of individuals' donations among their peers; generosity earns the private good of embarrassment avoidance. And the executive who delivers the corporate gift gets credit for his shareholders' largess.

Second, many individuals feel a spiritual, moral, or religious obligation to give. Indeed, tithing survives as an important institution in many churches. Some may help the poor as a way of memorializing relatives, enhancing their likelihood of salvation, or relieving guilt. And for many, helping others gives meaning to life. Third, some people just enjoy giving away money, and some donors are so rich that they will hardly miss the dollars they forgo.

Private philanthropy survives for an additional reason. People are creative in finding ways in which they can actually make a difference in helping the disadvantaged. They may focus their efforts on particular people, by being a Big Brother or Foster Grandparent or helping a family of recent immigrants who are not eligible for welfare. Or an individual, perhaps through a private organization, can become a public advocate, influencing others to generosity or even demonstrating how public funds for the poor can be spent more effectively.

Such activity is naturally more prevalent in small communities, including those defined by profession or ethnicity as well as geography. Private philanthropy has substantial advantages in target efficiency and in maintaining incentives. It need not maintain horizontal equity and can select beneficiaries on criteria the government could not employ. The ghetto teenager who shows character to the outside world will find many to aid him. His sleazy peer will be denied. Early intervention may shape values in time. One white New Yorker adopted an all-black sixth grade half a dozen years ago, promising scholarships to any student who was eventually admitted to college. Because of his initial promise and his continuing interest, these students have had extraordinary success in staying out of trouble and getting into college.[13]

Private giving to the income disadvantaged (a term necessary only because so many other criteria of disadvantage are in use) involves trivial dollar amounts relative to public expenditures for the poor. But because of its special advantages and benefits, it has survived and will continue. The major disadvantages of private giving are that it may be capricious, discriminatory, or ill distributed through simple inadvertence. There is no natural coordinating mechanism to ensure that private giving, however well intentioned, will not overlook some deserving recipients.

Public Assistance to the Poor. The public goods argument described above—an efficiency claim—is the principal justification for making assistance to the poor a government function. Some would add the claim that a society is better for undertaking this obligation collectively rather than individually. And some would argue that collective provision gives the mission dignity. Others would welcome the fact that public redistribution compels even a stingy minority to bear its share of the burden.

Public redistribution suffers three major disadvantages. First, and most widely cited, is the unsatisfactory nature of the process. In practice it is too indiscriminant, too restrictive on recipients, too much subjected to the whims of social workers, too vulnerable to the politics of budget cutting. These criticisms, coming from varying political directions, predominantly reflect substantial differences in views as to what should be done. No government approach seems likely to secure strong consensus.

The most salient consequence of the political pressures on public assistance efforts is that most aid to the poor comes through in-kind programs. Beyond the constituency of the poor—whose political power, though swelled by numbers, is limited by their resources and political inexperience—these programs are supported by the political leaders who create them, the public-sector workers who oversee them, the private contractors who provide them, and the intellectual and advocacy groups who believe in the particular merits of the item transferred. (In passing, it is worth noting that the more resources are required to meet mandated levels of benefits, the better off the overseers and contractors are likely to be.)

How do the poor fare under an in-kind redistribution scheme? Instead of being given a single cash transfer payment, do they do better by knocking on every door and receiving a little handout from each? I suspect not, for the nonpoor seem willing to spend only a certain amount of resources to assist the poor. We might call this the Iron Law of Redistribution. Since the nonpoor control the political process, whatever the poor secure in one area, say through the construction of subsidized housing, they will give up in another, say welfare benefits. If the Iron Law of Redistribution holds, then it is in the interest of the poor to have resources distributed in the most efficient way possible.

The law is overstated, of course. Tin is a more appropriate metal for the metaphor. But certainly some costs are imposed on the poor by a political process that pushes us toward in-kind contribution.[14] Indeed our income tax system, which has little effective progressivity, reflects a compensating stinginess with direct monetary transfers.

Second, government must strike an impossible balance between the competing objectives of compassionately redistributing resources and discouraging the undesirable behaviors that promote poverty. The basic difficulty is that because any government program must rely on objective, verifiable information and must respect procedural safeguards, it cannot reward the hard-working, responsible ghetto youth without giving as much to his or her shiftless counterpart.

Note as well our government's difficulties determining who is truly disabled and hence eligible for assistance. The balance between respecting beneficiaries' privacy and preventing fraud is no easier to achieve.

Third, public redistributional efforts end up promoting the wrong values. Poverty workers presumably have ambivalent feelings about increased welfare dependency, just as defense contractors do about enhanced Soviet military capabilities. Those who benefit from redistribution, and their political leaders, proclaim the justness of the mission and demand dignity for the recipient. As a consequence (though matters seem to be improving of late), there is a conspiracy of silence not to decry the styles of living that are likely to lead to poverty. A climate of acceptance of the roots of welfare dependency is created.[15]

Private redistributional efforts have advantages in all three areas. First, each private group may redistribute more or less as it wishes, for beneficiaries and service deliverers have no official claims against it. Second, private efforts can administer different levels of assistance depending on variables that public efforts cannot consider. Third, by focusing its efforts on the poor who most merit assistance, a private program can show by actions and reinforce by words the values of compassion and the rewards for effort.

If this argument is correct, it is unfortunate that the role of private redistribution in American society is declining. A society that wishes to be compassionate but not to encourage poverty must find ways to reap the advantages of private redistributional efforts in promotion of values and in the ability to make distinctions among potential recipients. The wisdom of Maimonides (*Charity's Eight Degrees*), distilled through nearly eight centuries, applies today: "Anticipate charity by preventing poverty; assist the reduced fellowman . . . so that he may earn an honest livelihood, and not be forced to the dreadful alternative of holding out his hand for charity. This is the highest step and the summit of charity's golden ladder."

Redistribution through Regulation

The further a redistributional item is removed from a straight budget expenditure, the safer it seems to be from political attack. Government expenditures in kind are safer than cash handouts. Programs that merge distributional and other goals, such as fostering mass transit or high-quality medical care, are more secure than strict re-distributional programs. Tax expenditures and loan guarantees are less vulnerable than direct government expenditures, particularly in these days of Gramm-Rudman. So too with government resources priced below market, such as grazing rights on western lands. And the safest of all are government programs that do not involve any dollars passing directly through the till, namely redistribution through regulation.

Through regulation, as pointed out earlier, the government can dramatically redistribute resources. Making osteopaths eligible for Medicare reimbursement benefits them at the expense of physicians. Import quotas shift resources from consumers to shoe workers. Such power has been exercised in a great range of government activities.

When an economic rent is available, whether for real estate or underground minerals, the government can control prices, say, to help tenants at the expense of landlords. A rent can be confiscated indirectly to serve other purposes, a function exemplified by local programming requirements on television stations. (This rent arises only because the government gives away rather than sells spectrum space, a valuable resource in limited supply.) Regulation can get the government into the prediction business—determining the extent to which age should be a factor in auto insurance rates, for example, or ruling that sex is inadmissible as an actuarial predictor for use in computing pension benefits. For protective regulation, such as EPA or OSHA activities, the administrative agency generates dose-response relationships and interprets them for policy. In such areas there is enormous scientific uncertainty, thus vast potential to manipulate multibillion-dollar benefits and costs. Any mandated program of cross-subsidy—be it of the sick by the healthy through health insurance or minority workers by whites in an affirmative action program—represents redistribution through regulation.

The Returns to Political Pressure. Regulatory statutes usually grant broad latitude to the agency. Hence political responsiveness typically dominates the ostensible purpose of regulation, which is often stated as restoring the outcomes that would be achieved if the market worked effectively (e.g., limiting factories to the pollution levels they would choose if they were forced to pay for the damage they imposed, making monopolists set prices as if they were behaving competitively). In environmental regulation, we become preoccupied with carcinogens to the relative neglect of other health effects, for in the political arena (though not in medical consequence) cancer counts many times as much as hypertension or respiratory illness.

Regulators cannot commit themselves not to respond to political pressures. Thus, for example, a power plant once constructed becomes a target for piecemeal expropriation if a future proconsumer regulatory commission refuses to authorize adequate rates (e.g., by not allowing a fuel adjustment charge). But such games become understood. And the ultimate loser is the jurisdiction hoping to have a power plant constructed, for it cannot plausibly commit itself to honor present commitments in the future.

Why Regulatory Redistribution? Why has the government chosen regulation of the private sector as a principal mechanism for redistribution? Why not redistribute directly? First, regulatory redistribution requires *no direct government expenditure*. Rather than taxing and spending the government merely oversees the turnstiles as resources and benefits flow from one group of individuals to another. This approach shields expenditures from the scrutiny of budget processes, avoids contributing to the deficit, and thus dampens the big-spending criticism. In fact, the government's impact in the regulatory arena is many times larger than the size of agency budgets would suggest.

Second, redistribution through regulation accords with *emotional proclivities*. The feeling is widespread in society that normal market processes do not yield a just distribution of resources. The government is the principal instrument of redistribution. Therefore, many find it appropriate that the government should seek to redistribute through its vast panoply of programs. And the popular appetite for tangible results is satisfied: The shoe factory remains open; more telephones appear in the countryside.

Third, regulatory redistribution reflects the society's multiple objectives. Few of the activities described above relate closely to the goals of *income* redistribution. If our objective were to assure the poor a greater share of resources, fairly straightforward ways of doing so are available. But society does not define its purposes and then set out to achieve them in the most efficient manner. Rather, it has many competing goals. Different ones are pursued with varying degrees of fervor in different circumstances. When our sights are set on one goal, we rarely stop to consider sacrificed opportunities to progress toward other valued goals. Our objective function is not only poorly defined but it shifts in shape from one decisionmaking arena to another.

Distributional goals are as compelling a rallying point for political support as is efficiency. They may be readily established whenever someone suffers relative to the status quo, preferably not because of personal culpability. The steelworker who loses out because of an overvalued dollar or an underinvesting corporation and the tenant who cannot afford market rents in his suddenly fashionable neighborhood both merit support under this rubric.

Fairness, Equality, and Equity. Many government programs attempt to promote fairness, equality, and equity in the consumption of particular goods. In the absence of clear-cut, unambiguous definitions, these terms carry adjustable meanings that can be designed to meet the circumstances. One possible interpretation is an *equal price for the same service.* This view has been influential in regulation of mortgages, auto insurance, and pensions. Its proponents argue that people who live in cities, where vandalism rates happen to be higher, should not be charged more for insurance than their country cousins and that women should not receive smaller monthly pensions just because they happen to live longer than men on average. Virtually no one is concerned about the loss of efficiency due to mispricing.

Rarely do we stop to ask whether the owners of urban autos and houses are wealthier than their rural counterparts, whether women are already advantaged by living longer, or indeed whether blacks might not benefit from attention to traditional predictors of mortality when annuities are computed. Much of the explanation is symbolic. We look at the urban and think of disadvantage, and forget that urban drivers are disproportionately affluent. And good actuarial pricing can be dismissed as unequal treatment if sex is the basis for distinction.[16]

Another possible interpretation of "fairness, equality, and equity" is *equal provision of service.* For a growing number of goods it is argued that equal price is not enough; there must be equal provision. This argument is made most strongly with respect to medical care, but it applies elsewhere as well. Some believe it is important to make mass transit available to the handicapped—at whatever expense, however few could use it, and despite the advantages, for most handicapped people, of alternative transit modes. Others oppose the development of the artificial heart because it might become a technology differentially available to the rich.

Many subsidies help people outside the groups that compassion would aim to benefit. Wealthy older people benefit from Medicare subsidies because we believe a means test would inappropriately create two classes of service for this population. Rich students benefit from the low tuitions at state universities. Moreover, if we did the calculations correctly, looking at lifetime incomes, we would discover that college students on average are much richer than those supporting them.

A third interpretation is *fair criteria in allocation.* Quite correctly, we believe it unfair to charge a black more for a commodity or to deny women an equal chance to secure a position. We extrapolate from such lessons in various ways, not all of them logically defensible. First, we may try to eliminate reliance on subjective criteria, which always carry the risk of biased interpretation, perhaps to serve as a secret means to discriminate on the basis of race or sex. Thus we may force loan officers to base decisions on observable numbers rather than on whether a business owner seems to have a well-worked-out plan. Even if experience proves that subjective judgment is a superior predictor, we may cling to the objective criterion.

Second, we frequently eliminate criteria that appear to favor one group over another. Thus, for example, objections to many forms of testing for admission to academic programs or for jobs relate to the fact that certain groups do better than others on these tests. The test, the messenger, must be shot. (A mispricing at the outset may be what makes the test significant. If police are paid above the market rate, as suggested by the thousands taking civil service exams for police positions, then a substantial prize is being handed out with an appointment to the force. Equity claims come to the fore.)

Summing Up. Why is redistribution through regulation so often the chosen method? To borrow a phrase from Willie (the actor) Sutton, because that's where the money is. Moreover, it is somebody else's money, and it is hard to protect. The costs of the redistribution are rolled in with those of other goods and services or jumbled together in an indivisible item. The price of a tariff or quota is not stamped on the product. The person who buys an insect repellent cannot know what proportion of its price arises from the costs that OSHA imposed on the production process. And few of us have any idea how many well-to-do individuals reside in rent-controlled apartments. The magnitudes of roundabout expenditures, however scrupulously calculated, can always be dismissed, just as cigarette companies can dismiss the notion of cancer causality.

WHAT IS TO BE DONE?

In America questions of the organization of society arouse little ideological passion. We have been spared the pains of careening from left- to right-wing regimes, from foolish cycles of nationalization and denationalization. Political sentiment by itself will not be sufficient to change the organization of an economic sector very much.

Economists might hope that our pragmatic nature would lead us to be flexible in drawing the line between public and private sectors, conceivably switching secondary education to the private sphere through vouchers while taking more direct public control of our river banks. (Such an exchange would reflect only comparative advantage. Many partisans would think both activities should be public or both private.)

Any such exchanges seem highly unlikely, despite the good sense of our citizenry, for changes in control come only from fierce pressures. We cannot expect to have much capital expended to privatize a potentially competitive industry, such as secondary education, for it will yield at best limited excess returns in the future.

Over the long term, an unyielding entropy, mixing public and private responsibilities on a sector-by-sector basis, may be at work.[17] In every area of responsibility, from health care to housing, there are voices and pressures on both sides. A compromise is struck in each sector. Since the players differ—and since cash-side payments are virtually excluded—there is little potential to trade off increased privatization of housing for more public responsibility in health care, even if such a swap would be beneficial on net. A parallel argument helps explain why, as we saw earlier, significant redistribution is carried out in so many different sectors.

Prescriptions

In what realms should the government be the agent for its citizens, and where should the private sector take that responsibility? In a hospitable world this might be considered as a question of effective service, of respect for the wishes of the citizenry. But the real world is hostile, for in many important sectors performance can be monitored only crudely if at all. Special or self-interests find ways to be served in both the private sector (through market power) and the public sector (through government's coercive power). Everyone suffers from these failures of agency. Assuming no shortage of sleaze, the shady used car salesman earns a competitive return, nothing extra. And if government bureaucrats' salaries are higher than warranted by their efforts on the job, some of the expected surplus will be frittered away in advance through competition for the position.

If a public purpose is to be served through government financing or subsidy to private production, the implications of this chapter are clear: Keep matters simple and foster competition. Simplicity implies directing payment, where possible, to final outputs, not factors of production or raw materials, and using single payments whenever possible for single purposes. Lump-sum subsidies let the public see what it buys and promote the lowest-cost production of valued outputs. Vouchers for education or capitation payments for health care score well on both simplicity and competition enhancement. Much of the opposition to voucher schemes arises among those who would not welcome an increase in competition.

Unfortunately, the private sector will be most vigorous in claiming or reclaiming turf in less than fully competitive sectors such as leasing oil lands or managing hospitals. The greatest benefits of private-sector production, in contrast, come from the exertion to efficiency that is prompted by stiff competition.

A discouraging conclusion of this chapter is that probably not much can be done to rearrange the locus of responsibilities for production of goods and services in the United States, even if it were agreed that the overall public-private breakdown would remain at roughly current levels. Too many identified parties have standing when it comes to a particular change. Those who would lose too much relative to the status quo will fight to prevent it. This leaves two options: (1) Make whatever minor rearrangements of responsibility are feasible or (2) improve performance within the present allocation of responsibilities.

Accountability

A major avenue to better performance is improved accountability. Today the principal mechanisms of control are reduction in profits or imposition of losses in the private sector (or conceivably an out-side takeover of control) and failure to win re-election in the public sector. They will undoubtedly stay the same. Given that incentives will remain unchanged, better monitoring becomes the most promising source of improved accountability. This does not mean sunshine laws for government or stricter SEC regulation for private firms. Such interventions are usually responses to specific failures, under-taken without much consideration of their broader effects. For example, sunshine laws may lead to fewer written records and more backroom dealing. SEC-induced warnings of risk may so drown corporate prospectuses in downbeat information that no meaningful inferences can be drawn. But surely we would be well advised in the long run to institute a more informative budgetary system for government, including a capital budget and a regulatory budget, so we could know how all our resources are spent, not just those that show up as dollars on this year's budget.[18] This analysis suggests a deeper problem with monitoring for many areas of the private sector. Given the government's intertwining activities in so many areas, we do not know how much we are paying for what we are getting. It is virtually impossible to compute the relative resource costs of an automobile, a coronary bypass operation, or an additional unit of low-income housing. Prices are distorted at every stage of the process, and the direct participants undoubtedly prefer the cloak thereby afforded.

The same concern holds for many direct public sector activities. Monitoring and accountability would be much improved if government subsidies, when desirable or inevitable, were simply paid in cash. This would also help straighten out incentives in some instances. No longer would we build new low-income housing in Boston at $70,000 per unit plus tax expenditures, when existing triple-deckers offer superior space for $60,000.

Time Myopia

The problem of short-term orientation seems endemic to most American institutions, though some, like Harvard University, seem to have escaped that affliction. If agents were merely reflecting the short-term orientation of their principals, there would be no problem. But because some outputs are readily observed and others — disproportionately long term — hidden, society's well-being suffers when attention is restricted to observable or predictable, hence mostly near-term, effects. If the manager could demonstrate that he had really developed a base for future sales, if the governor could establish that the long-term prosperity of the state had been bolstered, and if that is what their shareholders or citizens wished, then decisionmakers' time perspective would be lengthened.

An effective capital budget for government would diminish the enormous incentives to defer maintenance or to sell currently underutilized facilities that might be difficult to recreate later. And if balance sheets for firms included the now concealed value of research and development or personnel development, corporate managements would become more forward looking. Such innovations require no government action. The world will beat a path to the door of the accounting firm that builds a better information trap. If our public and private agents can find ways to inform their principals better, all will benefit.

Unmuddling the Public-Private Soup

I have invoked the metaphor of a lumpy soup of mottled hue to describe the American economy. Responsibilities have become muddled, and accountability has been lost.[19] There would be great benefit in sorting out this soup: distinguishing public and private functions and reassigning a few according to the principles of comparative advantage. The evolving political economy of our nation militates against such a feat, however. It will require forceful political leadership on a set of issues of great import but limited salience.

A quarter of a century ago, President Eisenhower warned us against "the acquisition of unwarranted influence by the military-industrial complex.... Only an alert and knowledgeable citizenry can compel the proper meshing . . . so that security and liberty may prosper together."[20] Today it is not our liberty but our prosperity that is at risk, threatened by ambiguous public-private complexes that secure the production not only of armaments but of automobiles, health care, and housing.

SUMMARY

The central arguments of this chapter are the following. (1) Traditional welfare economics arguments about how activities should be divided between the public and private sectors are not widely understood, carry little political weight, and except in the defense area explain little about the nature of government activities. (2) The convenient dichotomy between public production and private production applies in only a few cases. Ours is a mongrel economy, with public and private efforts jumbled together, particularly in the financing of activities. Even when the private sector produces on a privately financed, profitmaking basis and sells in the private market, the government may subsidize some factors, control the price, and oversee various aspects of the production process (not too many chemicals, not too few minority workers). (3) With responsibilities muddled in this manner, it becomes difficult to determine the true costs of various privately produced goods and services, such as a hernia operation, much less the benefits provided and costs imposed through a government intervention, such as one that leads to the hiring of an unemployed youth. Efficiency is lost because price no longer serves as a reliable guideline. Accountability is suppressed, and it becomes difficult for outsiders—budget committees or ordinary citizens—to determine what is going on. Often this obfuscation is deliberate. (4) Although much government activity is directed toward redistribution, little attention is typically paid to the actual *income* distribution implied. Distributional goals often amount to maintaining status quo arrangements, say for jobs or housing, and fostering equal consumption of particular goods. (5) Government often achieves redistribution through manipulation of private-sector activities. Such redistribution tends to be in kind and off the budget, and its costs per unit of benefit are often concealed. It may well be paid for not by the greater community but by participants in the same sector on a cross-subsidy basis. (7) Effective redistribution to the poor means helping the needy without encouraging the activities that lead to poverty—a delicate balance. Private redistributional efforts can employ screening criteria that will minimize the losses from this dread tradeoff. Procedural rules of equal treatment and the need to be objective hinder public efforts to be deft in this domain. Strongly articulated codes of values may inhibit poverty-promoting behavior. However, articulating such values tends to impugn the legitimacy of present assistance efforts. The leaders in public assistance muffle their voices. Private exhortations have less impact, because fewer dollars are involved.

The battle about the overall level of government and private sector activity will be fought in the hearts and minds of Americans and their leaders. The intellectual discussion might be better devoted to debating the appropriate composition within a specified level, a matter on which we can probably reach some consensus. Unfortunately, there is no automatic mechanism that strongly promotes a desirable or sensible division of public and private activities. If we lack an invisible hand, perhaps the inquiring mind has a role.

NOTES

1. On the appropriate redistributional role of government, the commentary of James Madison, one author of the Constitution, is instructive:

   > The diversity in the faculties of men, from which the rights of property originate, is not less than an insuperable obstacle to a uniformity of interests. The protection of these faculties is the first object of government. From the protection of different and unequal faculties of acquiring property, the possession of different degrees and kinds of property immediately results; . . .

   Alexander Hamilton, James Madison, and John Jay, *The Federalist* (1788); reprint ed., Benjamin Fletcher Wright, ed. (Cambridge, Mass.: Harvard University Press, 1972), no. 10, pp. 130–31.

   The Constitution also gives no indication that government is to play a role in transforming or enforcing values or uplifting the citizenry. Indeed, a strict interpretation of the Tenth Amendment might be thought to preclude such a role for the federal government. Yet in arenas from arts to abortion—a range beyond this chapter—the federal government now plays a central role in such activities and in values debates.

2. Paul Samuelson and William D. Nordhaus, *Economics*, 12th ed. (New York: McGraw-Hill, 1985), pp. 721–22.

3. The political process, with voting as its most visible manifestation, has two major deficiencies as a control device. One, much information is not elicited. For example, many issues are aggregated together, so that there is no way a citizen can indicate a preference for Reagan's economic policy but Mondale's foreign policy. Two, the preferences of the opposing minority, possibly intense, can be overriden without compensation. Leaving aside the potential trampling of values, inefficient decisions may be the result. Mechanisms have arisen in the modern political system to address these problems. Lobbying groups provide information and signal depth of feeling; logrolling takes account of intensities of preference; and campaign contributions reinforce these efforts. It is not obvious that on net these mechanisms produce a superior outcome.

4. Christopher C. DeMuth, "What Is Regulation?" in Richard J. Zeckhauser and Derek Leebaert, eds., *What Role for Government?* (Durham, N.C.: Duke University Press, 1983), ch. 3, pp. 262–78.

5. Despite economists' pleas, the body politic refuses to use pricing strategies (e.g., effluent charges) to deal with externalities. So we coerce through standards. But our society does not accept the use of coercion to provide benefits for others. Our aversion to pricing leaves us ill equipped to encourage positive externalities. Presumably we have too few kept bees (providing positive externalities through pollination) and too many unkempt lawns (radiating negative visual effects and weed seeds). Community pressure and competition with the Joneses helps with the lawns, and positive externalities appear to be more of a textbook nicety than a serious policy concern.

6. The malincentives problem arises in a different form, as we shall see below, if present decisionmakers value benefits to administrations of the future as Worcester might value those of Massachusetts as a whole, say at ten cents on the dollar.

7. See Oliver Williamson's thoughtful treatment in *The Economic Institutions of Capitalism* (New York: Free Press, 1985).

8. Given government's inability to commit, many government-supplied inducements, such as real estate tax abatements, must be given up at the outset.

9. The tort system, designed to assure trust where uncertainty is present, no longer functions effectively in many areas. Massive litigation costs get the media attention, but the greater losses may come from activities, such as day care centers, or products, such as the last nonchemical IUD available in America, that are forced off the market through excessive costs of insurance or litigation. More generally, litigation surrounding business contracts has induced some businesspeople to make legal safety as much a consideration in entering business relationships as economic justification.

   Society's difficulties with the tort system are part of a more general problem that arises because factors are rewarded by resources they shift from one party to another rather than on what they produce. The pork-barrel legislator or import-quota seeking lobbyist is a resource shifter operating in the public sector. Litigating commercial lawyers and hostile takeover artists who abrogate labor contracts play an equivalent role in the private sector.

10. Arthur M. Okun, *Equality and Efficiency: The Big Tradeoff* (Washington, D.C.: The Brookings Institution, 1975).

11. See the *New York Times*, February 17, 1986, p. A16. This calculation relies on work of Robert Crandall, Brookings Institution, on the increased cost per car, and a U.S. International Trade Commission study of the number of jobs saved through the Japanese Voluntary Restraints, each a difficult quantity to estimate. Alternative calculations might yield a substantially lower figure of annual cost per job saved but hardly a number that would seem desirable to most Americans.

12. A recent *New York Times*/CBS News Poll reported in the *Times* of February 25, 1986, pp. 1, A22, for example, shows that in these troubled times for farmers, 50 percent of the public supports an increase in federal spending to help farmers, up from 36 percent a year before. Moreover, "55 percent were willing to pay more taxes if an increase would help troubled farmers save their land."

13. *New York Times*, October 19, 1985, pp. 1, 50.

14. A countervailing consideration is that: " . . . designing equality into some individual programs is a way of creating a *sphere* for the realization of strict equality that is not practically attainable in society as a whole. . . . [This] consecrates the value of equality while keeping its scope within practical and desirable limits." Steven Kelman, *What Price Incentives?* (Boston: Auburn House Publishing Company, 1981), p. 85. I have argued elsewhere that the guilty or socially concerned affluent may be the major beneficiaries of such consecration.

15. Statistical studies based solely on economic variables have difficulty determining the causes of welfare dependency. Publicly announced values, virtually impossible to quantify and use in statistical analysis, may play a significant role. A similar linking of emergent public values and behavior patterns may be reflected in the recent substantial declines in marriage and childbearing rates of well-educated women; this development may also have long-term adverse consequences for society.

   I should make clear my belief that advocates for other beneficiary groups operate in a similar manner but with less harmful effect on values. Farmers, for example, have gotten into trouble by producing too much, and no one is fundamentally misled when the builders of housing proclaim the nation's need for more.

16. In certain circumstances we try to make people pay the costs they impose on the rest of society. When individuals engage in socially disapproved activities that we believe are under their control, charges seem appropriate, both to provide the right incentives and to restore equity. Hence cigarette taxes, through which smokers pay at least part of their excess health costs. Before embracing this argument, we should ask at least two questions: How effective are the incentives, and what are the net costs imposed on society by the offenders? If few smokers stop smoking because of higher taxes, the result of the charge will be random redistribution, and on that basis undesirable. Empirical investigations seem to show that expenditures on cigarettes are strongly regressive, with poor people spending absolutely more than the rich. If so, higher cigarette taxes would have adverse consequences for the income distribution. Such an outcome also suggests that smoking is more likely beyond the individual's control or only partially under his control, an affliction like diabetes. And what if analysis showed that smokers, with shorter life expectancies, actually save us money

through reduced pensions and Social Security and possibly even lower life-time medical expenditures? Would we be prepared to change our recommendation or just the basis on which it is made?

17. Joseph Schumpeter's celebrated assessment of the prospects for a capitalist economic system within a democratic context foresaw the destruction of the system's underpinnings and an inevitable slide toward socialism. Schumpeter, *Capitalism, Socialism, and Democracy* (New York: Harper and Brothers Publishers, 1942). With the benefit of a forty-five year retrospective, it appears that Schumpeter was correct in highlighting the importance of political and administrative factors in the future conduct of the economy and in predicting a much more substantial role for government in influencing the allocation of resources. But a socialist state of America seems significantly less likely than it did to him or in his time.

18. See Herman B. Leonard, *Checks Unbalanced: The Quiet Side of Public Spending* (New York: Basic Books, 1986) for a broad-ranging discussion of the loss of accountability in government spending and measures that might be taken to improve this situation.

19. Edward Banfield argues that the muddle results from the special character of the American political system, the easy access it gives to sharing political power. See especially the introductory chapter in Banfield, *Here the People Rule* (New York: Plenum Press, 1985).

20. President Dwight Eisenhower, "Farewell Radio and Television Address to the American People," January 17, 1961.

CHAPTER 4

Toward a Theory of
Social Assignments

Michael Walzer

H ow should we draw the line between the public and the private
sectors? What goods, services, activities, resources, and authorizations should we assign to the one and the other? Considerable
amounts of money are currently being spent (but in which sector?)
in efforts to elicit some wisdom about the proper balance of public
and private works. I shall begin, however, by questioning the categories in which the standard questions are framed and the simple
division of the world that they produce.

PUBLIC/PRIVATE

The term *private*, it seems to me, is especially unhelpful because its
use is too wide, extending from personal and familial life all the way
to the market, though the market is surely a public place, shaped
by public norms and legally regulated. The word casts a wholly un-
deserved aura of intimacy over the common business of buying and
selling. People come into the market for private reasons, of course,
but they also go to court for private reasons. If we focus on motive,
indeed, even the work of government officials is sometimes best
understood as private enterprise undertaken for careerist (rather than
professional or political) reasons. Self-seeking is as common in the
Congress or the Cabinet as in the corporation.

Public, then, is also unhelpful because its use is too narrow, extending only to the state. But there are many enterprises, undertaken in public for public-spirited reasons, that have nothing to do with the state—enterprises, for example, that are described as *nonprofit* to distinguish them from market activities but that are also, perhaps more important, noncoercive. These negative terms suggest that what we really have in mind when we talk of public and private is coercion, on the one hand, and profit-seeking, on the other. The two are very important, but they don't exhaust the social universe.

We need to mark out four sectors, not two. The first I shall simply mention and leave aside: that is the family, the genuinely private sector, whose characteristic mode of activity and interaction is intimacy. We do make assignments to the family—a certain degree of authority over children, for example (we have revoked the Roman law assignment of the power of life and death), and welfare payments of various sorts. We also depend upon the family for early socialization and, I suspect, for a great deal more. But in the current debates, family life is mentioned only occasionally, in moments of piety.[1] The major contenders for power and resources lie elsewhere.

The second sector is the market, the public setting for private commercial dealings, whose characteristic mode is the calculation of profit. And the third sector is the state, the repository of collective power, official representative of public purposes, whose characteristic mode is coercion.

We haven't yet settled on a name for the fourth sector, though I have already named it negatively: nonprofit/noncoercive. Perhaps this is a residual category—whatever is left in civil society once we have subtracted family, market, and state. I will call what is left the *social sector* and insist that it does have a positive quality; its characteristic mode is cooperation.

Calculation, coercion, cooperation: surely the last of these is preferable to the other two. Hence the anarchist dream of reabsorbing into the social sector all the activities of markets and states. The whole world organized cooperatively; relations among men and women friendly, open, harmonious; all activities voluntarily chosen, without selfish calculation or threats of coercion: This is the promise of a reintegrated civil society. Sadly, the promise won't be fulfilled; there are good reasons for the independent existence of markets and states. Scarcity, efficiency, coordination, law and order, minimal provision—we are all familiar with the reasons. But we should not forget the social sector, for important things still happen there. It is the setting for religious and philanthropic activities; for many educational, cultural, and political activities; for mutual aid and collective self-help (that last is an awkward phrase—once again, an appropriate name is missing, as if cooperation were a linguistic embarrassment). In theory, assuming the residual character of the social sector, these sorts of things require only the non-assignment of resources and authorizations to other sectors; whatever is not assigned remains in civil society. In practice, however, cooperation will flourish only if it is more directly supported.

How should we make the necessary assignments? How should we fix the location of particular activities? My general answer to these questions is that we have to begin by reflecting on the particular activities and the different sectors, on the meaning they have in our society, the energies and commitments they elicit, their characteristic aim or purpose. No single principle will divide up the universe of goods and services. Nor do the principles of justice, whatever they are, determine the division. Justice tells us something about what belongs where, particularly with regard to the market, where all participants legitimately seek to maximize their profits. But in the family, state, and social sectors a variety of distributive criteria come regularly into play, and assignment to one sector or another doesn't by itself resolve questions of justice.[2] In any case, I shall largely abstain from answering such questions in what follows. I am concerned instead with efficient, convenient, suitable, stable, and politically wise assignments; the sole constraint on the assignments is that they not be unjust.

THE MARKET AND THE STATE

I shall begin with the market and the state, partly in order to engage, if only indirectly, recent arguments about "privatization." Given current terminology, *privatization* involves assignments to the social sector as well as to the market, but most of its advocates are really market imperialists. They see profit-seeking, regarded as a voluntary if not a natural activity, as the only serious alternative to coercion and do not evidence any deep understanding of public-spiritedness. Indeed, the market is a useful place (so long as it isn't the only place). It makes for a largely noncoercive coordination of all those activities that Wordsworth meant to describe when he wrote about "getting and spending." I'll suggest a little later what Wordsworth may have had in mind when he said that "getting and spending, we lay waste our powers." For now, it is enough to say that we don't usually waste our money. Things get done in the market sector, and with efficiency; services are delivered, and with courtesy; products are invented, produced, and sold, and it is nice to be able to buy.

But not everything that we want to do fits under the rubric of getting and spending. And there are some things that we might not want to do, but have to do, because of the havoc that is wrought by getting and spending (most of it by getting). Noncoercive coordination is not the whole story of the market. There are other stories to tell—about social irresponsibility and environmental damage; about the tension and conflict bred by endless competition, played out sometimes at the individual, sometimes at the group level; about the people left behind in the competitive race, helpless and uncared for. I omit fraud, extortion, false advertising, and unsafe products. The market has its own remedies for that sort of thing, but those remedies work only over time, across numbers of people; so the state must step in to protect individuals. This is commonly granted, even by advocates of the minimal state.

The state must also be brought in to protect the community as a whole, not so much against particular crimes and local negligence as against the large-scale negligence of the market itself, the sum of its indirect and external effects. Getting and spending are not only self-interested activities, they are intensely and absorbingly self-interested activities. People involved in them don't have much time for anything or anyone else. This is the sense in which they "lay waste their powers"—for people have capacities, interests, concerns, and commitments that are not exercised or engaged by life in the market sector. But they also waste the powers of other people (people living and people yet to be born), *their* opportunities and resources, sometimes even their lives, unintentionally and indirectly in the course of everyday market business. So the state acts to save the others, protect the environment, establish safety standards, conserve energy, retrain workers, and so on, and this too is commonly granted—except, perhaps, by advocates of the minimal state.[3]

And finally, the state acts to provide those "public goods" that the market fails utterly to provide, whose consumers can't be charged for the benefits they receive and so must be taxed: national defense, public health, the economic infrastructure (a kind of market subsidy), and so on. I suppose there are libertarians who favor private armies, not quite on the feudal model, and regard the health inspector with stern disapproval, but the state's role in providing public goods is also commonly granted. It's not the case, however, that everyone who grants these three forms of state protection—against fraud and extortion, against the external effects of getting and spending, and against market failure—realizes the full extent of the grant. A great deal follows once "we" recognize the state as the protector of "our" society and environment, the source of "our" peace and security, "our" ultimate resort in time of desperate need. That recognition sets the stage for a variety of interesting and lively performances, and this is a stage where the performers need not waste their powers. If we are to understand why this is so, I must say a word about the first-person plural pronouns that I have put in quotation marks just above.

Market activity has coordinating but not integrative effects. The market is open to all comers, but while it brings individuals together—sometimes for brief encounters, sometimes more lastingly—it doesn't establish strong moral bonds or emotional attachments; nor does it give expression to such bonds and attachments once they are established elsewhere. The great virtue of a contract is that it connects two people only at the edges of their personalities. It stipulates this or that, and obligates the two only to the precise extent of the stipulations. Beyond the stipulations it doesn't touch their lives at all. But people do have lives beyond: Individuals have attachments to family and friends and also to wider groups of people with whom they share language, history, and culture. It is these attachments that determine the use of first-person plural pronouns. They define the *public* in *public good*, insofar as it can be defined; they set the boundaries of the society within which people seek protection and acknowledge some obligation to protect one another. The market exists, in part, within this society and to some extent reflects its norms. But only the state is its agent, actively expressing and imposing those norms. For just this reason, the state opens to its citizens a range of opportunities for actions more expressive of their attachments and commitments, their social personalities, than getting and spending can ever be.

I don't mean to suggest that men and women don't express themselves in economic activity. But they express only themselves, their private interests and individual talents, and these last only so long as they are conducive to the business of the market. Once we recognize the state as an agent of redress, protection, and provision, we enter a larger arena, in which interests are more broadly conceived and common human talents—for rational argument, moral engagement, and political organization—are more widely deployed. Below I will discuss three characteristic features of this larger arena, which I will usually refer to as the state sector but sometimes, when I have in mind its background conditions, as the political community. (The latter term does not commit me, however, to any strong version of communitarianism: There are many different sorts of political community, some of them, like ours, very loosely structured.) All three features depend, if only in the last analysis, on the availability of coercive power.

Solidarity

The first feature of the state sector is *solidarity*. Though we argue with one another, we act together; we disagree about what to do, but we are all implicated in what finally gets done. More than this, when we consider making assignments to the state, we think about our fellow citizens as well as ourselves; we are led to understand our interests as permanently intertwined, though they are clearly not identical. Here we express the extent and force of that understanding; there is no other place to do so. Solidarity can, of course, be spontaneously expressed (in the social sector), as in the outpouring of grief for the astronauts killed in the *Challenger* explosion. But would the nation have grieved in the same way had the launching of *Challenger* been a strictly private enterprise? What made it a national enterprise, and the astronauts national heroes, was the assignment of space exploration to the state sector. We declare ourselves committed to exploration by spending tax money on it, as if it were a public good. (Perhaps it is: Certainly the men and women moved by the drama cannot be charged for their excitement, their pride, or their grief.)

When we argue about welfare policy, we are testing a different and more fundamental commitment—to one another. How far should we extend the state's role in protection and provision? What are our obligations to our fellow citizens? Should we regard education or unemployment insurance or health care as a public good, benefiting the political community as a whole and not just its individual beneficiaries? How we answer questions of this sort depends on what we think about the political community and the relations of its members—the extent to which we are *members*, not islands only but, in Donne's phrase, "parts of the main." The more we are bound up with one another, the more obvious it will appear that the education of my neighbor's child is something in which I have (and therefore ought to take, even be made to take) an interest.

Solidarity begins—in theory, not in history—with market failure, with public goods strictly speaking, but it extends also to what we might call constructive public goods. What makes for the construction is an acknowledgment of the mutuality of membership. Of course, individuals can buy education for their children in the market; historically, the private tutorial probably precedes every sort of public instruction (though it comes after familial instruction). But if we conceive instruction as a public good and want to make sure that everyone is instructed (and instructed along certain lines, with reference to a determinate set of subjects), we must deploy the coercive powers of the state. We express solidarity by coercing one another, and the expression is possible only if the coercion is. If we could not argue about assignments to the state sector, we could not commit ourselves or measure our commitment to a particular project or policy or even to the community as a whole.

These arguments, I should stress, resolve the problems of assignment only in a broad, theoretical way; the details are resolved more opportunistically. A decision in favor of public education, for example, does not prevent us from inviting private contractors to build the schools or private publishing companies to provide the textbooks. But one would not expect the design of the buildings or the actual choice of the books to reflect economic calculations alone. School buildings should be aesthetically pleasing and physically safe as well as efficiently constructed, and textbooks must express communal values: Here political as well as market decisions are called for. So long as the state reserves its decisionmaking authority, however, it can contract out a great deal of its actual work. This kind of privatization is probably desirable and certainly harmless, no threat to solidarity.

Democratic Responsibility

The second feature of the state sector is *democratic responsibility*. When we jointly develop some particular program of redress, protection, or provision, we are trying to control our common destiny; we are trying to avoid, as far as possible, indirect and unwanted effects (at least, effects *on us*—there are international externalities that are hard to control without cooperation among states). We take responsibility for state coercion because, according to democratic theory, it is only our responsibility that legitimates the coercion— but also because our responsibility sets limits on the agents of coercion. They report to us (they are *our* agents), and we must judge what they do: confirm the assignment, shift the agents, change the policy, and so on. Coercive activity must be defensible in public. We have to be able to look at one another and say, yes, this is what we should be doing, and these are the reasons.

Here is a crucial limit on privatization: We cannot privatize any coercive activity unless it loses its sting in private and becomes wholly voluntary. Coercion is barred in the market sector. I have argued elsewhere, on the basis of this simple rule, against the privatization of the prison system.[4] Rules for punishing people are established in a democratic state by legislative enactment—that is, by laws passed in the name of all the citizens, future criminals included. We are collectively responsible, else the punishment is unjust. Criminals are fellow citizens, and when we punish them we presume upon the fellowship. (When we punish aliens or visitors, we presume upon a kind of guest fellowship.) If this is right, then it is morally and politically necessary that the agents of punishment be agents of the citizens. Though it may sound paradoxical, the criminal is punished by his own agents—who are ours too. Private punishment is ruled out; it is all too likely to be arbitrary, lawless, and vindictive. Only some public purpose that we are prepared to acknowledge as our own justifies the coercion, the detention, the pain of confinement, the everyday power of prison wardens and guards, and so on. Wardens and guards are our representatives, directly responsible to an elected officialdom.

If prisons were privatized, however, their officers would be responsible in the first instance to the owners and stockholders of the prison companies. That would set up what is surely a dangerous incentive system, exposing the prisoners to private or corporate rather than democratic purposes. All the internal rules and regulations of their imprisonment, the system of discipline and reward, the hundreds of small decisions that shape their daily lives, would be open to a single, unanswerable question: Is this punishment or economic calculation, the law or the market? Similar questions would arise if we contracted out of the state sector for police work or public health inspections (unless we made compliance voluntary), or if we farmed out the collection of taxes. Wherever coercion is necessary, so is democratic responsibility.

But there are also cases where we choose coercion for the sake of responsibility, because we want the control of outcomes or the guarantee of participation and coverage that only the coercive mode allows. This is the rationale, for example, for the British National Health Service, where doctors are effectively conscripted for public service—though private practice is still allowed at the margins. The quality of ordinary care, annual investment in hospitals and clinics, rate of technological innovation, and amount of money devoted to research all have been turned into matters for democratic decision.[5] Patients badly served by the system have a complaint, ultimately, against their fellow citizens. But there is this difference between prisons and hospitals: The prisons, sadly but necessarily, belong to the people; hospitals are nationalized by choice. If we sentenced people to hospital (as we might quarantine them in time of plague), the choice would vanish, and democratic responsibility would be a requirement, not an option.

Public Performance

The third feature of the state sector is *public performance.* I return now to the notion of the state as a stage. Men and women who speak up at meetings, who agitate or demonstrate for a cause, who campaign for elective office, who act (as officials) in the name of the people, are performing before their fellow citizens. Democratic politics requires performances of this sort; ideally, all or almost all of the business of a democracy would be carried out in this way. We are suspicious of privacy in the state sector—of mysteries of state, state secrets, private intrigues, cabals, and every sort of offstage wheeling and dealing. No doubt, some of this privatization of democratic business is both unavoidable and useful; it humanizes an otherwise impersonal bureaucracy. But some of it is corrupting, more or less dangerous depending on what is at stake. In general, solidarity can be expressed, the common interest (rather than some "special" interest) served, and democratic responsibility sustained, only if ordinary citizens, and activists and officials, perform in public.

It would be wrong, however, to value public performance only in instrumental terms. It is a value in itself. In every political community there are people who want to perform in public, and there are people (sometimes, in the healthiest communities, the same people) who enjoy watching the performances. Aristotle described the life of a democracy as "ruling and being ruled in turn" because for him the most important political performance was officeholding: Democratic citizens rotated through the chief magistracies of the community.[6] But we can speak more generally of taking turns as actors and spectators. For us, officeholding is not the most common political activity, even if we leave out voting, which is a private (secret) performance, except at meetings where we raise our hands in the midst of our fellows. We engage more frequently in arguing and organizing, and these two are only sometimes functions of office. Some people take great delight in arguing and organizing, and there is a sense in which the state sector is made for them—also, in part, by them. The sector grows through a kind of bureaucratic accretion, but it also grows because we value good public performances and because the performers value our evaluation. They seek honor and glory, or at least approval and recognition, which are not so readily available in the market. Celebrity, which is available in the market, particularly in the entertainment industry, is sometimes confused with political honor—actors and athletes with politicians—but the two are in principle distinct.

Should we expand the activities of the state sector in order to provide more opportunities for political participation—and then for honor and glory? Only if the activities are themselves worthwhile, that is, if they serve the requirements of solidarity and responsibility. We can't just pencil in performances that the plot does not allow. In this case, however, the performers work out the plot, and they work it out as they go along. A democratic political community requires, then, the largest possible number of motivated and skillful performers, accustomed to acting in the eye of their fellows, to taking the interests of their fellows into account, and to seeking honor as well as profit. This argument has been cogently made by John Stuart Mill in his review essay on Tocqueville's *Democracy*.

The main branch of the education of human beings is their habitual employ-ment; which must be either their individual vocation, or some matter of gen-eral concern, in which they are called to take a part. The private money-getting operation of almost every one is more or less a mechanical routine: it brings but few of his faculties into action, while its exclusive pursuit tends to fasten his attention and interest exclusively upon himself, and upon his family as an appendage of himself; making him indifferent to the public, to the more generous objects and the nobler interests, and, in his inordinate regard for his personal comforts, selfish and cowardly. Balance these tenden-cies by contrary ones; give him something to do for the public, whether as a vestryman, a juryman, or an elector — and, in that degree, his ideas and feel-ings are taken out of this narrow circle. He becomes acquainted with more varied business, and a larger range of considerations. He is made to feel, that, besides the interests which separate him from his fellow-citizens, he has inter-ests which connect him with them; that not only the common weal is his weal, but that it partly depends upon his exertions. Whatever might be the case in some other constitutions of society, the spirit of a commercial people will be, we are persuaded, essentially mean and slavish, wherever public spirit is not cultivated by an extensive participation of the people in the business of government in detail. . . .[7]

All this would require an activist, and also a decentralized, state—though Mill's purposes might also be served by a lively social sector. They are not served by the market, and so Mill has framed an argu-ment against privatization as it is usually understood. If we restrict the range of public performance, we also restrict the mental and moral reach of our fellow citizens. It might be said in response that the less the state does, the less we depend upon the mental and moral reach of our fellow citizens. At the limit, why should we care? Even in a minimal state, however, politicians would make important deci-sions and compete with one another for honor and glory, and both the decisionmaking and the competition would be hazardous for ordinary citizens if they lacked political knowledge and skill. Demo-cratic responsibility cannot be sustained unless citizens are capable of public performances, whether or not they actually perform in any particular case. To switch the metaphor, the great capitalists of power must be balanced by an enterprising petty bourgeoisie. That means, as Mill suggests, that a significant number of state activities must be open, available, and attractive to men and women who might otherwise concern themselves only with economic profit. If they did nothing but get and spend, they would lay waste their powers.[8]

THE SOCIAL SECTOR

Activity in the social sector is also marked by solidarity, responsibility, and performance in public, but the communal background to all this is wholly determined by voluntary association. It is not the political community but more particular communities that come into play. Men and women agree to cooperate on the basis of shared ethnicity, religion, political orientation, professional interest, or philanthropic purpose. Insofar as there are many such agreements, as in our own society, the social sector is pluralist in form. And because it is pluralist, it provides opportunities for a more focused and particularized version of a public life.

The state provides a great variety of goods and services for a fixed constituency, the body of citizens. Its program and budget are the outcome of a complex political process that involves struggle, negotiation, and compromise. Most of my tax money (perhaps even my conscripted service) goes for things in which other people take a greater interest than I do. But in the social sector, in the world of churches, parties, unions, movements, philanthropic organizations, and so on, I can devote money, time, and energy to things in which I take a special interest. Special interests are legitimate here. I can join with others, a subset of my fellow citizens, to pursue some limited aim, to work for some single purpose, that I share only with them. I can express an identity short of citizenship (or an identity transcending citizenship) that can't be expressed in the state sector.

Why do we need to take account of such voluntary activities in a theory of assignments? The first reason is an obvious one: A residual category like the social sector is determined by assignments elsewhere. It is also determined by the repeal or reversal of assignments elsewhere. The argument for privatization is an argument for reversal in the name, chiefly, of the market. An argument can also be made for what I will call *socialization*, that is, reversal in the name of the social sector. This second reversal can be made at the expense of the state or the market, replacing public officials or private entrepreneurs with freely associated citizens. Replacements of this sort might be both complex and incomplete—as they would be, for example, if we were to foster the development of factory cooperatives. The cooperative as a whole would still function in the market, but its internal life would be more like that of an association than a company. Hence we might talk of socializing productive activity.

Socialization also figures in the theory of assignments because it often depends upon state subsidies. The dependence arises from the nature of the particular communities that take shape within the social sector. Because these are voluntary communities, without coercive power, they are likely to be constituted by activists at the core, free riders at the periphery. They can collect a certain amount of money; they can mobilize time and energy, which are better than money; but they can't always afford to pursue the full set of activities in which they are interested. And so, if the rest of us think that their interests are legitimate and important, we may decide to subsidize them—with tax exemptions or matching grants or some such assignment of state resources. Thus, for example, we socialize the welfare system, and sponsor an alternative to state provision, when we assign matching grants to religious or philanthropic organizations that run hospitals, old age homes, or day care centers. Half the money is tax money, but state bureaucrats do not follow, as they usually do, in the wake of the expenditure. The managers of these hospitals, homes, and centers are responsible in the first instance to their own organizations and to the more particular solidarity (of some religious community, say) that those organizations express.[9]

When there are many organizations of this sort (in the United States today there are some 300,000 organizations functioning, one way or another, in the social sector), there are many opportunities for individuals to find "something to do for the public." The relevant publics, of course, are smaller than the political community itself; performances are less dramatic than in the state sector; honor and glory take on a more limited character. Still, the social sector offers a "more varied business and a larger range of considerations" than the market does for most people. So it substitutes for the state not only in the services it provides but also in the activities it opens up.

Associational pluralism doesn't substitute for democratic responsibility. Any decision for which the body of citizens is responsible, including the decision on whether and how to subsidize the associations, must be made in the state sector and overseen by state officials. In practice, however, citizens who are socially involved are likely also to be politically involved and to play a large part in state decisionmaking. The first involvement serves as a kind of training for the second. State and society are competitive for activities—not, apparently, for activists. The market, I think, is competitive for both. When Wordsworth complained that "the world is too much with us," he was thinking chiefly of the economic world and of the pressures imposed by the pursuit of profit.

But if a strong social sector strengthens democratic responsibility, a strong state sector doesn't necessarily enhance social liveliness. Associational life requires subsidy, as I have argued, and so it cannot dispense with the state; moreover, even a very large number of associations cannot guarantee universal coverage in the provision of goods and services, and so the state cannot in general be dispensed with. But the stronger the solidarity of the political community as a whole and the wider the range of its commitments, the less important assignments to the social sector will be. Imagine a state different from our own, one that is also a nation-state, whose collective life reflects a single ethnicity, a single religion, a common history. It is unlikely that the more particular communities that develop within that nation-state will play a major role in its public affairs. Class division may take the place of ethnic or religious division and produce intense and particular solidarities, as in the case of European Social Democracy in the late nineteenth and early twentieth centuries, with its wealth of educational and welfare institutions. But these institutions have not shown much staying power; nor were they originally intended to do more than anticipate a future state sector. The voluntarism they generated was supposed to be replaced, and has to a large extent been replaced, by the coerciveness of the contemporary welfare state.[10] In the absence of ethnic or religious pluralism, voluntary initiatives are intermittent or weak—and then the state sector probably has to be relatively strong. By contrast, the stronger pluralism is, the larger the number of associations, the more assignments to the social sector serve to underwrite significant voluntary initiatives—and then the state can be, perhaps should be, relatively weak.

In a society that has neither a single, overarching political solidarity nor a strong set of social solidarities, the market is likely to be especially busy and expansive. Conversely, an expansive market undercuts solidarity of every sort. Beyond a certain level of affluence, at least, getting and spending are individualizing activities. In the past, both work and consumption were social and familial concerns. Today work has been significantly individualized, so that men and women are only marginally committed to the firms and factories where they work. They are highly mobile, individually responsive to market forces—exactly the sort of people the market "needs" and tends, over time, to create. Consumption too is individualized, as more and more people live alone and as families multiply their possessions. The picture of parents and children gathered together around the family radio or phonograph evokes a quickly fading past.

But individualizing tendencies of this sort are dangerous, since the market too requires subsidy for the sake of the economic infrastructure and so depends on the existence of a state capable of mobilizing the loyalty and resources of its citizens. Similarly, because it requires a certain sociability—we might say, a moral infrastructure—the market depends on state schooling, religious training, and familial socialization. All of these help ensure that minimum of honesty and trust without which the calculation of profit is only erratically reliable. Pure calculation does not create a social world: Here is another limit on privatization. The market can pick up the slack when state and society falter, but beyond a certain point it only makes the faltering worse.

The social sector is especially vulnerable to market forces. Virtually all of the hospitals, private schools, old age homes, and day care centers that the social sector provides could be profitably provided by the market. But there are heavy costs involved in this substitution, for its effect would be to disengage the energy and resources of ordinary men and women from associational activity and press them into ever greater getting and spending. Then their only resort in the face of unwanted externalities and market failures would be to the state; there would be no social alternatives.

But the communal basis of the state is also undermined by market forces. And the state is a wholly satisfactory resort only when it reflects a strong and coherent community, only when it can enlist a wide range of performances from its citizens. Solidarity, democratic responsibility, and citizen activism sustain and legitimate its coercions. When state power is naked it is also unappealing. Calculation and coercion do make a social world, but not the best possible social world. Given the pluralism of our society and the relative weakness of our political community, they need to be supplemented by cooperation.

BALANCING ASSIGNMENTS

Social assignments should play to social strengths. When the political community is effective and coherent and its citizens are committed to "extensive participation . . . in the business of government in detail," then it makes sense to assign many activities to the state sector. When there are lesser communities whose members are prepared to work together to advance their special interests, it makes sense to assign activities and resources to the social sector. When society is highly individualized and the market is expansive and effervescent, privatization is a sensible policy.

But social assignments should also aim at a balance of sectors. Sometimes this can be achieved through various sorts of mixed regimes—as with matching grants that join states and associations; corporatist arrangements that give legal or quasi-legal force to policies negotiated among the representatives of governments, corporations, and trade unions; or the commercial sponsorship of cultural activities, itself sponsored by the state with tax benefits. But the pursuit of balance also involves restraining one sector in the hope that another will grow. So social assignments play to *potential* strengths, to the sense that there are entrepreneurs, volunteers, or citizen activists waiting in the wings. If they are waiting, they should be brought on stage. Once again, different balances will be appropriate in different times and places, depending on our assessment of both actual and potential strengths. There is no "correct" balance.

We have to feel our way, and I think this is the case in theory as well as in practice. Theory-in-itself, if there is such a thing, is no guide, though it is helpful to have some theoretical understanding of the three modes; it is also helpful to have some practical understanding. Each mode, of course, has its own ideology (a kind of prepackaged theoretical understanding): Libertarianism is the ideology of calculation, statism or state socialism of coercion, anarchism of cooperation. And each ideology describes its own sector as if it were self-sufficient and potentially all-encompassing. But all such claims are false. One quick way of revealing their falsehood is to list the victims of each sector when it stands alone, with no balancing activity from any other. The victims of the market are the unemployed and the poor and, very often, the sick and the injured. The victims of the state are political and religious dissidents, members of minority groups, guest workers, and aliens. The victims of the social sector are the unassociated, all those men and women incapable, for one reason or another, of joining together or of enlisting the sympathies of those who are already joined. Taken in combination, however, the three sectors provide opportunities for each other's victims. Members of minority groups prosper on the market; parties, movements, churches, and civil liberties unions, organized in the social sector, proclaim the rights of dissidents and minorities and offer them a home; the state provides social security for unemployed and unassociated citizens, and so on.

I said at the outset of this chapter that assignments of resources and authorizations should not be unjust. When we argue about such assignments, then, we should attend to the victims of the market, the state, and the social sector. The ultimate point of fostering and balancing sectoral strengths is to protect individuals and groups of individuals against exclusion and neglect, to open the way for their participation in public performances, in voluntary initiatives, and even in getting and spending. That is also the path, it need hardly be said, of political wisdom.

NOTES

1. Patrick Moynihan is a significant exception here: For some twenty years he has championed the assignment of significant resources to the family. See, most recently, his *Family and Nation* (New York: Harcourt, Brace, Jovanovich, 1986).

2. The four sectors intersect and overlap with what I have elsewhere called *the spheres of justice*, but it's not my purpose here to provide a map. See my *Spheres of Justice: A Defense of Pluralism and Equality* (New York: Basic Books, 1983).

3. Some libertarian theorists would allow state action through the courts but not through the legislature or the regulative agencies of the executive—a distinction I find quite bewildering. See Robert Nozick, *Anarchy, State, and Utopia* (New York: Basic Books, 1974), especially ch. 4.

4. "Hold the Justice," *The New Republic*, April 8, 1985, pp. 10–12.

5. For a useful account stressing the importance of planning, see Harry Eckstein, *The English Health Service: Its Origins, Structure, and Achievements* (Cambridge: Harvard University Press, 1958).

6. Aristotle, *Politics*, 1275a.

7. Marshall Cohen, ed., *The Philosophy of John Stuart Mill* (New York: The Modern Library, 1961), pp. 140–41.

8. On the other hand, they might also devote themselves to their families or sit home and write poetry or listen to music or build cabinets. Mill probably undervalues intimate and personal activities; he focuses too narrowly on "private money-getting" rather than on private life more generally.

9. Compare the interesting case of state-financed political campaigns. Because we don't want parties or candidates to be heavily dependent on a small set of wealthy supporters, we support them (in part) with tax money. The money is spent for particular purposes, which include opposition to the government that makes the allocation.

10. There is some evidence now of a desire to reverse this process. See, for example, Roger Hadley and Stephen Hatch, *Social Welfare and the Failure of the State* (London: Allen and Unwin, 1981).

PART III

THE MIND AND
THE SPIRIT

CHAPTER 5

Environmental Management

Michael O'Hare

I n 1636 or 1936 a book about public and private responsibilities would not have had a chapter on the physical environment. Though the policies of those times produced environmental consequences, those effects were seen as mainly incidental to some other stated goal. We have learned something important: Among the many environments we inhabit (the market, politics, social structures, and so on) none more deserves self-conscious and responsible care than our physical surroundings. They injure us if we mistreat them, and they confiscate our attention and restrict our options every waking minute even more implacably than the tax system takes our money.

Environmental policy is as ubiquitous as environmental consequences. In fact, my wife and I confronted almost every major environmental policy issue when we painted our house last year.

The project was motivated by the refusal of the old paint, peeling and flaking with age, to protect the building structure from rain. Typically, *the physical environment is modified incidentally, even if thoughtfully, by people trying to do something else.* Of course, we would have had no house if its prior owners hadn't taken good care

The research giving rise to this discussion was partially supported by the Alfred P. Sloan Foundation under contract #70-711-9281-2-30. The conclusions presented here are not necessarily the position of the foundation. I have benefited from formal comments by Peter Schuck at the conference; from Richard Zeckhauser, Mark Moore, Robert Reich, and Win Knowlton; from the conference discussion; and from presentation at two faculty seminars at the Kennedy School.

of it. They used only the best paint—which so dosed the backyard soil with lead that we had to replace several cubic yards of it to grow vegetables safely. *The environment is a medium for intergenerational transfers, both positive and negative.*

Choosing a color was complicated. At first, we just wanted it to "look nice." But at least one neighbor thought "nice" meant a peach-pink that made it easy to find the street but required teeth-gritting politeness to admire. There seemed not to be *an objective measure of environmental quality.*

The local historical commission offered advice: Authentic colors for our 1893 house were muted tones with the trim darker than the body color. White was never used. Since every house on our street had been built within a ten-year period and none had suffered exterior remodeling, we felt responsible to preserve a significant environment. But only three or four of our neighbors had thus far painted with "correct" colors. Would one more authentic house make the street meaningfully more correct? We seemed to be responsible for a *common-property resource that would be protected only if almost everyone did his part.*

Furthermore, a few of our windows had been replaced with un-paintable white vinyl-covered sash, so authenticity would not be cheap. And we couldn't help noticing that the world had changed its views during the last eighty years on how houses should look. There had been some progress in chemistry, too. What would the Victorians have done with modern paints? The authentic houses, we had to admit, seemed a little gloomy. Apparently, *historically correct environments are in some conflict with modern life.*

Then there was the matter of latex versus oil-base paint. On grounds of durability, oil-base seemed to have a slight edge, but it dries by evaporation of a hydrocarbon solvent. (The solvent of latex is water.) The solvent doesn't go away, of course, since there is no such place; people would breathe at least a little of it. If paint-thinner-induced cancer has a linear dose-response curve with no threshold, someone would eventually get cancer from our paint job; if there is a threshold, we would probably do no harm. *The consequences of environmental tampering are uncertain and likely to remain so.* We decided it would be better for the world not to breathe more hydrocarbons. The environment, after all, is *a determinant of public health* and *the risks it imposes are often invisible and insidious.* Instead, we treated everyone to a small dose of the mercury-based fungicide that protects latex paint from mildew. *Environmental risks are inescapable; the best we can do is trade one for another.*

We put on some test patches, and several neighbors stopped by to cheer the project along. All agreed that painting our house was going to be "good for the neighborhood" aesthetically and financially. Our paint was increasing the value of their houses, providing *an external economy* that extended quite a way down the block and around the corner.

Now that the painting is finished, people pass by with only an occasional glance. But while ladders and scaffolds were up, a small audience watched the operation. A house being painted is apparently even more attractive to look at than a newly painted one: *The process of environmental change itself can be of value.*

Of all the interested parties, our neighbor across the street seemed most interested in our color choice. Our house is the principal visual element in her outdoor environment, comprising most of the view from her front windows and greeting her as she leaves home. It's only a minor presence for the folks two houses away. *Not all environmental externalities are pure public goods.*

It occurred to us that the outside of our house was invisible to us almost all the time—indeed, we only saw it when coming home in daylight. So we were about to let our facing neighbor choose the color when we saw a television commercial urging us to "express ourselves" with the sponsor's brand of paint. We are a cheerful bunch—sunshine yellow to all we encounter—and if she chose a gloomy shade of brown, it would mislead our friends. *The environment is not only a consumption good but also a communication channel.*

All in all, we felt quite intimidated by the public obligations attached to managing what seemed to be everyone's castle. Especially surprising was how little direction we got from the public sector and how little information was provided to us by price mechanisms. Something else is protecting the environment of my street. In this chapter, I will try to prescribe a formal and informal policy environment that would influence us, and everyone whose actions affect the physical environment, to do the right things. First, I will present the qualities that make for a good environment. Then I will describe the main features of a policy environment that furthers them. I will close with (quite abstract) recommendations to guide the renovation and maintenance of the formal and informal policy structure.

ENVIRONMENTAL VALUE

What it is that makes an environment good defies generalization in the terms we use to describe particular places. Even devising a few simple categories like "city" and "country" doesn't help much.[1] What we try to protect in the rain forest is its diversity of species; what we protect in New Zealand is an extreme poverty of organism types. It might seem that, at least in the natural environment, we want to keep things as they were before human influence. But many landscapes worth caring for are artifacts, like the farm country of New England that returns to unbroken forest as soon as cultivation stops, the hedgerow fields of England, or (the polar case) the gardens of Versailles (Figure 1). No general prescription can be made that environments should be either actively maintained or left alone.

Rather than ask what is good for the environment, we might ask what makes an environment good for people. Certainly the environment shouldn't be dangerous, so we suppress toxic discharges, prevent construction of wobbly buildings, build railings along precipices, and exterminate the smallpox virus. Difficult questions arise immediately, however. We are not so quick to straighten rivers for flood control as we used to be, we don't build fences at the edge of Big Sur, and we protect grizzly bears from people even though people would be safer if we enjoyed all the bears as rugs. And many people seem to seek out intrinsically dangerous environments, like coral reefs, whitewater rivers, or the Chicago Board of Trade.

Uniform, antique, ordered, random, natural, safe—no qualities described at this level of abstraction will provide a basis for policy. Nor will consideration of the moral justification for caring about the environment in general.[2] Whatever is precious in valued environments must be either so circumstantial as to be circular ("I love the boulevards because they are so Parisian") or must be characterized more abstractly. I believe there are such abstract qualities and that they can be protected purposefully.

To find them, I first note that the origins of the environmental movement—then called the conservation movement—suggest economic productivity to be an important dimension of environmental quality. Gifford Pinchot was little interested in preserving wilderness when he organized the Forest Service in 1910; he wanted to be sure there would be trees for us to build our houses with. If we take a broad enough view of the noun *good* (that which people will give up

Figure 1. This rural environment deserves protection, but everything in the picture is a consequence of human intervention. [Michael O'Hare]

something to obtain), we can characterize environmental value in this fashion. The recent history of environmental consciousness can be understood as an expansion of the kinds of goods society wants to include in a grand optimization of environmental productivity, first in Pinchot's time as market products in the future came to be balanced against market products in the present, and lately as we try to include goods not traded in markets.

The economic model provides the critical signpost in the present exercise: It is built on the idea that prices are *behavioral* evidence of a *willingness* to exchange. The idea of value is apparently inseparable from what people do and how they feel about it. We will find environmental value in the relationship between environments and people, not in environments by themselves. I find five qualities that favor positive interaction between an environment and a person. They are *coherence, complexity, honesty,* evidence of a *process*, and *significance.* I will discuss these in turn, with examples, to argue that their advancement is a reasonable guide to action.

Coherence

Everyone hates a mess. Even people who lack the self-discipline to keep their surroundings neat feel better if someone picks up after them. Tidiness makes it easier to find our keys, but it is more important as a way to make an environment comprehensible—to get it into an observer's head so it can be used. Often this is achieved simply by having few things at hand—a single chest of drawers rather than dozens of articles of clothing. But coherence is more complicated. It means the existence of perceivable or inferrable relationships between the elements of an experience.

A conventionally furnished office is coherent: one sits at the desk in the chair and writes on the paper. A single concept comprises three major elements. The humor of the fraternity prank in the movie *Animal House* lies in the dead horse's incoherence with the dean's office; the horse has nothing to do with anything around it, and the joke is enriched by the appearance of a chain saw, which has the same non-relationship to the horse in conventional expectation as the horse to the desk.[3] I mention a humorous example here for two reasons. First, it is notable that humor pales quickly. We cannot savor a joke for an extended period, and it is no accident that architecture is the art form worst served by humor. A funny building becomes irritating outside the evanescent experience of a roadside or an amusement park. Second, it is only the coherence of the dean's office that makes the horse funny. A dead horse on a junk pile, or even in a bustling marketplace where some coherence has been obscured by complexity and process, is just a dead horse. Rather than beat it further, let us turn to the individual consumer's contribution to environmental coherence.

If we try hard enough, we can nearly always see some relationship between two or more things. What makes an environment coherent is that the relationships be deep or meaningful. Surely one of the most coherent, integral environments in the world is the tropical rain forest. Not only are the links among its inhabitants, climate, and soil profound, having to do with nourishment and reproduction, but they are also astonishing and instructive. These links reveal themselves to an observer who has an idea what to look for, even one whose training consists of a few "Life on Earth" episodes. But the unprepared observer, after a gasp of awe at the density of vegetation, will just see a mess. Unless we have some idea of what relationships exist or might be sought, a complex environment will be off-putting or trivial, much as the dean's office would be incoherent for a Martian who never sat or wrote.

Coherence is thus a joint product of the observer's sophistication and the environment's intrinsic properties. At least some incoherent environments become coherent without physical alteration as we come to understand how they work. To preserve or create environments that are potentially coherent in this sense requires that environmental policy be made and implemented by environmentally knowledgeable citizens or through a conscious deferral to expertise. But to experience coherent environments, we must acquire some expertise ourselves. Ignorance of this principle leads to a demand that "the environment itself" be coherent, and for an unsophisticated consumer this can only be simulated, usually by trivial relationships between the parts. The novice at home decoration buys everything in the same two colors; the novice planning board demands all buildings to be in what is called a single architectural "style"; the novice city planner ordains neighborhoods of a single kind of land use; and the novice civil engineer tries to make everything flat and dry (Figure 2).

Figure 2. Coherence without complexity: This environment is boring because the relationships between its parts are few and simple. [Stock Boston/Peter Menzel]

Complexity

Environments in which coherence is sought by suppressing variety rather than furthering meaningful relationships are boring because they lack complexity. Complex environments allow an extended and challenging interaction with their users and are not easily or quickly "used up." The rain forest will serve again in the narrowest economic sense: It's worth protecting if only because so many different things live in it that might yield materials, chemicals, or scientific knowledge. But even an environment that probably can't be exploited for market goods can be valuable on account of complexity; scarce as life is, and like each other as sand grains are, we know that careful attention to a desert will show us more and more illuminating interactions and relationships between its elements.

Architects and critics have long recognized the importance of complexity in the built environment[4] even as they deplore the unplanned growth of cities. Note that coherence and complexity are not poles between which to seek a happy medium, but complements. Good environments are strong in both dimensions. As an illustration, it is appropriate on this anniversary to note the Harvard campus, with all its wrong turns and bad guesses still one of the best in the world. It is for the most part a set of courtyards, formed by brick buildings of similar (walk-up) size (Figure 3). So is the nearby Cambridge housing project Washington Elms (Figure 4). Why is Harvard wonderful and Washington Elms mediocre?

In essence, the difference is that Harvard's underlying coherence is a background (1) that can be perceived per se and (2) against which differences and variety are perceived, while Washington Elms is nothing but background. Harvard's buildings are alike enough in materials, scale, and texture for differences to be meaningful, and different enough to be worth attention. The variety among buildings visible from a single place signals the viewer that this environment will deliver a new, but not incomprehensibly different, message from the next place, and the cornerwise connection of the courtyards makes every view from one space to the next a challenge: "There is something interesting here that you can't see unless you come over and have a look."

The visual complexity that enriches the campus is, furthermore, present at several scales. Not only do we have the contrast of distinctly different brick walk-ups (Figures 5 and 6), but the buildings also exhibit remarkable variety in their use of similar elements.

Figures 3 (above) and 4 (below). Harvard Yard and a nearby public housing project. Both superficially an arrangement of brick walkups around courtyards, but the former exhibits the kind of complexity that makes the built environment worth attending to. [Harvard News Office; Michael O'Hare]

Figures 5 and 6. Sever and Massachusetts Halls, Harvard University. Both function as background through consistency of materials, size, and concept with the other yard buildings, but each offers a distinctive experience. [Harvard News Office]

Figure 7. All these Harvard windows are apertures in a brick wall, and are glazed with multiple lights, but the ensemble displays an extraordinary complexity. [Michael O'Hare]

a   b   c

f   g   h

Figure 7. continued

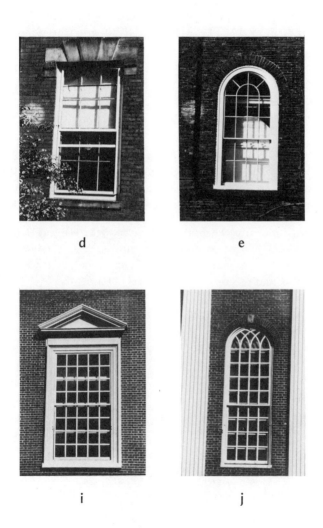

d

e

i

j

Floors are detailed differently; window sizes change; roofs pop up and down; chimneys are now close, now far apart; brick courses corbel out and panels withdraw (Figure 7). Even the bricks manage to present both long and short faces in the typical Flemish bond, and no two are quite alike in color or shape.[5] Finally, a few special cases punctuate the pattern by departing from it in many dimensions at once. Some of these high-stakes experiments fail, like William James Hall; some succeed brilliantly, like Memorial Hall and the Science Center.

The complexity that enlivens Harvard isn't merely visual: The middle of the Harvard campus is a tangle of commercial, civic, and academic activities that has both a sharp division from the academic environment (along Massachusetts Avenue) and a fuzzy one (to the south).

In summary, the variety of things people do at Harvard is mirrored by the physical fabric. This reflection is sometimes deliberately suppressed in favor of other environmental virtues, as at Northeastern University (Figure 8). Whether a physical environment completely

Figure 8. Northeastern University, where the architects of the Harvard Houses (Shepley, Bulfinch) have emphasized coherence, perhaps too much, and hidden the variety and complexity of college life. A commuter school, Northeastern may be well served by this emphasis on unity. [Michael O'Hare]

reflects the society it shelters is usually, but not always, an indicator of environmental quality. It may be appropriate to restrict an environmental message to a few important dimensions of behavior or values. But an environment that misrepresents its source, or accurately reflects a dishonest life, lacks the third environmental merit in my list.

Honesty

An overgrown garden and the City of Mahagonny are complex but certainly not admirable; we must distinguish an environment that we don't understand completely yet from one that we don't want to understand or can't. The latter cases usually evidence what I call dishonesty, choosing the word to emphasize the importance of environments as communication processes.[6] We want to trust an environment to yield some benefit, and not a trick or disillusionment, if we attend to it. In natural environments, honesty is usually a matter of authenticity or originality; because of the inexorable pressure of natural selection, unspoiled environments are what they reveal themselves, to a sophisticated observer, to be. In the built environment, honesty is a more complicated idea.

A relatively unexamined part of my professional training was the interpretation of modern architecture as a reaction against a dishonest and reprobate Beaux-Arts tradition. Like most of my cohort, I became uneasy with this view as we came to appreciate the wit and complexity of the few Beaux-Arts buildings we Americans have, especially when they were at risk. The destruction of Pennsylvania Station called forth no joyous mob of architects to help demolish an infamous lie. Certainly the visual vocabulary of Stanford White was an anachronism, either five or twenty centuries wrong, and the load-and-support relationships in a Beaux-Arts facade had nothing to do with the steel beams that actually held it up. But these mismatches and dissemblings aren't that different from painted wood or from the organization of a facade into windows of the same size serving varying room sizes—surely not grounds for moral outrage or a revolution. Also, the visual vocabulary of the Beaux-Arts tradition could capitalize on its coherence with a long-familiar tradition and with its neighbors to make visible a complex reinterpretation of the convention.[7]

Only when I eventually saw Vienna did I realize what Josef Hoffmann and Adolph Loos were about.[8] Nineteenth-century Vienna mirrored the fundamental dishonesties of the empire it glorified. A desperate mishmash of borrowed styles was troweled across buildings that had nothing to do with the originals—here a multistory municipal office building in the garments of a Gothic cathedral, there a Parliament building wrapping democratic behavior in the skin of a temple (what could be more autocratic than a Greek God?) (Figure 9), down the road a theater where acoustics and sightlines were abandoned so the auditorium plan could be lyre-shaped in honor of Greek theater. (The troweling wasn't merely figurative, either; much of the stone is stucco and paint. Unfortunately, the illusion is so skillfully achieved that once the fakery is discovered in a single case, all buildings, real and simulated, are suspect. The material dishonesty in this case debases the entire architectural currency.)

What I saw was a stage set in which the environmental authorities tried to give a crumbling alliance of fumbling leaders the appearance of empire, civic stability, and temporal clout. Franz Joseph had

Figure 9. Parliament Building, Vienna; 1873–83, Theophil Hansen. The visual language of this building is completely detached from its function, its symbolic intention, and the buildings with which it forms an urban environment. [Michael O'Hare]

plenty of clothes; it's the fact that he wasn't really an emperor that made his parade ludicrous. The contrast between Vienna and contemporaneous official London characterizes the difference between a dishonest and honest urban environment at a level beyond atomistic verity. The anachronistic, symbolically confused, British Parliament building is tolerable where the anachronistic, symbolically confused Austrian one is not because nineteenth-century London generally manifested the reasonable aspirations of a city that governed a real empire rather than the insupportable illusion of ceremony.

I don't want to push this example into serving as a proof. Modern movements were under way in other countries and other media. Still, what made the Viennese pioneers admirable was their ability to see the *fundamental* dishonesty of their visual world at the time, and without having Professor Sekler[9] to explain it to them. Rachel Carson's contemporary insight that the air and the water were becoming a lie is exactly analogous.[10] Chemicals that were supposed to make the environment better serve us were making it dangerous to breathe or swim and denying us the birds that made the natural environment worth attending to. Exactly as the deception of the stage changes from delightful to outrageous when it becomes inescapable, pesticides that usefully interrupted the food chain of life under the sink became outrageous when they made the prey of falcons poisoned bait rather than food. It is not only the literal danger of pollution that drives current toxic waste policy, but also the invisibility of the risk and the consequent threat that the environment will become dishonest.

Process

It is impossible to think about the Harvard campus apart from the idea of walking around in it. The process of experiencing an environment is surely an intrinsic part of a place. Equally important is the process of creating an environment; insofar as "how this happened and what will happen next" can be perceived from a place itself, that environment is allowing an interaction that we value highly.

The little town of Rothenburg-ob-der-Tauber in Germany somehow escaped not only the massive destruction of the Thirty Years' War but also most events of the ensuing three centuries. It has been restored to the last nail and cobblestone as a tourist attraction—a

Figure 10. Rothenburg-ob-der-Tauber, a town "restored" to the late Middle Ages. Halting the process of environmental evolution paradoxically undermines the illusion intended. [Michael O'Hare]

"living museum"—with deeply paradoxical effect. What the visitor sees is a brand new late-medieval town (the Renaissance was slow to affect rural Swabia); not a Disneyland fake, but the "real" thing (Figure 10). But what is a brand-new medieval town?

It is, oddly, like nothing that has ever been. It is especially not like medieval Rothenburg, for two reasons. (These do not include the presence of tourists or even the yellow Kodak signs and tour buses, which are easy to tune out.) First, at any moment in the Middle Ages, Rothenburg had some new parts and some old ones. Among the shiny new masonry houses with sharp-cornered stones and crisp mortar joints were wooden houses a hundred years old, weathered and splintery. Some streets had newfangled paving stones, but most were mud tracks. The new church was under construction, but down the block was the Merovingian one, steps already worn smooth and walls soot-blacked above the candles. What has been preserved in Rothenburg is only those parts of that complicated tapestry that survived—as is true in the old parts of any city—shorn of the new parts that would have replaced the old as they disappeared had the town enjoyed a continuing economic life. Furthermore, the restoration has made everything the same age (new): the result is a sort of conjecture of what a medieval boomtown would have looked like, all built at once. Finally, time has been stopped; nothing else will be permitted to happen. The restoration, in trying to preserve an environment, destroyed it by (1) concealing the process by which it came to be, and (2) preventing the future in which it would become something else.

The second reason the experiment fails—why Rothenburg isn't a real anything—is that we could not see what the Rothenburger of 1550 saw, even if the restoration *had* magically recreated it as it was. We note what is different from what we know—the small windows, the stone carving, the narrow streets, the peaked roofs. He saw all this as background, unremarkable components of the generic idea *town*, and noted instead the wide new main street, the disappearance of Frau Wittel's sow at Christmas time, and the remarkable grandeur of the mayor's windows. The use of an environment is a process that inseparably combines the experience of the user with the "objective" stimulus, and it occurs inside the user's head. Many alumni who love Harvard's Memorial Hall could not name its architects, and some haven't noticed the degree of its departure from the campus pattern; what makes it valuable to them is their association with it on characteristic occasions like taking examinations, giving blood, and registering for courses (Figure 11).

Both notions of process—developmental and experiential—also inform the idea of value for the natural environment. The round, water-tumbled stones in a riverbed, the broad leaves of the understory shrubbery, and a rabbit's big ears evidence processes that connect once to now and now to the future. In the rain forest of the Pacific Northwest, trees sometimes grow in perfectly straight rows a hundred feet long: They are the tombstones of their grandmother, on whose fallen trunk their seeds found a ten-foot head start toward the light that allowed them to overshadow their cousins who had to start growing on the ground (Figure 12).

But just knowing about a nurse tree or being told "all about" the rain forest won't do. We want also to be able to go there, walk around in it, step on the moss, see the sun barely reach the ground, feel the rain fall, and know ourselves to have come out of the woods (or the desert, or Central Park, or Trafalgar Square) changed somehow by the experience.

Figure 11. Memorial Hall, Harvard University, Ware and Van Brunt 1872. Experiences like this examination are an intrinsic part of the building in the recollections of alumni. [Harvard News Office]

Figure 12. Nurse tree, Washington State. Seedlings growing on this trunk will outcompete neighbors starting on the ground, producing a row of trees that manifest the process of light-competition in the rain forest. [Mark Harmon]

Significance

Such a change is the result of significance. An environment, as I have argued, speaks to us. But what does it say, and so what? An environment can signify in three ways, depending on whether we are thinking about it (or using it to think with), experiencing it, or are part of its process of change. As to the first, consider that most seductive and poignant environment, the seashore. We can hear

> . . . the grating roar
> Of pebbles which the waves suck back, and fling,
> At their return, up the high strand,
> Begin, and cease, and then again begin.[11]

Sophocles thought that sound spoke of the "ebb and flow of human misery," and told Matthew Arnold; Arnold hears the "melancholy, long, withdrawing roar" of the sea of faith and tells us. Johnny Green covered the waterfront at his most wistful;[12] Nevil Shute describes the end of the world there.[13] It is the place of beginnings and endings, of the amphibious conquest of land and of shipwrecks. It puts our footprints in the perspective of something awesome and measures our time against a cosmic rhythm.

The environment here is not only a source of meaning, but a language and thus to be prized, like all languages, as our most precious common property resource. As metaphor, it provides a set of experiences widely shared that help us use paint, poetry, even music to communicate with each other. It is Arnold's direct experience of Dover Beach and Sophocles' walk along the Aegean that allowed Sophocles to get his message to the nineteenth century. At the least, we may wish to protect our access to such common experiences for this reason.

A second communicative role is played by the built environment and our stewardship of everything else: The environment tells us about each other and ourselves. The mine tailing heaps of Appalachia are as eloquent as the most self-conscious Viennese prince's palace facade (Figure 13). We didn't "mean" to make a wasteland, just to keep our houses warm. But perhaps if we make a point of keeping warm without making wastelands, we will not only seem like better people, but be better. It is in this sense that the significance of an environment ought most to bear on our valuation of it.

Figure 13. The environmental process described by this landscape is strip mining without restoration. The result tells us how we feel about energy, amenity, and our children. [Stock Boston/Elizabeth Hamlin]

124 / THE MIND AND THE SPIRIT

Finally, an environment tells us, if we listen, how it should be modified or used. This third set of signals should be heeded by coal operators, architects, and house painters as both a moral and a practical guide. It was the kinds of variety, and the kinds of consistency, that already existed on our street that showed my family what options for painting were appropriate to choose among. It is the ensemble of completed buildings on the Harvard campus that tells the next architect what vocabularies, in that place, will be understood, what will be gibberish, and what innovations in the existing language would enrich the opportunities of the *next* next architect. Paradoxically, creation requires an environment in which, because some properties are present, others are not. If anything is possible, nothing is worth doing; if you didn't have an environment, you couldn't have a self! [14]

The natural environment is every bit as communicative. To put summer houses on barrier beaches, whose coherence is in their form and not their location, which changes from year to year, is to turn a deaf ear to the guidance a sand dune provides about its own relationship to human welfare. Massive irrigation of the desert, which leads to salinization and costs a fortune, and clear cutting of the tropical forest, the fertility of whose soil depends on a cyclic transformation of the trees, are only two more examples of the sort of mistake the natural environment warns us against.

PUBLIC AND PRIVATE RESPONSIBILITIES

Among the five qualities of good environments that I think we should further, two—process and significance—highlight the means by which to do so. Since our interaction with the environment affects it, ourselves, and each other, we should treat it as a "social sector" in the sense described in Chapter 4—a control and coordination mechanism intermediate between formal government and individual, self-regarding competition. It follows that the influence acts both ways; the title of this chapter is intended to describe management both of and by the environment. We have a duty to guide the development of the environment through both our myriad kinds of collective public actions (building codes, antipollution laws, and all the rest) and equally important private contributions (no conceivable collective action alone could create Harvard Square, though many wrongheaded collective policies could prevent it). But we have an exactly equivalent duty to be guided by the environment as it stands now, listening carefully to the messages it transmits from other people (in the built environment) and from something larger (in nature) and trying to discern the messages it is best equipped to carry from us to the future.

Though atrocious environments have been created, Americans live in a richer variety of excellent physical surroundings than anyone in the world and have constructed—or preserved—this cornucopia in only three centuries (just one in the far West). The state of the environment allows us to exploit the valuable resource of "no crisis." We can take the time to develop environmental policies for a splendid 500th Harvard birthday. What should their essential qualities be? What would make the physical world more complex, more significant, more coherent, more honest, and more eloquent about its future, its past, and us?

I will call the guiding principle for our public and private actions a *managerial* style to distinguish it from command, technocracy, passivity, and preservation. I mean to encompass management of both the physical environment in which we go about our various business and the policy environment in which we act upon the physical world.

Three characteristics define a managerial style by reference to the relationship between a manager (person or institution) and individuals in an organization. First, the central activity of management is information transfer that has only partly predictable effects on what a polity or its members produce. Second, choices are made with conscious attention to their implications for a dynamic future (not arrival at a finished world) and the constraints of a dynamic past (not correction of particular errors). Third, policy is directed not only at an environment but also at its inhabitants; the managerial task is to make better people and a better people, not just better environments.[15]

I see five especially important opportunities to observe these principles better.

Cost Focus. Instead of managing the environment through a continuous flow of information to and from the people who affect it and will go on doing so, we frequently try to ordain a specific result. This teleological-command fallacy focuses our attention on changes that can be described confidently and precisely, and these tend to be avoidable costs rather than latent benefits. Our attention is riveted on apparently exclusive choices between making "mere" economic goods like food or timber and protecting something already in place. Largely as a result of overreliance on regulatory mechanisms, we seem endlessly preoccupied with preventing people from building too close together, stopping wasteful use of public funds, avoiding forest fires, protecting ourselves against pollution or floods, and arresting neighborhood decline.

These are worthy goals, to be sure. But it is not possible to create something glorious, especially something new and glorious, by avoiding harm. We are sacrificing the good we haven't thought of yet, but could if we tried, in deference to the bad we are almost too good at conjecturing. This is so for two reasons. First, virtually any innovation involves some risk of bad outcomes. Frost-protective bacteria could help feed us and create attractive agricultural environments beyond their current climatic range—but they might do all sorts of scary things if they were to get loose.[16] Cost obsession systematically inflates the importance of these risks. Second, preoccupation with damage diverts attention from new possibilities and engenders misallocation of the most fundamental scarce resource, which is human thought.

Health Primacy. The cost most overemphasized by public policy is damage to physical health. (Private behavior is better balanced.) Occupational exposures certainly put specific, rather small, groups of people in unnecessary danger, and to hurt people for no reason is deplorable. But average life expectancy in America is so near the point at which diffuse aging processes dominate everything else that no major advances in average environmental health can be expected, even if we could magically cleanse the earth, air, and water of all pollution and hazards. Indeed, once the drinking water is separated from the sewage and the cigarette smoke excluded from the lungs, aggregate environmental health improvements are very hard to make; we always have to give up something that makes life worth living to get a little more life.

Americans are already paying too much for physical safety in some cases. The Riva degli Schiavone is a wide street (sidewalk) in Venice, bordered on one side by hotels, restaurants, and shops and on the other by the lagoon (Figure 14). Occasionally a cruise ship will tie up right at the curb. It has no railings; there are a couple of slippery stone steps and then water. You can sit in a cafe and watch

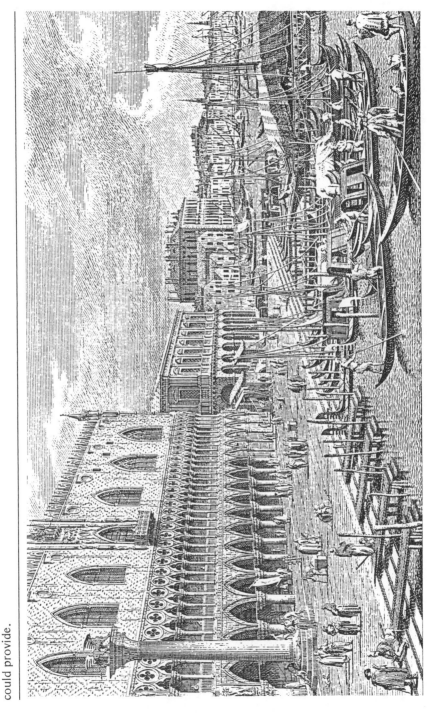

Figure 14. The Riva degli Schiavone, Venice, in a Canaletto view engraved by Visentini in 1742. (The broad sidewalk has since been extended several blocks to the east.) Here, the aesthetic experience of the lagoon is preferred to the safety a railing could provide.

the strollers, the boats, and the lights on the water; it's one of the most beautiful streets in the world. In this country, such a public hazard would be abated by a railing or parapet at least waist-high and dense enough to contain a suicidal child, at significant aesthetic cost.

As far as I can tell from a survey of shopkeepers and two *carabinieri*, no one ever falls off it. But I think the experience of the Riva degli Schiavone on a summer evening, for Venetians and tourists alike, is worth the chance that someone will fall in, and the further chance that he or she won't be pulled out in time. I hope I will be in Venice again to take that chance, even when I am old and infirm. This view may seem harsh. But if you would sacrifice the view for the safety, consider whether any safety is really obtained. Perhaps people now recognize the risk and protect themselves, by being careful where and how they walk, just as well as a fence could.

Might not a fence be even more dangerous than the curb? People lean on railings by habit and railings eventually rust out and become weak. We can endanger people by seeming to promise that the built environment will always substitute for private caution. Would we be safer from coastal flooding, for example, if homeowners knew that they built on barrier beaches at their own risk and would not be given groins, sea walls, and disaster loans?

Defining the appropriate level of protection from environmental hazard is even more complicated if we consider the cost we really want to minimize to include not merely accidents and injury but also anxiety about them.[17] Just as the coward dies a thousand deaths, environmental hazards injure us every time we are reminded of their presence. The railing is reassuring, of course, obviating concern about the slippery steps. But it replaces a simple hazard, which can be dealt with subconsciously by a resolution not to walk too near the edge, with a set of more complicated and persistent fears: Will my child try to climb on it? If I lean over (as railings always invite one to do), will a prankster push me from behind? Is it strong enough to lean on? for three of us to lean on at once? Protection against risks we can handle alone are much like warnings we can't use ("Beware of low-flying planes") and may be directly costly.

But there is a more important reason not to overvalue physical health. Asked why we should care whether we all die in a nuclear exchange, Einstein is said to have replied, "We could no longer listen to Mozart." To care overmuch about our bodies for their own sake expresses a philistine small-mindedness that reverses the proper relationship of mind (and heart) to body, like going to the ballet to see seminude pretty girls. At the same time, to prevent people from controlling their own risks is disrespectful of autonomy and individual differences. We need a much more careful discrimination between hazards that cannot be foreseen, which are plausible candidates for public protective policies, and hazards that someone might not perfectly foresee, or that most people would like to avoid, which are much more questionable. More important, I hope we can put uncountable, unmeasurable, awkward, uncertain, aesthetic benefits in the place of honor in our environmental cost-benefit calculus and relegate the simplistic counting of expected life years to the subsidiary, albeit important, role it deserves.

Uniformity. The idea that government's job is to make a good environment, rather than to make it possible for people to make good environments, leads us to suppress complexity in many contexts. For reasons of administrative simplicity, a misapprehension of the equal-protection ideal, and possibly oversimple cost-benefit comparisons, our environmental policies are too consistent across circumstances calling for variation. No river should be filthy—but not every river should be kept or made swimmable. Los Angeles probably should have quiet, clean cars—but perhaps the fun a teenager in a small country town has with a fast, polluting car outweighs the damage she does.[18] Massachusetts has a single state building code—but some people live in houses too far apart to endanger each other.

Beyond its economic inefficiencies, this leveling has two more important consequences. First is a systematic suppression of environmental complexity and communication. The New York City zoning law that allows building owners to trade the rights to build and to exchange specific amenities for increased density shows that even a regulatory policy can accommodate variety and texture if we want it to.[19]

The second cost is more troubling. Most of us can't identify a good environment without seeing it; the Eiffel Tower, when first proposed, was condemned as an assault on the amenity of Paris.[20] Both wonderful things and big mistakes are conceived by visionaries, but we can't tell which are which without some samples. Unfortunately, when we regulate behavior to a uniform standard, we cripple the experimentation, with both environments and policies that affect them, necessary for progress. Static efficiency notwithstanding, I think the strongest argument for emission charges in place of minimum standards is that charges encourage experimentation with ways to reduce pollution or to trade a little pollution for a lot of something else.

Process Ignorance. Deliberate experimentation and multiple right answers are difficult to account for in the legal system. Another challenge to governmental ability to act fairly and predictably is the existence of processes with uncertain results and those that continue indefinitely with no result. Inevitably, neighborhood change and pond siltation bring circumstances in which the best thing that can happen next is quite different from the best thing that could have happened ten years ago. Processes are troublesome to both legislators and engineers, who prefer to describe the solution to a problem, figure out how to get there, and do it. As a result, we get technical interventions like stream-straightening and beach stabilization, and legal instruments like zoning ordinances and "best available technology," all of which throw out the baby of environmental evolution with the bathwater of current defects.

A sophisticated understanding of process is especially important when we want to interrupt a bad process, such as racial "tipping" of neighborhoods away from integration. It is indispensable when we want to direct a basically good process so as to avoid nonessential injury, as when we intervene to protect historic buildings or streetscapes from economic change without trying to stop the change itself.

Cost-hiding. Improving environments without trying to improve polities and citizens presents the constant temptation to present actions worth taking as though they were even better than they are. Possibly for this reason, many of our most important environmental policies incorporate devices that conceal cost. Regulation, for example, conceals what we are giving up for its beneifts, since no independent accounting system keeps track of the value of what a regulation prohibits. Implementation of any regulatory program implies at least an implicit judgment that its costs are less than its benefits, but the regulatory reformers of the last few years claim that these judgments are often erroneous, and they are probably right in at least some cases.

Cost-hiding is not limited to regulatory policies. The New York City zoning program I admired above originates in an unpriced seizure of the right to build beyond certain limits, called a *zoning envelope*, from among the property rights landowners held before the basic zoning ordinance was enacted. In what may be the most influential wrongheaded decision of the century, the Supreme Court held this seizure not to be a "taking" for which a government would have to compensate landowners,[21] and local governments have used the opportunity to hide the cost of zoning controls for sixty years. The fatal attraction of the device, of course, is that because the seizure need not be compensated, lots of environmental protection seems to be available for free.

Hiding the cost of environmental protection has a bad consequence and a very bad consequence. The bad one is that we are buying too much or too little protection as a result of not being able to analyze the cost-benefit balance explicitly. The very bad result is a denigration of environmental values. All we know about benefits obtained at unknown cost is that they are better than nothing. If we had to confront the sacrifices demanded by responsible environmental stewardship, we would show each other that we care significantly about our surroundings. We would also force upon ourselves an informed and lively debate about the environment and what we want from it—one that (since the environment *is* precious) could only increase our collective appreciation of the environment we have and our valuation of the amenity we could obtain.

What positive effects can we expect from environmental policy that corresponds to the managerial principles stated at the beginning of this section? On this point, I will necessarily be rather abstract. As a preface to the following points, I should note that this discussion has repeatedly identified cases in which the environment itself functions as a policy—a mechanism for social influence over individual action—and not only as the consequence of nonphysical policies like laws and habits. This symmetry suggests that the criteria for environments, and my recommendations for policy conventionally defined, may both be applicable beyond the present context. Some of the discussion here is probably relevant to legal and social environments.

Information and Indirect Influence. The manager's influence is exerted by information transfer, and it operates through other people's thoughts. What is produced depends on the people through whom the manager acts. Instead of ordaining a defined result, the manager empowers others to find better outcomes than they or the manager could reach alone. Because different people stand between management and particular outcomes, the manager's unitary intention produces a variety of results.

The environmental result is complexity and coherence. Complexity emerges from the differing information and values brought to the task by the various people engaged in it—from what we *each* know. Using the environment to communicate and to solve our own housing problems, my neighbors and I are making (and the builders of a century ago made) no two of our houses alike. Coherence within this variety results from the things we *all* know. The historical commission's advice, the restrictions of the building code, the neighborhood gossip about lead paint (and the prohibition against its use), and the existing streetscape itself are signals we all receive alike, and to which our responses are generally, but not perfectly, aligned.

Linking Current Choices to the Future and the Past. If actions are consequential, what we have done restricts what we can do, and what we do affects what will happen. One of management's fundamental duties to an organization is to discover and describe this intertemporal linkage. Focus on the causal relationships between now and then, rather than on a particular state of affairs to be pursued, distinguishes management from technocracy and from command.

To manage the environment in this spirit protects both evidence of process and significance. Making the history of environments more recognizable places process in the consciousness of the organization's members, where it improves their experience of the environment and their actions upon it. It also motivates environmental decisions that make processes apparent. Although the current environmental management system is especially weak in this quality, my family depended at least on a structure of laws and social conventions to assure ourselves that our house and street had a future in which to think about our paint job.

Significance, as we have seen, is closely linked to process. Public consciousness that environments result from purposeful acts of people or the operation of natural laws makes it possible for environments to say something about who or what made them. Here it is often looseness, rather than constraint, that serves effective management. It is precisely because our historical commission's powers were only advisory and our local government had not appropriated building exteriors[22] that our paint job could mean something about us and that we could mean something to the (physical) environment of our street.

Capacity Building. The third distinguishing quality of managerial style is attention not only to outcomes of the organization's efforts, but also to its capacity to accomplish things as yet unperceived. The freedom to decide what color our house should be and whether it would be preserved for another hundred years created an accountability to the neighbors and to the next generation that focused our attention on the physical environment of our street. Having responsibility for that decision made us more attentive environmental consumers and stewards. Paradoxically, the constraints of social convention, the colors already chosen by others, and the consistency of the street's underlying architectural style were equally important in this regard, because it is just as trivial to decide among an infinity of indifferent alternatives as to decide among one.

Our policy environment thus made us incrementally better environmental participants by obliging us to choose, making the possible choices meaningfully different, and allowing us to choose wrong. Like everything of value, this betterment has a price; on our street, it was the peach-pink house. Perhaps we can take the occasional disaster as an environmental quality indicator: seeing someone paint a house pink, drain the wrong wetland, or even puff out an occasional dose of poison is a reassurance that environmental management capacity is growing.

NOTES

1. But see the thoughtful discussion of *uniqueness, irreversibility of damage, beauty, support for human life,* and *naturalness* as criteria of value for preservation of natural environments in Harvey Brooks's chapter, "Environmental Decision Making: Analysis and Values," in Laurence H. Tribe, Corinne S. Schelling, and John Voss, eds., *When Values Conflict* (Cambridge, Mass.: Ballinger Publishing Company, 1976). The discussion is in the context of balancing a new dam against the injury it will do to an unspoiled river.

2. For discussions of this question, focused on protection of the natural environment against development and regrettably little attentive to the built environment, see Donald Scherer and Thomas Attig, eds., *Ethics and the Environment* (New York: Prentice-Hall, 1983).

3.   The reader with no time for lowbrow movies can consider instead the ass on the piano in Luis Bunuel's *Un Chien Andalou.*

4.   Christopher Alexander, "A City Is Not A Tree," in Gwen Bell and Jacqueline Tyrwhitt, eds., *Human Identity in the Urban Environment* (New York: Penguin, 1972).

5.   Steven Kelman has pointed out to me the interesting, albeit rather abstract, parallel between the foregoing discussion of complexity and coherence and the utopian framework of community variation under the ordering consistency of a minimal state in Robert Nozick, *Anarchy, State, and Utopia*, Part III (New York: Basic Books, 1974).

6.   For a discussion of a physical environment serving as a language that communicates a theology, see Ernest Panofsky, *Gothic Architecture and Scholasticism*, Meridian Books No. 44 (Latrobe, Penn.: Archabbey Press, 1951).

7.   For a discussion of this conventional language and its evolution, see John Summerson, *The Classical Language of Architecture* (Cambridge, Mass.: M.I.T. Press, 1963).

8.   Josef Hoffmann and Adolph Loos, with Otto Wagner the founders of modern architecture in central Europe at the turn of the century. See Eduard Sekler, *Josef Hoffmann* (Princeton: Princeton University Press, 1985).

9.   Eduard Sekler, distinguished Harvard architectural historian and my professor of modern and ancient architectural history.

10.   Rachel Carson, *Silent Spring* (Boston: Houghton Mifflin, 1962).

11.   Matthew Arnold, "Dover Beach," in John Hayward, ed., *Oxford Book of Nineteenth Century Verse* (New York: Oxford University Press, 1964).

12.   (Johnny Green with E. Heyman) "I Cover the Waterfront," Warner Bros. Music, c. 1933.

13.   Nevil Shute, *On The Beach* (New York: Ballantine, 1979).

14.   Compare the vitiation of artistic innovation caused by too-ready embrace of anything as art, described in Chapter 6: if everything is art, making art is vacuous.

15.   The discussion in this section is much influenced by curriculum development activities and exploratory research by colleagues at the Kennedy School. Most of this material is circulating as notes and drafts, but see M. O'Hare, "The Manager's Role," *Governance* (Fall–Winter 1985–6); Herman B. Leonard, "Theory S and Theory T," unpublished paper, Kennedy School of Government, Harvard University 1985; and Mark H. Moore, "A Conception of Public Management," unpublished paper, Kennedy School of Government, Harvard University 1983 and "Realms of Obligation and Virtue," in Joel Fleishman, Lance Liebman, and Mark H. Moore, eds., *Public Duties: The Moral Obligations of Government Officials* (Cambridge, Mass.: Harvard University Press, 1981).

16.   M. Sun, "EPA to Approve Testing of Gene-Altered Bacteria," *Science* 230 (November 29, 1985): 1015.

17. Michael O'Hare, "Bargaining and Negotiation in Risk Management," in Howard Kunreuther and Paul Kleindorfer, eds., *Transport, Storage & Disposal of Hazardous Material* (New York: Springer-Verlag, in press).

18. David Harrison, "Controlling Automotive Emissions: How to Save More than $1 Billion Per Year and Help the Poor Too," *Public Policy* 25, no. 4 (Fall 1977).

19. Jonathan Barnett, *Urban Design as Public Policy* (New York: Architectural Record Books, 1974).

20. Jean Keim, *La Tour Eiffel* (Paris: Editions Tel, 1950).

21. *Village of Euclid v. Ambler Realty Co.*, 272 US 365, 388.

22. In Rome, for example, and many historic districts, it is forbidden to alter or to fail to maintain the outside of a building. This prohibition extends to paint color, which is why Rome is brown-orange.

CHAPTER 6

Members of the Audience: Public and Private Responsibilities to the Arts

Winthrop Knowlton

F or more than a quarter of a century there has been waged in this country a fierce, if intermittent, debate on the question of whether or not the U.S. government should endorse and fund a program of direct public support of the arts: in other words, whether or not we should have an arts policy.

By now all the "lofty" and the "vulgar" and the "economic" arguments[1] about whether or not art is a "public good" have been heard, and it is clear that those who think it is, and that therefore we should have an explicit program of support, have won.

This victory manifests itself in the ability of the National Endowment for the Arts (NEA), the most substantial instrument of such a policy, to withstand what one arts advocate has described as "the ordeal by politics" to which it has been subjected by the Reagan administration. Funding for the Endowment and its state counterparts has held its own in constant dollars since the beginning of the 1980s—this despite the fact that increases in private giving to the arts during this decade now nearly equal the public funding in question. (In other words, such public funding could have been virtually eliminated and the arts would have been no worse off.) The ability of the programs in question to survive the twin threats of political animosity and financial redundancy is testimony both to the stamina of

I am grateful to my colleagues Michael O'Hare and Richard Zeckhauser for their helpful comments on this chapter.

public programs once established and to the fact that even those most opposed to these subsidies enjoy the arts, long to be perceived as doing so, and thus increasingly tone down their arguments with expressions of mea culpa and regret.

Proceeding, then, on the assumption that public programs of support are here to stay, I wish here to address the question of whether the arts policy we have is either the right or the best one. This policy advocates more of a great many things: *production* of more art, particularly more excellent and innovative works of art; more *participation*, that is, more people creating art; more *access* to art by more people; more *diversity*, with encouragement given especially to regional and ethnic categories of art; and more *conservation* of works of art, great ones and merely good ones if they are unique. This list of values, or goals, has been articulated by many proponents of an active arts policy in recent symposia.[2] It also closely resembles the land mark 1978 *Statement of Purpose* of the NEA.[3]

To explore whether this emphasis on more of virtually every aspect of art is appropriate, I will discuss, first, the role of art in society today; second, the question of whether and how we might best help individual artists and arts institutions; and, finally, what our own responsibilities as arts lovers or arts consumers (depending on one's terminological bent) might be if we are to enhance the role art plays in our lives. In so doing, I hope to distill a more precise sense of where individual and institutional, and public and private, responsibilities lie.

THE ROLE OF ART IN SOCIETY

Perhaps the first thing we ought to recognize is that art is never what it used to be. In the Middle Ages and early Renaissance, works of art (I refer primarily to visual works) were almost always renditions of holy stories produced by artisans delivering stipulated goods for a fee. In the Enlightenment, and perhaps more vividly in the Romantic Era, society becomes more self-conscious about art, more anxious to define it and to formulate unifying theories about it. The word *aesthetic* crops up for the first time in the mid-eighteenth century. Toward the end of that century and through most of the following one, art is pursued for truth and beauty. It is cherished for its content and for the feelings it evokes, this combination of certitude and exaltation providing (at least in the minds of scholars) partial substitutes for the solace of church and the ardor of state.

With the advent of our own century and the collapse of traditional ideas about the structure of the universe and of ourselves, art becomes something different again and something more—but exactly what? It does not now shed its didactic role but, like the twentieth-century world itself, is newly configured and more complex. Sometimes it is abstract, disembodied, fragmented, jagged; at other times, as in the case of modernist architecture, it is pristine, cool, "pure."

Along with new forms (and, of course, materials) come changed attitudes. In its various twentieth-century manifestations and manifestoes, art is, by turns, transcendental and therapeutic; it is high endeavor, shock, and prank. In short, it is many kinds of things at once. It is, above all else, *new*, with its newness taking an almost infinite variety of forms.

As in previous artistic epochs this change has been engendered by vast social, political, technological, religious, and commercial transformations. These influence not only what art is but how it is delivered. Never before has art been on display in so many different kinds of places—in museums, concert halls, and bookstores; in executive suites, shopping malls, bars[4]; on airwaves and cassettes; even on spacecraft.

New technologies make it possible, furthermore, to enjoy reproductions of the visual and plastic arts, and to watch and listen to theatrical performances, opera, ballet, and concerts in the home. There has been much argument about whether access to these various derivative forms should count as exposure to "true" art. Whatever the ultimate outcome of that (exceedingly heated) dispute, these new delivery and facsimile systems would appear, at the very least, to provide a stimulus to the curiosity of novice arts consumers as well as a supplementary form of enjoyment for those already exposed to the real thing.

It is also worth noting that these new technologies know no national borders. To list a dozen or so artists who have enriched our lives during the past hundred years—Ibsen, Joyce, Proust, Faulkner, Eliot, Bishop, Beckett, Balanchine, Graham, Stravinsky, Matisse, Picasso, Johns, Le Corbusier, Chaplin—is both to acknowledge the extent to which twentieth-century art is international and to make us ponder what exactly, in this context, a national policy is. In a world of traveling orchestras and satellite communications, we benefit as much from Austrian policy toward Vienna's music institutions as Austrians do from ours toward Lincoln Center. When we talk of diversity in terms of our own (presumably neglected) regional and ethnic specialties, we sometimes forget that these must now find their way in competition with Persian miniatures, Japanese kimonos, and Nigenian masks. In this setting, support of disadvantaged local groups in the name of equality or participation may have parochial and protectionist aspects we have not yet adequately addressed.

Finally, while still considering art in the aggregate (so to speak) and in its newer aspects, let us not forget that "old art" has not gone away. Indeed it is very much on the move. It is newly mined for marginal exotica, newly restored, newly packaged, and it, too, is newly delivered by the technologies described above. In addition, we constantly redefine and re-animate it by the ways in which we respond to it, our responses influenced by changes in our values and modes of perception (these, in turn, being shaped by the times in which we live). There is, for all these reasons, a kind of generational struggle in progress in which old and new art vie for viewing and listening and reading space, but with the old (in my judgment) increasingly compelled to redesign itself in order to attract our attention.

Is it possible that our arts policymakers, like our generals, are busy fighting the last war? That we already have more art available to us, new *and* old, than we can realistically absorb? That its diversity, especially if we consider its international dimensions, is awesome? And that innovation reigns supreme, so much so that it occasionally acts as a surrogate for art, making it difficult to determine what art actually is?

If the answer to these questions is affirmative, and if, accordingly, policymakers' emphasis on encouragement of more production of art of particular kinds (new, innovative, and so on) is ecologically unsound, then are there elements of existing policies on behalf of specific segments of the arts community (e.g., individual artists, arts institutions, arts consumers) that make more sense? Present policies, after all, presume that aspiring young artists should be helped, that arts institutions should be helped, and that more people should be given access to art and should participate in the making of it as well.

ASSISTING THE INDIVIDUAL ARTIST

Let us consider the question by starting with the individual artist, for it is he or she, in conjunction with and in response to the above-described broad shaping social forces, who creates the works we deem precious.

The job of identifying the artist who is worthy of support has always been difficult and is made even more so today because of our very insistence on equating worth with works that are "new" or "innovative."[5] More demanding even than finding an artist capable of producing an individual meritorious work is the task of identifying those with the capacity to create an oeuvre. Why would one want to do so? Because it is the artists whose work evolves over time who make the most distinctive and lasting contributions to art.

George Balanchine was once (surely more than once!) accosted by the mother of a young applicant for the School of the American Ballet who asked, "Will my daughter dance?" Balanchine paused to reflect; the question came again, and he responded, "La danse, Madame, c'est une question morale."[6]

While talent (itself an elusive concept) may be a necessary condition to successful artistic endeavor, it is not a sufficient one: Also required is character, one (and only one) aspect of which is an obsessive and prolonged dedication to one's craft.

Describing Balanchine's attitude, Lincoln Kirstein has written: "Two epithets he particularly detested, though they were frequently invoked to qualify his 'genius', were 'creative' and 'original'. The first, he thought, was the more false; only less offensive was 'original' or its twin 'authentic'. Any unique explosion of initiative was usually mutation, but, more often, dilution."[7]

If there is wisdom here, and I believe there is, then the matter of selecting worthy individual candidates for public (or even private) subsidy at the *outset* of their putative careers is even more difficult than we might have supposed. Like management consultants or venture capitalists exhorting clients to be entrepreneurial, all the while overlooking more subtle and demanding virtues, our benefactors may have their essential standards essentially wrong.

Another case made against support for individual artists (one that leaves me uneasy) holds that the artist needs to work *against* something. Lack of friction (or even of suffering) inadvertently dulls creative impulse.[8]

What I am arguing is a good deal less complicated—namely, that the artist whom we may wish ultimately to support cannot be officially "found" in the early stages of his career because his virtues are indecipherable. It follows from this quite practical consideration that he must necessarily be thrown upon his own resources—courage and endurance and evolving skill—with assistance limited to those nearby: family, friends, and idiosyncratic patrons whose obsessions match his own. Later, after talent *and* character have begun to be demonstrated, there may be more reasonable opportunity for other forms of support—a foundation grant, say, or a prize—but this is essentially a strategy of *recognition* and not of *discovery.*

There is an immense difference between those two strategies. The arts policy we have now, whether we consider its efforts to support art in general or artists in particular, is rhetorically and emotionally driven by the urge to stimulate, and even to induce, discoveries. These are, obviously, *new*, and they add to the stock of what we already have. Recognition, on the other hand, involves the granting of rewards for efforts that have already been made. Recognizers discriminate from a stock of objects or activities already in existence. Recognizers are driven less by the need to be ahead of the times than by a desire to sort out the times. Implicit in recognition is the notion of conservation.

What I am suggesting is that a realistic appraisal both of the overall state of the arts *and* of our limited ability to discover individual artists leads to the conclusion that arts policy might usefully move in just this direction: toward conservation. I refer to conservation not in the sense of finding art and storing it in archives but in the more active, indeed creative, sense of selecting, preserving, and presenting works of art to a variety of audiences, with the caveat that these works be created by artists who are already, to some extent, established.

THE ROLE OF CONSERVATION

Let us explore the possibilities of such a policy by turning to the world of arts institutions, for an arts policy that has *conservation* as its central theme necessarily calls for the support, perhaps almost exclusively, of museums, orchestras, theatrical companies, and other such organizations. They, after all, are our means for the selection, preservation, and presentation of art.

While a policy devoted largely to helping arts institutions may seem relatively simple compared with the wide array of efforts now in vogue, it may, in fact, involve many of the same pitfalls. It can be just as tempting to discover "innovative" or "new" institutions—in the performing arts, say—as it is to discover emerging new individual artists. And indeed, existing arts policies, which provide a good deal of financial aid to institutions, do just that, supporting a wide range of "experimental" groups. And in supporting large, established institutions, like urban museums, policymakers may simply be delegating existing policies downstream, for some of these institutions have agendas as broad as the public agencies from which they derive help.

The approach I wish to explore will provide more focus than do existing efforts; and it will be, I hope, more strategic, taking more explicit account of the role of other (private sector) players and acknowledging that we are dealing with dynamic forces—life cycles, if you will—that gradually force changes in priorities (indeed the priority of conservation will itself ultimately change) and in targets worthy of support.

There is, first and foremost, the life cycle of the artist, who must struggle alone most of the time but especially so at the outset of his or her career. As that career unfolds, the web of support, individual and institutional, from galleries or publishers, from foundations and museums, gradually widens and takes a greater variety of forms.

Arts institutions have cycles too. Let us return to the case of George Balanchine and the New York City Ballet to illustrate the point. When Balanchine came to America in 1933 there was no ballet in this country—not only no resident company but no audience to speak of and no discernible interest. He established, first, a school for dancers and then a small company, which for years was generously supported by Lincoln Kirstein and James Warburg, two idiosyncratic patrons who recognized Balanchine's genius and shared his passion for the dance. There were other, lesser known individual supporters too. As time passed and word spread, an audience grew and the sources of support expanded to include the Rockefeller and Ford Foundations, corporations, more individual donors (large and small), local government (which helped house the company at the City Center and then the State Theatre), and then the NEA and the New York State Council on the Arts.

From the mid-1930s until his illness in the late 1970s, Balanchine had an unusual ability to turn hardship into triumph. A budgetary imperative like lack of scenery became part of the Balanchine aesthetic (an example of the constructive effect of restraints on art). He also ran a tight ship. By insisting there be no "star system," he helped put a cap on operating costs. In later years, after musicians and dancers had been unionized, he was able to limit their demands by threatening, persuasively, to close up shop and move to Switzerland. Box office prices were kept low, which helped attract an audience and more particularly to *hold* it. Attending performances several nights a week for years on end, a remarkable number of the members of this audience came to understand, not merely appreciate, the works they saw.

Today the New York City Ballet is part of the arts establishment. But with Balanchine gone, the enterprise has moved into another stage of its artistic and financial life cycle. Costs are rising rapidly. Despite increased financial assistance across the entire range of public and private benefactors, deficits are larger than ever. There is virtually no endowment. The question of whether support is still merited, or merited in traditional forms, is far more problematic than before.

Meanwhile, the dance has become an accepted part of the American arts scene. Like the successful assimilation of art itself into the cultural mainstream, this was made possible not only by the brilliance of individuals like Balanchine, Merce Cunningham, and Martha Graham but also by the impact of other forces: our greatly improved ability to film or tape dance and to broadcast it (the technological contribution); the extraordinary success of a movie, *The Turning Point*, that made ballet glamorous (the commercial contribution); and the spectacular defections of Rudolph Nureyev, Mikhail Baryshnikov, and Natalia Makarova from the Soviet Union (the political contribution).

If these cycles exist (and they obviously do), then can we devise a philanthropic strategy that takes them into account and in so doing avoids fighting wars already won or intervening before the artistic stamina of promising individuals or institutions can be convincingly demonstrated?

As the story of the New York City Ballet demonstrates, cultural institutions, like individual artists, attract support from different sources as their lives unfold. There is no museum or orchestra or arts institution of consequence (with the exception of the formally public ones in Washington, D.C.) that has not received its initial financial impetus from individual patrons whose passions match (or indeed define) its own and whose tolerance for start-up hysteria cannot be emulated by institutional decisionmakers in thrall to committee and compromise. With recognition and gradual acceptance of artistic merit there come for these institutions, as with commercial ventures, managerial and financial perils of different scale and sort. It is in these middle years that institutional philanthropy, both public and private, can probably play its most useful conserving role, enabling the enterprise to hold onto what it has already produced, to permit it to evolve, and *to preserve itself* as a going concern.

What exactly should that role be?

I cannot answer that question with precision for the reply will vary greatly from institution to institution. I can, however, suggest some lines of inquiry and some new emphases that may help make existing policies more effective over the long run.

There are, to begin with, some broad questions regarding support for various genres of art. Clearly some require institutional support more than others (the performing arts, for example, compared with the visual). In addition, it may be that certain genres of art are at a stage of their life cycle that requires particular kinds of institutional bolstering. Is modern music, for example, an instance where much work of merit has already been done but where adequate conserving methods have not yet come into being? Does modern music need the kind of institutional support that the Museum of Modern Art has given modern painting and sculpture? Do we need an Orchestra of Modern Music? (Our present arts policies, with their emphasis on innovation, are likely to encourage the composition of more new music without acknowledging that the new music we already have goes unheard.)

Continuing in this vein, does the modern tempo of absorption— that is, the relative speed with which we take things in—favor certain arts over others (the visual arts, say, over literature)? And does this require some adjustment? The National Endowment for the Humanities' and the Ford Foundation's support of *The Library of America*, a definitive version of our literary classics (a project that could not have been undertaken by any commercial publishing house), is an exemplary undertaking of this sort, as well as of the kind of conservation appropriate to the times.

We come next to questions that are institution-specific. Does a potential institutional recipient of public support have "character" analogous to that of the worthy individual artist? Arts institutions, after all, are made up of individuals. And it is individuals like Alfred Barr, Arturo Toscanini, and George Balanchine that give these organizations aesthetic vision *and* managerial drive. Should we ever provide public support to arts institutions that lack such kinds of demonstrated leadership?

Do we want to help a given institution because it plays a specific conserving role (would we support the New York City Ballet henceforth if its sole mission were the preservation of the Balanchine oeuvre?) or because it helps keep a variety of aesthetic options open, of which conservation might be an important but not necessarily an exclusive component?

What standards of accountability should recipient organizations be held to, and how can these standards be implemented without demoralizing creative spirit? How do we judge when funds are being squandered, when costs are rising more than they should, and when it is time, either because we have succeeded or failed, for additional funds to be withheld and public support gradually withdrawn? (We are woefully inadequate, in all of our programs of public subsidy, in articulating and implementing *exit* policies.)

Finally, there are questions relating to collaborative efforts with private-sector donors. As the descriptions of life cycles suggest, corporations, foundations, and public agencies are all likely to—and I believe should—enter the life of an arts institution at the same stage of its development.

I take it as a given that there will continue to be an important role for the American corporation in this philanthropic process. Indeed, recent statistics indicate that corporations have become the largest single institutional donor, public or private, to the arts.[9] These gifts will undoubtedly continue to be made under the rubric of self-interest, with an understandable temptation to support art that is attention-getting (blockbuster museum shows are a conspicuous case in point), for visibility enhances corporate image, and enhanced image makes philanthropy worthwhile to shareholders, or so executives assume. But it must be visibility of the right sort. And so there will also be a temptation for corporations to play it safe. Neither the tendency to be flashy nor to be bland is calamitous. Of greater significance is the transient nature of corporate interest.

This is particularly important if the policy of conservation is to include contributions toward endowment. Such support is not only consistent with the notion of institutional preservation but is today acutely needed—perhaps more so than ever before. It appears that only two dozen or so American arts institutions have endowments capable of generating annual income equivalent to three months' operating expenses. The great majority of the rest have virtually no endowment at all. These figures may be testimony to the fact that arts benefactors of many kinds have become more beguiled by the pleasures of supporting arts transactions—events and exhibitions— than by the task of building institutional durability.

If this is so, then there may be opportunities for the public sector, through matching or contingent grants or other collaborative efforts, to encourage its private sector counterparts to shift a portion of their resources to endowment-type gifts. Certain companies may be in a better position to do this than others. For example, a major New York life insurance company recently assumed all of the capital and operating costs required to open and operate a branch of the Whitney Museum in its new headquarters building. Here, visibility and endowment would appear to walk hand in hand. In instances where these kinds of gifts are less appealing to corporate donors, perhaps the public sector can compensate by shifting its own resources (and encouraging foundations to shift theirs) to endowment-type forms of giving.[10]

There would also appear to be opportunities for the two sectors to work together more imaginatively on another form of endowment: the human one embodied in systems of governance. Active participation by experienced and effective private sector executives, working more closely than has traditionally been the case with public arts administrators or their surrogates, may well be the key ingredient that makes new systems of institutional accountability work.

None of this will be easy. Bits and pieces of it have been tried. The programs of the new National Arts Stabilization Fund, building on the work of the Ford Foundation over several decades, is a pioneering attempt to knit public and private funds into a coordinated effort that includes elements of accountability. But it is still a small program and very much alone.

No single gift to the arts is perfect. Each is bound by silken (or steel) threads to a donor's ego or aesthetic sensibility or hunger for public acclaim. But if there is an intensified focus on conservation and if collaborative efforts are applied at the right time in the cycle— when needs are still great but quality and character persuasively established—then we may enhance our chances of weaving these various strands into a supportive web that is coherent and strong.

I have suggested that existing public policies in the arts have an anachronistic and sentimental quality that manifests itself in an agenda that is both unnecessarily and unrealistically broad. I have explained why the emphasis on more—especially more production of the *new*—is no longer appropriate, if indeed it ever was, and why recognition rather than discovery may provide a more useful philanthropic frame. The policy to be put in the frame would then be one, essentially, of conservation, institutional in character and with strong elements of accountability. In describing the life cycles of individual artists, of genres of art, and of arts institutions, I have suggested where various public and private responsibilities might lie and a few ways in which the two sectors might work together to meet those responsibilities more effectively.

MACRO POLICIES, PERSONAL RESPONSIBILITIES

However, as one observes the fantastic abundance and variety of art in our society, one cannot help but wonder if I have not left out a few important matters. What I refer to are policies that are not "arts" policies at all. The list of artists provided earlier in this chapter is testimony to the importance of freedom of expression in making art possible and of freedom of movement in making it broadly available to us from a diversity of places. These are, in a sense, the macro policies that go with the micro options I have been discussing. So too are educational policies that teach children how to read and write and to understand that the past has value. These seem to me more significant than specialized kinds of arts education designed to help students participate in the arts. (The two, of course, are not mutually exclusive.) Important, too, are macroeconomic policies that produce the levels of private disposable income that are the wellsprings of philanthropy and the building blocks of audiences that can partly, if not entirely, pay their own way. The responsibilities implicit in these various public philosophies and programs are central to our artistic endeavors.

And what of *our* responsibilities—those of us who are, as economists tell us, the ultimate beneficiaries of whatever subsidies are proffered? If conservation is to be a vital force, then the works of art preserved by the institutions we help must be conserved on our behalf. Public and private philanthropies help *us*, influencing the kinds and quality of art available to us, as well as its price.[11]

We would appear to be giving art a great deal in return. After all, we worship it. Exactly why is not always clear: perhaps because art is wonderful or it is so well marketed or we lack other forms of solace and status. We may even worship art too much, expecting that it be all the things it has ever been over the centuries: visualizer of holy stories, exemplar of civic and moral virtue, therapist, entertainer, explorer. And our idolatry may be more ritualistic than we admit. We may utter the right prayers, but often we apprehend the objects of our adoration mechanically and on the run. Perhaps what is required of us is not reverence but affection and skepticism and most especially an abiding interest and concern.

Critic Robert Garis, one of the ardent followers of the New York City Ballet to whom I earlier referrred, has written movingly of attending performances of *Liebeslieder Waltzes* over the decades, each time seeing and hearing it differently. He tells us that dancers, musicians, members of the audience must all continue "to define works of art . . . to keep our minds open to new performers or critics who modify our ideas about the identity of a work of art, or show us that we were in fact wrong before, and that the new experience we've been given is finally, at last, the *piece* [emphasis mine].[12]

Surely we must take the time to sort, to savor, and to re-explore works of art, redefining them and renewing ourselves. When all is said and done, is not the quality of these individual experiences at the core of what we are trying to preserve? If, as a result of these experiences, we become conservers too, and if institutions are needed to deliver art to us and to help us engage in this process, then it may be more appropriate than our economist friends would have us think to subsidize these institutions and, in so doing, to subsidize ourselves.

Are *we*, then, the ultimate conserving instrumentality? Are we, through the application of our individual tastes and judgments, the ones who determine which works of art will last or even what art itself will be? An affirmative answer makes for a pleasing ending, one in which we conclude, after examining various public and private responsibilities, by congratulating ourselves on our own importance. But sadly, I do not believe it is so. We can and should play a part here, as I have already said. It can be active and explicit; or it can be by default, leaving discriminations to others, in which case art will be more academic than it might otherwise be or more commercial.

In much the same way as we refine our own aesthetic sensibilities, we should fashion arts policies that are helpful and attuned to our times. Of course, neither arts policies nor individual sensibilities are as significant as the freedoms we bestow on individuals to do their work; the creations of gifted artists evolving their craft through difficult, prolonged, and even tormenting effort; personal philanthropy, zany and sublime; or the broad shaping forces of society such as scientific discoveries, political revolution, religious revival, and economic upheaval. If, for instance, we were today in a period of artistic slackness—if the above described cultural ferment were in fact a "cover," as some allege, for lack of genuine creativity—then we might ask ourselves: How could we "pump up" the arts? The answer is, we probably couldn't, no matter how enlightened our policies or discriminating and heartfelt our aesthetic judgments. We would have to wait. To be patient. To let inexplicable events happen. Some things that are important are also mysterious. Some are important *because* they are mysterious. That is one of the essences of art. Recognition of our limitations in influencing the creation of essential "pieces" of art will not come easily to activist policymakers genuinely concerned with the public good. But this may be one of our abiding responsibilities, too.

NOTES

1. The terms are Professor Ronald Dworkin's. The "lofty" argument claims we ought to subsidize art because we can't be a great society without it. The "vulgar" argument says we ought to help art because it benefits taxi drivers and waiters near Lincoln Center. The "economic" argument claims art is a marketable good that should pay its own way.

2. See especially the background paper by Professor Paul DiMaggio of Yale for the forum "Can Culture Survive the Marketplace?" held at the Institute of Politics of the John F. Kennedy School of Government on April 21, 1983, under the sponsorship of the Kennedy School and the Massachusetts Council on the Arts and Humanities. The paper was published in a Special Issue of the *Journal of Arts Management and Law* that spring.

3. From *Statement of the National Council on the Arts on Goals and Basic Policy of the National Endowment for the Arts*, adopted June 17, 1978, Washington, D.C.

4. Henry Geldzahler, former curator of twentieth-century art at the Metropolitan Museum in New York, acted as arts consultant for the 1985 opening of the Palladium, a disco gallery in downtown New York.

5. It is made more difficult, too, by the immense quantity of new work being produced. Take the case of book publishing, where editors are annually confronted with thousands of unsolicited manuscripts by aspiring writers

who think it important and even fashionable to write novels. This flow of material makes it more time consuming than ever before to find the good piece of work, to publish it well, and to fight for it, against thousands of other words, in the marketplace.

6. Lincoln Kirstein, *Portrait of Mr. B: Photographs of George Balanchine with an Essay* (New York: Viking, 1984), pp. 15–16.

7. Ibid., p. 18.

8. Art critic Mark Stevens puts the broader cultural paradox as follows:

> However wild, unsuccessful, radical, or misunderstood a young artist may be, he is now a cultural insider; universities, the press, museums, government, foundations— and most important discotheques—treat him respectfully. Yet this same young artist typically regards himself as an outsider. Or wants to, for he is steeped in a modernist ethos that positions the artist heroically above and apart from a corrupt society. This inside/outside perspective is part of the slow melt of modernism into mainstream culture. What was edge is now center.

"The Trend in Torment," *The New Republic* (March 10, 1986).

9. This is true if one ignores the role of indirect public support through tax-breaks. These, in a sense, are a kind of matching grant for private gifts. A number of policy questions are associated with this indirect support. See Alan L. Feld, Michael O'Hare, and J. Mark Davidson Schuster, *Patrons Despite Themselves: Txapayers and Arts Policy*, a Twentieth Century Fund Report (New York University Press, 1983).

10. While the NEA's challenge grant program helps further these aims, these grants account for only 12 percent of its total appropriations. The overall impression left by the NEA's 1985 Annual Report is of an extraordinarily diffuse grant-making effort that stands in dramatic contrast to the notion of functional and life-cycle focus endorsed here.

11. Whether enough of "us" have access to art is a question I cannot adequately address here, at least in conventional quantitative terms.

12. Robert Garis, "The Dancer and the Dance, Balanchine: Change, Revival, Survival," *Raritan Review* (offprint).

CHAPTER 7

Whose Business Is Good Behavior?

T. C. Schelling

T his chapter is about the behavior of people as persons—not as
teachers, scientists, artists, public officials, or corporate executives but as human beings. It is about responsibility for their good or
bad behavior. The subject relates to poverty, but more specifically to
the behavior affecting individual poverty—holding a job, staying with
one's family, becoming pregnant with a child one does not want or
wants but cannot afford. It relates to the environment—littering,
being careless with fire, being inconsiderate about the volume of
one's radio or the transmission of communicable diseases. It relates
to education—going to school, taking school seriously, dropping out.
It relates to politics—campaigning, contributing, going to the polls
on election day. But the unit of analysis is not a system or a sector,
though any sector of private or public activity may be sensitive to
integrity or corruption at the level of the individual.

Criminal law defines particular bad behaviors and assumes some
responsibility for prevention and control, even retribution. But I
shall not consider criminal behavior; the allocation or assumption of
formal responsibility for that kind of behavior is fairly straightforward. Overt criminality aside, there is no accepted definition of my
subject. It could include all behaviors that lead toward crime, but
there is no close agreement even on what those behaviors are. The
subject could include the use of addictive and intoxicating substances, sexual activity, idleness and work habits, seatbelts, hygiene,

nutrition, exercise, civility and good manners in public, charity, or kindness to animals. For some it would include reverence and worship and the verbal and other expressions of attitudes toward race, sex, or handicap or attitudes about patriotism or civil participation.

Two questions arise before the question about the locus or distribution of responsibility for appropriate behavior. The first is, who has or should have or claims to have responsibility for deciding which of these behaviors are anybody else's business? Second, once we know which behaviors belong on the agenda, who is or should be or claims to be responsible for determining just what is good or bad? There may be a few nearly universal answers to these two questions: family, school, and, for some of us, our churches would be noncompeting candidates for authority. But disagreement on what constitutes bad, acceptable, and good behaviors can be acute and divisive.

Teenage unmarried sex offers an example. Some among us see the conscientious and reliable use of contraceptives as an exemplary behavior and a social goal of utmost importance; others see it as a sordid precursor to a most abhorrent behavior. To some among us the conscientious and reliable use of contraceptives appears to be the only solution to the dreadfully divisive issue of abortion, while to others it is part of the problem, not a solution. Issues like this usually hinge on where one is willing to compromise; and compromise is hard when moral and religious values are at stake.

In an earlier era contagious diseases had to be somebody's business; people with scarlet fever were regularly quarantined. Recently the problem has become hideous again with AIDS. The pertinent behaviors are sexual promiscuity, the selection of sexual partners, the nature of sexual performance, perhaps submission to testing for the virus, and the sharing and sterilization of needles for intravenous drug injection. Here again there are trade-offs and compromises. Is the conscientious and effective sterilization of a common-use needle before each use in a group of heroin users a "good behavior" in which we all have an interest because it may retard the spread of AIDS, or are sterilized needles merely a counterdeterrent to the use of heroin? Is the use of condoms by male homosexuals a "good behavior" to be encouraged through public health education, or would such education be complicity in an offense?

I raise these questions to make two points. The first is that dispute over what is good or bad, let alone what is anybody's business, is inevitable. The second is that we are unlikely to find any universal or even widely applicable principles governing where responsibility belongs for encouraging good behavior, discouraging bad behavior, providing incentives or education, or assuming some disciplinary command.

Consider advertising. Advertising on television and in magazines is probably a major contributor to dental hygiene, encouraging both youngsters and their parents in the regular cleansing of teeth. Advertising is certainly a powerful influence on the prevention of under-arm perspiration. It is alleged to be an influence on the consumption of beer by young motorists. And it must be a negligible influence on the use of contraceptives among unwed teenagers. Evidently advertising can be, but is not necessarily, a significant influence on behavior. It can encourage behavior that is good, behavior that is bad, and behavior that is inconsequential.

Unable to provide a single analysis of responsibility that would cover the entire universe of behaviors, I shall choose the opposite extreme and investigate one behavior. It may serve as a case study, generating a checklist of potential loci of responsibility. Moreover, it can demonstrate that different responsibilities toward any given behavior may be at different loci. The responsibilities for determining what constitutes good behavior, for informing the public about the behavior and its consequences, for rewarding good behaviors and punishing bad behaviors, for regulating the behavior in different locations among different parts of the population, and even for providing attractive alternatives to the bad behavior may be widely dispersed among public and private agencies and the marketplace. In some cases responsibility may be accorded to a public agency, assumed by a private institution, promoted by a commercial enterprise, and taught in the schools. This diffusion of responsibility and influence will emerge clearly in the particular behavior that I examine, namely, the smoking of cigarettes.

A case study of a particular behavior will be most useful if it illuminates the many loci in American society where responsibility might be assumed or assigned. It can then serve as a guide or checklist of where to look for some exercise or failure of responsibility. And in addition to the exercise of responsibility toward good behavior or the avoidance of bad behavior we should be alert to the exercise of influence—sometimes in the name of responsibility—that goes contrary to what we might consider good behavior.

In some respects the behavior I have chosen, the smoking of cigarettes, may lack richness and nuance. It is a precisely defined activity, unlike being kind to animals, dutiful to one's parents, or considerate of the handicapped. And the main choice is binary: to smoke or not to smoke. Quantity is important, inhaling is important, tar and nicotine may be important, but to the extent that the behavior is a matter of choice it tends to be smoking or not smoking. Going to school or dropping out has that quality, but there are more variations in school performance and behavior than in smoking behavior. Smoking is usually a public, not a clandestine, activity and for most smokers it is continual, even more so than eating, not episodic, like getting drunk, and it can be done almost anywhere (except for fire hazard) and done simultaneously with most activities (except while taking a shower). Finally, it requires a well-defined commodity that can be purchased from stores and vending machines almost everywhere, and a pack-per-day habit costs about fifteen minutes' work at the federal minimum wage.

A comparison with poverty may be useful. Government policy is much more, and more easily, directed at the consequences of smoking and poverty than at the behaviors: medical care for smoking, assistance in cash and in kind for people who are poor. Much less is known about how, and much less is effectively done, to keep high school students from smoking or to keep them from getting pregnant or to give them the values and motives that will make them good workers, good parents, and good neighbors. Smoking and the behaviors associated with poverty are conditioned by the cultures in which they are embedded; people who grow up where hustling is more admired than working tend to perpetuate the tradition, and people who grow up where smoking is the tradition tend to smoke. Both behaviors are affected by socioeconomic status, level of education, and sex.

Because smoking is ubiquitous it is potentially susceptible to encouragement or discouragement at home and at work, in vehicles and public buildings, in stores and restaurants, and in schools. Because it depends on a marketed commodity, it is subject to regulation or influence through the market.

Smoking is one of those behaviors that affects the quality of other people's environment. Until recently the offense was limited to cigarette butts and the ignition of fire, but the smoke itself is increasingly deemed the offender, especially with the growing evidence and publicity that, in the concentrations in which it typically occurs indoors, sidestream and exhaled smoke may be harmful to anybody who breathes it.

So let us examine in detail where influence is brought to bear in our society on the smoking of cigarettes, why smoking may qualify as a "bad" behavior and a proper subject of public concern, and what case can be made that, if necessary, some responsibility might properly be assumed by or assigned to some of our public institutions.

SMOKING AS "BAD BEHAVIOR"

I take smoking to be "bad" behavior; the corresponding good behavior is not smoking, or attempting to quit. (To avoid any connotation of evil, guilt, or fault we can substitute "undesirable.") It is a behavior that most readers will concur with me in deploring. We hope that young people do not become regular smokers and that smokers will try to quit, and succeed.

I identify two main reasons why we should deprecate smoking, although when we come to discuss whether there is a public responsibility, we shall consider a few more. The first reason is simply that smoking has been determined to be hazardous to the health of those who smoke. The surgeon general of the United States regularly publicizes an estimate that about 350,000 people die prematurely each year as a result of their habit. The estimate can be disputed, but even dividing it by two leaves it an impressive figure. Most of the people who die as a result of smoking do not die young, but they die when more than a decade of good living would otherwise remain. In addition to death there is sickness: heart disease, cancer, chronic lung disease, and unhealthily low birth weight.

A quite different reason for treating cigarette smoking as undesired behavior is that in this country *most of the people who smoke wish they did not.* Surveys show that nearly all smokers know that cigarettes are a major cause of cancer and heart disease.[1] In 1980 more than half of all young smokers, aged 21 to 24, of both sexes had unsuccessfully attempted to quit within the preceding twelve months.[2] Most people who smoke become regular smokers by age 21 and most of them quite promptly regret it.[3] About two-fifths of all the people in this country who ever smoked have quit; and, while some of them are still at risk of relapse, most of those who relapse will try to quit again.[4] It is therefore pretty conclusively established that smoking is considered a bad behavior by a large and relevant part of the American adult population—most of those who have ever smoked.

And most adults who have never smoked, especially the parents among them, dislike smoking by the people they care about. (I leave for later the people, mostly nonsmokers, who are offended or affected by others' tobacco smoke.)

Smoking is somewhat unusual among the behaviors we may deplore in that it is deplored by the people who engage in it. But there are other behaviors that share that quality. Many people who abuse alcohol wish they did not, and many who enjoy alcohol wish they could restrain some of the behaviors they engage in when intoxicated. Wife and child abusers often deplore their actions (which often occur under the influence of alcohol). Many people abuse drugs other than nicotine and alcohol and wish they did not. Many people neglect to fasten seatbelts and wish they did not. Many people eat too much, exercise too little, and skip their medicine and wish they did not. Many people kill time at the television and wish they did not. The list goes on.

A few demographic and social trends provide background. One of the more stunning social trends in the United States since World War II, one that was still not noticed or predicted even in the late 1960s, is the decline in the prevalence of smoking. Among the cohort of men who were in their twenties during the 1940s more than 70 percent smoked; in the comparable cohort today—and age twenty to thirty has always been the peak age of smoking prevalence for men in this country—the corresponding percent is about 40.[5] In 1965, 52 percent of adult men and 34 percent of adult women reported themselves to be current smokers; fifteen years later the percentages were 38 for men and 30 for women and declining.[6] The absolute number of cigarettes sold in this country—the product of per capita smoking and population size—peaked a few years ago and turned down.[7]

The prevalence of smoking is higher at lower incomes (but not at the very lowest), strikingly higher among high school graduates not expecting to attend college than among the college bound.[8] Among senior noncommissioned officers in the military services more than 60 percent smoke; among junior commissioned officers fewer than 25 percent smoke.[9] Cessation of smoking among women lags the cessation among men by a decade.[10] Smoking has virtually disappeared among people who will read this book, especially male readers. The good news, then, is that the trend is strongly against smoking in the United States. The bad news is that it is declining with a half-life of more than a generation, and is increasingly a habit of the less-advantaged classes.

A newer trend is that smoking has become less fashionable. Despite the advertisements, smoking is no longer generally perceived as a graceful, sophisticated activity. Nonsmokers in some sectors of society have become aggressive; smokers in many walks of life have become apologetic. Ashtrays are disappearing from corporate boardrooms, and smokers at conferences, if there are any smokers, are often clustered, voluntarily or by direction, near the ventilator outlets. Recent surveys among corporate employees indicate that even smokers believe there should be some explicit regulation of smoking in the workplace (if only to identify smokers' rights more clearly, as well as the rights of nonsmokers).

That smoking is bad for people does not necessarily establish it as a candidate for public-policy attention. It may be easy to establish a governmental responsibility for ascertaining and publicizing the nature of the health hazards, the benefits of quitting, the synergy of cigarette smoke with coal dust or cotton dust or worksite chemicals, the effect of smoking on a human fetus, and the nature of damage due to sidestream smoke. But controversies in several states on legally requiring that seatbelts be fastened in private vehicles show a lack of unanimity on whether people should be compelled to protect themselves from physical injury. (The absence of controversy on laws requiring appropriate restraining for small children is a pertinent contrast.)

THE CASE FOR PUBLIC POLICY

Various justifications have been adduced in support of public policies toward smoking. Three of them entail a kind of paternalism; three are based on alleged negative externalities; one focuses on social harmony. Each has merit, but whether any among them can win a policy argument will depend very much on what policy is being argued. Income-tax deductibility for the cost of a quit-smoking program may be more easily justified than raising the federal excise tax from sixteen cents to a dollar a pack. And some arguments for the assumption of public responsibility for smoking behavior may be policy-specific—that is, they may relate to taxation but not prohibition, to public buildings but not private, to school programs but not worksite programs.

Paternalism

The simplest argument in favor of some public responsibility is the one called "paternalism," a somewhat sexist term. People who smoke do not know any better; they make wrong decisions; they cannot control themselves; they need to be protected from social pressure. The Food and Drug Administration can forbid the sale of products containing dangerous ingredients, especially carcinogens. Cigarettes contain carcinogens vastly more potent than any that have been detected in commercial foods; people need to be denied the opportunity to consume cigarettes.

I do not know of any proposal to prohibit the sale or consumption of cigarettes. The weaker version of the argument would be that people cannot inform themselves about the hazards of smoking and so need to be told (as most of them have now been told repeatedly); that people need small obstacles put in the way of their smoking, like an excise tax higher than might be justified on revenue grounds; that people should be prevented from smoking where public bodies have appropriate jurisdiction, as in public buildings or health care facilities; or that public authorities should advise physicians and teachers on effective means of intervention in the smoking of their patients and pupils. Mandatory seatbelt and motorcycle helmet laws are examples of paternalistic regulation.

Self-Paternalism

More subtle is the justification that is sometimes referred to as "self-paternalism." This is the principle that people not only need to be protected from their own waywardness but want to be. They may welcome measures that make it more difficult for them to smoke, that remind them of the hazards of smoking, that support their efforts to quit, and that remove or reduce temptations and stimuli. An example of self-paternalism would be the deliberate purchase of an automobile that does not function if seatbelts are unfastened or if alcohol fumes are detected over the driver's seat. Clients of a faculty club or corporate dining room might vote to eliminate high-calorie desserts or at least not to keep them on display. There is evidence that many who smoke, and especially many who are trying to quit, would welcome an imposed environment in which cigarettes were simply unavailable; and that could be interpreted as establishing the legitimacy of a public policy of denial.

Parentalism

The third version of paternalism, which might better be called "parentalism," emphasizes that people become habituated as regular smokers at an age when they should be considered children and when they are treated as children for certain purposes in some jurisdictions. Alcohol is again forbidden to people under twenty-one in most states. The regulation of alcohol is at least partly justified by the hazards that young drunk drivers pose to others as well as to themselves and could equally fall under the heading of externalities, discussed below. The sale of cigarettes to young children is indeed forbidden in most states, though the restrictions are little enforced (and especially difficult to enforce on vending machines).

The parentalist case for government intervention can often be legitimized by reference to the acknowledged public role in schools, where smoking may be forbidden or where antismoking education and training may take place. And a special argument could be made that several hundred thousand young people each year enter military service, where the government should have an obligation at least to minimize the stimuli that may lead them to become regular smokers. (Since at least the First World War the federal government has had policies on smoking in military service, but of a perverse sort: Cigarettes were included in rations in both world wars; cigarettes are tax exempt and otherwise subsidized and touted as a fringe benefit in commissaries, post exchanges, and ships' stores.)

Externalities: Contagion

Next are three quite distinct concepts of externally imposed costs. The first is that cigarettes are (or contain) addictive substances, addiction to which spreads like a communicable disease. People smoke because other people smoke; people learn to smoke because they grow up in a society in which older people are already smoking. Furthermore, people learn to smoke before they fully appreciate that once they are habituated to regular smoking they will be unable to change their minds and quit. They learn to smoke when the publicized hazards of smoking make an inadequate impression, perhaps because the health consequences are beyond any youngster's planning horizon, perhaps because the publicity is from sources youngsters have learned not to trust, perhaps because the immediate motives for smoking have a captivating or blinding effect. Some adults report that they became regular smokers when they took a first job and found themselves surrounded by smokers. There is evidence that people quit more successfully if family, friends, and colleagues at work are also quitting or do not smoke. According to this analysis smoking has a "multiplier effect"; if a certain fraction of the smokers in a given social environment can be induced somehow to quit, another fraction will eventually quit as a consequence, and vice versa.

Smoking is "catching," like bad colds and many bad habits. This addictive communicable disease argument ties in with the parentalistic argument: If enough young adults, or perhaps adults of any age, can be induced to avoid or to quit smoking, fewer children will become regular, addicted smokers. Government, according to this argument, has an obligation to search for ways to protect children from the influences that will make them become regular smokers who cannot quit; among the main influences is the smoking that goes on around them. Government thus has an obligation to discourage any smoking that can influence the smoking of youngsters.

Externalities: Medical Costs

An altogether different externalities argument is that smoking is a voluntary individual activity that causes many people to become gravely ill, inflicting excess medical costs on the taxpaying public through Medicare and Medicaid and on the general public through medical and hospital insurance. The costs of medical care associated with terminal lung cancer—and most victims of lung cancer die within a year of diagnosis—are on the order of $15,000.[11] Most of these costs are not paid for by the patients themselves. The argument is that the government has a right and an obligation to discourage behaviors that inflict high costs on other people. (This argument was occasionally explicit in congressional discussion of the federal excise tax in 1985.) Strictly interpreted, this is an argument for making cigarette smokers pay more for their smoking, perhaps through special federal and state cigarette taxes identified with Medicare and Medicaid and higher health insurance premiums for smokers. But if health insurance discrimination is infeasible, getting people to quit may be the next best response to the argument about external costs.

Externalities: Passive Smoking

The third externality, only recently publicized in the medical literature, is that one person's smoke may harm another's health. More broadly, one person's smoke may be offensive and disagreeable to others. The two interact: People who were previously unaffected by the cigarettes smoked around them may have come to associate cigarette smoke with ugliness and disease, and now they not only are offended by the sight and smell but even suffer psychosomatic symptoms.

Conflict Management

Finally, it is argued that smoking in certain locations ought to be regulated simply in the interest of conflict resolution. If some people want to smoke, some do not mind smoke, and some despise the smoke they breathe, orderly arrangements may be needed to separate smokers from nonsmokers or to let smokers know when and where they can smoke least offensively and also to help adjudicate disputes when smokers and nonsmokers need to occupy the same space.

Smokers can claim they are "handicapped" by addiction to nicotine and that if no provision is made for their smoking they are subject to severe symptoms of withdrawal. Nonsmokers may claim symptoms from secondhand smoke. Within the family and among friends these conflicts may be settled informally, but on passenger aircraft and trains, in shops and offices, and in lobbies and waiting rooms these conflicts may be better resolved at a higher level of organization.

There is increasing evidence that smokers as well as nonsmokers appreciate the need for rules. This is not yet a case for government responsibility: Wise corporate executives, successful managers of restaurants and theaters, and the people who manage airlines and passenger trains might be expected to do a better job if they were free to adopt the rules best suited to their customers or employees. Still, the argument is made that a coercive push from government authorities may speed things up. Possibly an initial push by government can get a process moving that will sustain itself uncoerced. (In government buildings, of course, the government itself is the "local" manager or employer.)

THE EXERCISE OF RESPONSIBILITY AND INFLUENCE: THE PRIVATE SECTOR

What have been the responses at the different loci in American society to the unmistakable evidence, the substantial publicity, and the widespread opinion even among smokers that smoking is a severe hazard to the health of those who smoke, the "single most preventable cause of death in the United States" in the words of the U.S. surgeon general, and the most deadly commodity on the market "when used as intended" in the words of the dean of Harvard's School of Public Health?

Saving government for last, we can begin with the private sector, and within that sector "the market," and within the market, the market for cigarettes.

The Cigarette Market

Cigarette manufacturers responded early with filters. The efficacy of filters is not attested by any regulatory authority; filters do little to nicotine and do not remove much tar. The difficulty is primarily that filtering out tar or nicotine filters out flavor. But customers wanted filters, primarily to remove harmful substances; and the existence of filters may remind smokers that smoke contains something that needs to be filtered out.

More important, the tar and nicotine in cigarettes have steadily declined to an average only half that of a generation ago. Customers want low tar and nicotine for the protection of health; hardly anybody thinks cigarettes low in tar and nicotine taste better.

Interestingly, there is no evidence that any cigarette has been introduced that is low in tar and high in nicotine. (For agricultural reasons the tar and nicotine in tobacco tend to be strongly correlated; high-nicotine, low-tar tobacco is apparently not available or, if available, does not taste good.) There is evidence that people who smoke the low-tar, low-nicotine cigarettes compensate in various ways—by smoking more cigarettes, inhaling more deeply, holding the smoke longer in the lungs, even by holding the cigarette so that less air dilutes the smoke and more tar and nicotine get delivered. It is conjectured that the blood-nicotine level is being maintained by this compensatory smoking. If that is the case, smokers might be offered the nicotine they demand in less dangerous form by reducing only the tar in cigarettes, not the nicotine. If necessary, nicotine could be added to tobacco low in both tar and nicotine.

This possibility was mentioned in a report of a committee of the National Academy of Sciences a few years ago. There is no regulatory authority to prevent the sale of such a cigarette, although advertisements for it could be kept from making health claims. There is strong opposition to the mention of such a cigarette among people concerned with smoking and health, but most of that opposition seems ideological. Possibly cigarettes with nicotine as an additive are at a flavor disadvantage. Collectively the manufacturers might expect sales to fall as smokers received the nicotine they demand from less tobacco. Whatever the reason, here is a product that the market has not successfully called forth.

A competing tobacco product has enjoyed some market penetration within the past half dozen years. Known in the public health community as "smokeless tobacco," it is a moist snuff that is used the way old-fashioned chewing tobacco was used (and still is by several million people, mostly rural), namely as a source of flavor tucked between the back teeth and the cheek. Its reported use is chiefly among young people, especially well-to-do youth, and may be at least partly a reaction to the publicized health hazards of smoking and the lack of comparable publicity about smokeless tobacco. Only in the last few months has federal law required a health-hazard label on smokeless tobacco.

Smokeless tobacco is generally considered to be carcinogenic, affecting the oral cavity, not the lungs, but it is too soon to have good epidemiological data on the extent of the hazard and especially the consequences of using smokeless tobacco for a brief period of years. It is also too early to know whether young people obliged to give up the habit on taking an indoor job, because of the continual spitting it requires, will have become addicted to nicotine and require cigarettes to meet their needs or, alternatively, will have survived the period of susceptibility to cigarettes and escaped a lifelong habit.

The Anticigarette Market

Whereas the snuff is a competitor to cigarettes, a new pharmaceutical product is an antismoking commodity. Trademarked Nicorette, this is a chewing gum that contains amounts of nicotine calculated to meet an addict's most urgent need for this substance without inhalation of smoke and on a nonaddictive schedule for tapering off. The marketing strategy was to seek FDA approval as a prescription drug. One of its special advantages is that physicians, many of whom would like to help their patients quit smoking but do not know how to help, have something now that they can do—write a prescription. (This makes Nicorette something like a placebo that works on the physician.) The gum is chewed according to schedule with declining dosages over a period of about three months. It is too early to know how successful it will be with smokers, but Nicorette has enjoyed an initial success with physicians.

There have been reports that other devices that deliver pure nicotine may appear on the market. Whether they are intended to be lifelong substitutes for cigarettes, without the tar and the carbon monoxide and other poisonous gases, or aids to people who want to taper off is not yet clear. (The former would offer more enduring profits.)

Not many years ago smoking-cessation clinics, of which Smokenders was most widely advertised, were a budding industry. Currently, several health promotion packages are being marketed to American corporations, many of them with antismoking components and some of them focused on smoking; but the market for such help for the individual consumer has never burgeoned. It is difficult to gauge the efficacy of those commercial programs since the necessary follow-up research has not been possible. There is a very small market for hypnosis, acupuncture, aversive conditioning, and a few other therapies; most of them are generally considered to work, but none especially well. So the market may have failed to respond to the demand for a cure for the cigarette habit for the same reason it failed to attract customers to a cure for the common cold, namely, that no one has succeeded in devising an effective cure. But possibly the failure is one of marketing; few people who wish to quit smoking appear interested in therapy, commercial or other.

Aside from nicotine chewing gum, the main market response to the health-hazard publicity has been a steady downtrend in tar and nicotine content. We usually look to the market to produce what consumers demand. If lower tar and nicotine do not make smoking significantly safer, the fault, if any, is the consumer's erroneous belief in the efficacy of lower tar and nicotine; and this belief may be induced by (perhaps misguided) policies of the federal government. The surgeon general has never sought either to publicize the benefits of lower tar and nicotine or to denounce the idea of a safer cigarette. The evidence is unclear and the correct advice is probably a compromise: Lower tar and nicotine may benefit most smokers but not as much as the reduction in those two substances would suggest, and more for some smokers than for others, depending on how they smoke and perhaps on how important nicotine is in their need for cigarettes. This may be too many words for a warning label.

By requiring that tar and nicotine figures be displayed in cigarette advertisements and on cigarette packs, the Federal Trade Commission certainly is responsible for a powerful suggestion that tar and nicotine are what matter and that lower tar and lower nicotine make a difference worth the smoker's attention. Perhaps the market is responding to consumer demand that in turn is responding to a public health message it receives from a trusted federal agency by default rather than by intent.

Insurance

The market for insurance has made at least a nominal response to the evidence on the health effects of smoking. Some life insurance and fire insurance companies offer slightly reduced premiums to nonsmokers. Whether these reductions are based on any quantitative evidence of reduced mortality and fire hazard I do not know but consider unlikely. The reductions may simply be price discrimination to attract nonsmokers. I know of no attempt to monitor the veracity with which applicants check the no-smoking box on the application form.

It is often proposed, sometimes in the U.S. Senate, that health insurers should discriminate in their premiums against smokers (that is, in favor of nonsmokers). It is also sometimes proposed that health insurers should cover the cost of antismoking therapies and programs. Generally these insurers do not discriminate, and there may be several reasons for not doing so.

One would be the difficulty of distinguishing smokers from nonsmokers, handling minor relapses, distinguishing heavy smokers from light smokers, even making allowance for tar and nicotine content. A second would be the difficulty of dealing with obesity, exercise, alcohol, automobile use, and a variety of other health-related activities and environments that might equally claim attention as bases for discrimination.

Probably most decisive is the delay in the health consequences of smoking, coupled with the tendency for people to change health insurers when they change jobs. The medical care costs to be borne by an insurer in consequence of the smoking of a thirty-five-year-old whose health insurance goes with the job will be nearly inconsequential unless the occupation is one of exceedingly low turnover. Most lung cancer occurs after age sixty; most heart attacks occur after age fifty. If people subscribed for their lifetimes to a single health insurer and took the subscriptions with them as they changed jobs, the insurer would have a much stronger incentive to reflect the discounted value of future medical costs in current premiums.

The relevance to behavior, of course, is that if a person can be charged for the social costs of smoking, his or her smoking may be deterred. But the elasticity of demand for cigarettes is low, and the premium penalty for a smoker is not likely to be a large fraction of the cost of the cigarette he purchases, so the economic incentive might not prove powerful. Still, the publicized existence of a life insurance or a health insurance penalty premium for smokers might provide a dramatic reminder, reinforcing the surgeon general's message.

Legal Services

The market for legal services has recently responded to the health consequences of smoking. In this era of burgeoning malpractice and product-liability damages, several score suits have been filed around the country in behalf of victims of smoking-related illness or death. Whether the courts will eventually find in favor of some of the plaintiffs and, if they do, whether large punitive damages of the kind associated with, say, asbestos, will be assessed against defendant companies, nobody can predict with confidence. One difference between cigarettes and asbestos is that, pursuant to federal requirements, cigarette companies have been attaching health warnings to cigarette packs and advertisements. And juries may be less sympathetic with people who smoke themselves to death than with people who worked with asbestos in naval shipyards during World War II.

The courts are public bodies, a branch of government; but in civil cases their role is to resolve disputes that arise in the private sector. Civil suits against the government have in recent years been an important part of the policymaking process of government, as in the challenges to the financing of schools through the local property tax. The courts may yet impose something like a tax on the cigarette companies, if their liability insurance rates or self-insurance costs become substantial.

Advertising

Despite the federal ban on television advertising, advertising outlays for cigarettes have more than doubled in real terms in the past dozen years.[12] The power of advertising to lure young people into the regular habit of smoking and to keep adults loyal to their smoking habits invites strong opinions. Virtually all cigarette advertising is brand-specific, although R. J. Reynolds and Phillip Morris have done some generic advertising of an editorial nature. Reynolds, for example, financed the familiar large-print editorials on smokers' rights, on the "controversial" health hazards of smoking, and on smoking as an "adult habit."

Accused of using advertisements to entice people, especially young people, to smoke, spokesmen for the cigarette industry have argued that the advertising is aimed at brand loyalty, not at increasing the aggregate market. Opponents of cigarettes and of their advertising emphasize the portrayal of smoking as youthful, healthful, and romantic. People concerned with smoking policy usually assume that cigarette companies know what they are doing when they advertise and would not spend $2 billion per year unless they were getting their money's worth. Even the fact that many ads are nominally focused on youthful smokers, however, does not prove that the money is being spent to enlarge the market rather than to hold and attract smokers to the brand advertised. (Controversy in the Congress about the effects of advertising, especially about the efficacy and constitutionality of restrictions or prohibitions on advertising, may itself heighten awareness of the health effects of smoking.)

Much more important, and quite aside from the perfunctory warning attributed to the surgeon general in advertisements, cigarette advertising may have been the primary vehicle for publicizing the health hazards of smoking. For two decades a central theme of cigarette advertising has been the tar and nicotine content, the importance of combining good taste with the reduced delivery of these hazardous substances, and competitive debate over whose cigarette is safer. New brands are continually introduced that are "lighter" in tar and nicotine and advertised accordingly. We are invited, if we must smoke, to try Carleton. Some ads for low-tar cigarettes have quite blatantly shown handsome young men who acknowledge their awareness of the connection between smoking and health and aver that they just would not smoke if they could not find good flavor in a cigarette with less than five milligrams of tar.

The message being sent is that lighter cigarettes are safer. But the message received must also be that smoking is inherently unsafe. Airlines do not tout their individual safety records and invite comparison with other, less safe airlines; one might have guessed that cigarette companies as a group would try to avoid public competition over cigarette safety. But evidently there has never been a secure enough oligopoly to police itself against self-destructive advertising or to keep new entrants from coming into the market with great tar and nicotine fanfare.

In its zeal to protect the consumer the Federal Trade Commission may have somewhat dampened this tar and nicotine competition. The commission will not allow health claims in advertisements unless the product has been demonstrated healthful; somewhat perversely, the commission has attempted to apply this principle to tone down the health claim implicit in the claims of "lesser danger."

Advertising is a major activity, whether measured by the money spent or the fraction of our visual environment that consists of happy people, rugged people, healthy people, and sophisticated people smoking. But it is anybody's guess whether its cumulative impact is to entice people into smoking and to keep them smoking, to drill home the deadly message about tar and nicotine, or merely to support a thriving advertising industry. (It may be worth keeping in mind that the primary business of advertising companies is to sell advertising, not cigarettes.)

The Media

Although television, magazines, and newspapers are market commodities, their message content often reflects editorial or artistic judgment rather than a direct response to consumer demand. Thus their treatment of smoking as a health problem may not be exactly a response to consumer demand. And it may even be susceptible to dependence on advertising revenues. It is certainly no coincidence that *The Reader's Digest*, which pioneered the campaign to bring venereal disease to public attention in the 1930s, rejects cigarette advertising and has been a strong public voice on the health hazards of smoking. Even a cursory comparison of most magazines' treatment of the health effects of smoking with, say, their treatment of vitamin C invites suspicions of reticence. Magazines like *Parade, TV Guide, Family Weekly, Penthouse,* and the *National Enquirer* get a quarter or more of their advertising revenue from cigarettes.[13]

Considering the space that magazines have devoted over the past fifty years to techniques for weight loss, there is remarkably little in print on ways to quit or cut down on smoking. More has been published on how to housebreak a pet than on how to help your spouse quit smoking. One magazine publisher told me explicitly that she would not consider running a series of articles on the health hazards of smoking or the best ways to quit and avoid relapse because of her absolute dependence on cigarette advertising revenues. A magazine devoted to science recently published an article of several thousand words on ways to enhance longevity by controlling one's own behavior. It had room to mention hanging by your heels to let gravity straighten your spine, in the interest of longer life, but not a word on smoking. That issue actually had no cigarette ads, but it was a new magazine venture, substantially supported by advertisements for Scotch whiskey, and may have been anticipating cigarette revenues that it did not wish to jeopardize.

Cigarette advertisements have been banned from television since 1972. In 1969 the Federal Trade Commission determined that under the fairness doctrine antismoking time had to be provided on television broadcasts. The antismoking programs came from several sources, but the stations generally were compensated for the time by cigarette advertisers, which now had to buy extra time for the rival publicity. There is statistical evidence that these antismoking broadcasts were effective—extremely effective in relation to cost, considering the few tens of millions of dollars that they cost each year. They were so effective that the tobacco interests offered little opposition to the proposed ban on advertising.

If the advertising was essentially market-share competition, one might have expected the cigarette companies to welcome the ban on television advertising as a way to save expenditure on a zero-sum game. But advertising outlays more than doubled in real terms in the following decade, suggesting that the ban was either inadequate protection or irrelevant. But the ban did protect the television industry from direct pressure from cigarette advertisers on their treatment of smoking in programs. The networks might still be susceptible to potential withdrawal of advertising of other products—cookies, canned vegetables, or beer—produced by subsidiaries of cigarette companies. But it is probably harder to perceive implicit threats about the treatment of smokers from the advertisers of canned peas, and explicit threats may be strongly inhibited.

And this has made a difference. Except in old movies, smoking has virtually disappeared from most television. Panel discussions on public television used to be viewed through graceful columns of pipe and cigarette smoke; the studios no longer even put out ashtrays. Newscasters and commentators used to smoke if they wished; now they do not, and maybe do not wish to. These impressions are confirmed by a recent study of "cigarette acts" in television dramas and situation comedies. Some tens of hours of television dramas and situation comedies were examined in each of four periods, the first 1950–63 and the final one 1981–82. Each smoking act was tabulated and the data converted to an hourly rate. In the earliest period, just before the first surgeon general's report, there were four or five such "acts" per hour on average; in the latest period the average was about one act for every three hours of drama. The decline was tenfold. In situation comedies the rate had dropped to less than one-sixth what it was in the earliest period. I take this trend to be simultaneously a *reflection* of the lowered status of smoking and an *influence* on it. And it very likely reflects some combination of network policy and the personal smoking habits of television professionals. (There was an opposite trend in the portrayal of "alcohol events.")[14]

The Health Professions

The American Medical Association has until recently been quiet on smoking, even on physicians' responsibilities toward their patients' smoking. Only in early 1986 did the AMA publicly call for severe restrictions on the advertising of cigarettes. A few of the medical journals conscientiously addressed the subject of smoking; in December 1983 the *New York State Journal of Medicine* devoted its entire

150-page issue to the subject, not just to medically pertinent facts but to social and public policy.

None of the major medical associations has embarked on any kind of campaign, even to enlighten, educate, and motivate its own membership toward a more effective intervention with patients. (I think it likely that the American College of Obstetricians and Gynecologists will shortly face up to the issue more resolutely as a result of recent evidence and publicity on the hazards of smoking to a fetus.) Physicians are among those who have shown the greatest trend toward cessation of smoking themselves, but they are diffident about their patients' smoking. And they have reason to be. Most of their smoking patients have already tried to quit, unsuccessfully; a little more advice may seem futile to the physician; and the physician's success rate is usually discouraging. Most physicians had little education in the behavioral sciences and no specific training in how to help patients quit—even where to send them for help—other than merely advising them to quit if they can.

Hospitals have not been in the vanguard of institutions that regulate when and where people may smoke. Registered nurses are beginning to join the professional trend toward less smoking but have often claimed that the stresses of their job make rules against smoking on duty a stressful privation. Still, some example is set. Most people's physicians no longer smoke, and patients recovering from a heart attack are attended by fewer nurses who smoke in their presence.

Employers

Executive leadership in many large corporations is being attracted to policies that forbid or regulate smoking in the workplace. This trend may reflect the declining prevalence of smoking among senior corporate executives themselves (although on the executive floor of many corporate headquarters the support staff still smokes). It often reflects concern with some potential future legal liability for a "safe workplace." Smoking policies in a corporation can be a delicate matter. Organized labor, for example, possibly inhibited by fraternity toward organized workers in the production and distribution of cigarettes, has been negative on the subject. Paternalism, especially emanating from upper middle-class executives who recently quit smoking themselves, can be resented by employees who have no private offices where they can retreat for a private smoke. Nevertheless, with care and patience many corporations have succeeded in discussing, experimenting with, and eventually adopting policies that let smokers know where they may smoke and where they may not and procedures for resolving disputes, monitoring the rules, and hearing complaints. The R. J. Reynolds Company in one of its recent editorial advertisements reassured the corporate public that there is no need for and no serious trend toward corporate responsibility for the indoor environment and that barely more than one-third of the largest corporations have policies on smoking! More than one-third and growing. . . .

Church

Fifty years ago in this country the Protestant and Catholic churches strongly and quite effectively disapproved of smoking. There was widespread moral disapproval especially of smoking among young women, and my grandfather refused to hire anybody to mow the lawn who had ever been seen smoking. None of the great religious leaders of today has thrown any weight behind the surgeon general, though one might have thought that pro-life and antismoking had something in common.

Smoking is almost nonexistent among Mormons, Seventh Day Adventists, and Christian Scientists. So a church that is a powerful institution in a person's life can have great influence on smoking behavior. This influence is both direct and indirect—direct in its disapproval of smoking, indirect in creating in localities, like Brigham Young University, where the church is influential, a social environment in which smoking is so uncommon as to offer little stimulus to those who might be susceptible. Interestingly, the Seventh Day Adventists successfully operate quit-smoking programs all around the world.

The "Voluntaries"

Until a very few years ago the American Cancer Society, the American Heart Association, and the American Lung Association behaved more like rival candidates for contributions than a coalition bound by a common interest in the prevention of smoking. Now those three organizations support a new Coalition on Smoking or Health, with a lobbying headquarters in Washington. On matters like the cigarette excise tax and, potentially, on any further action against cigarette advertising, this Coalition has proved remarkably effective. Like so many medically oriented organizations, these "voluntaries" have tended to think first of research into the diagnosis and cure of disease. As with polio, muscular dystrophy, and birth defects, the tradition is a medical one, and preventive behaviors, while appreciated, have been outside the disciplinary boundaries. (Contrast the dental profession.) The American Lung Association does offer help to those who want to quit, and in many large cities it can respond to telephone calls. All three associations participate annually in the Great American Smokeout, a one-day ceremony that gets media attention.

The Personal Sector

Before turning to the public sector, we should spend a moment on the individual smoker and the family as a locus of responsibility. In this country it appears that one of the strongest influences on whether a young person takes up smoking is the smoking behavior of parents, siblings, and closest friends. It may be no exaggeration that the most effective thing parents could do to keep their children from smoking is simply not to smoke themselves. A pediatrician who advises parents against smoking in the nursery—and apparently few pediatricians ever discuss the subject—might reasonably add that the long-run health of the newborn may be influenced more by whether he or she grows up with two smoking parents than by the indoor pollution during the first months of life. I shall not discuss the moral authority and effectiveness of the family as a locus of responsibility for good behavior; but parents' behavior seems to have a strong direct influence on children's behavior with respect to smoking.

What people can do personally to abet their own attempts to quit smoking is a saddening subject. We can find excellent help on how to control our dog's behavior, but nowhere in our school systems (with the possible exception of a psychology elective for college sophomores) can we learn about the skills needed to control appetites and compulsive behaviors. People are on their own and substantially without help when it comes to dealing with the fingernails they bite or the cigarettes they smoke. Diet for weight loss has been well represented in the literature for fifty years, often on the bestseller list;

just about everything written on what helps in quitting smoking, or in helping a spouse or parent to quit, would make a very small book.

It undoubtedly helps to be a person of decisiveness, determination, resolve, and strong character when trying to kick an addictive drug like nicotine or a habit like smoking. The most decisive determinants of success, however, may be skills and strategies for coping, an understanding of relapse and how to cope with it, skill in gaining support from friends and family, even skill in deciding when and how to quit, and what the more auspicious occasions are.

Here I offer a judgment. Much more is known that could help than is readily available to the people who try to quit. Perhaps this knowledge is not available because they will not accept it; most efforts to quit may be impetuous, allowing no time for study and planning. Perhaps what is known, though potentially helpful, is not decisive enough to gain a reputation for efficacy that will draw in the customers.

But the field of self-discipline, or "self-command" as I call it, is underdeveloped and goes substantially unacknowledged in the formal training we provide youngsters as they grow up.

THE EXERCISE OF RESPONSIBILITY AND INFLUENCE: THE PUBLIC SECTOR

The federal government has had to be ambivalent about smoking because the states of North Carolina, Kentucky, and Tennessee have a tradition of heavy dependence on tobacco cultivation and cigarette manufacture. Tobacco accounts for only about 3 percent of farm products by value in this country, but its regional concentration makes it a political force. The surgeons general, who have a little moral authority and some access to the media, have been soldiers against smoking for at least twenty-two years; the cabinet secretaries they work for have included some who supported them to the hilt and some who offered no support at all. Presidents and their wives can make the war on addictive drugs a favorite campaign, but the single addictive drug that accounts for more premature deaths than all the other drugs together has never received sustained attention from the White House. (The number of people dependent on tobacco for a living is smaller than the number estimated to die every year because of smoking, but no one can make powerful electoral arithmetic out of that.)

The federal government's assumption of responsibility has taken several forms. Most important has been research, much of it supported through the National Cancer Institute and the National Heart, Lung, and Blood Institute. Here as in the private voluntary agencies one sees the focus on diagnosis and cure rather than on behavior. It is to the credit of the National Cancer Institute that it recently began to finance research on smoking as a behavior that needs to be brought under self-control. Very recently the National Institute on Drug Abuse put smoking on its agenda as the most deadly drug of abuse in this country. (Those institutes cannot help looking over their shoulders at tobacco-state senators and congressmen on appropriations committees.)

In the field of information and education, the federal government relies substantially on a small Office on Smoking and Health in the Department of Health and Human Services, which serves as a clearinghouse for information about smoking and is responsible for compiling the surgeon general's reports on *The Health Consequences of Smoking.* This is the main publicity thrust of the federal government. There are no federal programs in the schools on the subject. Eventually the National Cancer Institute may try to train some thousands or even tens of thousands of physicians in how to be effective with respect to ending their patients' smoking, but that will not happen until it knows how physicians can be effective and how they can be motivated.

The federal government restricts the advertising of cigarettes. The 1972 ban on television advertising had the unfortunate effect of cutting off the financing for antismoking TV spots. Labels are required on cigarette packages, and recently the standard "hazardous to your health" label was replaced by four more specific labels to be rotated periodically. (Ironically, the warning labels may have protected cigarette manufacturers from liability for deaths and illnesses caused by cigarettes, and may even have been so intended by some legislators.) It appears that the federal excise tax will be kept at sixteen cents, where it has been since 1983, having been steady at eight cents for the preceding thirty years. The Food and Drug Administration exercises no authority over additives to cigarettes. When the Civil Aeronautics Board disappeared there was apprehension that the mandatory separation of smokers from nonsmokers in commercial aircraft might disappear, but the Department of Transportation continues to enforce the segregation.

There has been talk in the Congress about federal legislation to require or induce health insurers and life insurers to offer discriminatory premiums for smokers and nonsmokers. And very recently—potentially of tremendous importance to the nation's health—the Department of Defense has begun to show concern and acknowledge responsibility for the rather dismal record of smoking within the armed forces. What can be done to curb the smoking of young servicemen and women, if anything, remains to be seen.

State governments are increasingly putting limits on smoking in buildings and vehicles under their jurisdiction and in places where health care is delivered to the public. There is a very modest trend toward municipal policies that regulate smoking, that oblige worksites to have policies, or that require restaurants to separate smokers from nonsmokers. In most states it is illegal to purchase cigarettes before a certain age, but there is nowhere any sign of enforcement. A few school systems are beginning again to experiment with rules against smoking. States (and some cities) have cigarette taxes, but mainly for revenue, not to discourage smoking.

In my judgment the increasingly pervasive public and private restrictions on smoking and separation of smokers and nonsmokers are powerfully effective reminders that smoking is a hazard to health and that it has become unfashionable and offensive. Their role is educational as well as regulatory.

CONCLUSIONS

The striking conclusion is that with no strong assumption of responsibility anywhere regarding smoking, the prevalence of smoking has declined dramatically during the past two decades. I have not been persuaded by any of the efforts to determine statistically, through time-series analysis and cross-section analysis, just what has influenced this trend. Something has happened that we do not understand, that we probably never will disentangle, and about which we can all make our own guesses. Maybe the surgeons general and their various reports had far more influence than anybody could believe; maybe the tobacco industry shot itself in the foot with its advertisements in response to the health-hazards publicity. Maybe the greater interest in exercise, nutrition and diet, and the avoidance of cholesterol along with the recently noticed decline in the consumption of hard liquor represent some pervasive trend of which the decline in cigarette consumption is a part. It is hard to know where to give credit for bringing this about, and maybe no great credit is due anywhere.

A second conclusion is that influence and responsibility with respect to smoking behavior is widely dispersed among federal, state, and local agencies, voluntary associations, the health professions, the information and entertainment media, churches, employers, parents, and the market. Many of the institutions that one might have expected to claim or assume responsibility and to exercise influence have been remarkably inactive.

A conclusion that I reach, but that does not emerge from what I have written here, is that there are no easily recognized, highly effective policies at the federal level, of a kind appropriate to a democracy, just waiting to be adopted and implemented as soon as the health agencies of government can be mobilized or the tobacco-state interests bought off or overcome. There are still over 50 million smokers in the United States, the large majority of whom are old enough to vote. To attempt the equivalent of a prohibition on smoking or a prohibitive federal tax is not only politically out of the question but would certainly be a divisive interference with personal behavior.

But the trend is away from smoking. Here is some behavior that is actually getting better. May it continue!

NOTES

1. American Lung Association, *NEWS*, December 5, 1985.
2. *The Health Consequences of Smoking: Cardiovascular Disease,* a report of the Surgeon General (Rockville, Md.: Health and Human Services, Office in Smoking and Health, 1983), Table 6, p. 373.
3. Kenneth E. Warner, "Consumption Impacts of a Change in the Federal Cigarette Excise Tax," *The Cigarette Excise Tax, April 17, 1985* (Cambridge, Mass.: Harvard University Institute for the Study of Smoking Behavior and Policy, 1985), Table 3, p. 95.
4. *The Health Consequences of Smoking,* Table 1, p. 367.
5. Jeffrey E. Harris, "Cigarette Smoking among Successive Birth Cohorts of Men and Women in the United States During 1900–80," *JNCI* 71, no. 3 (September 1983): text-figure 1, p. 475.
6. *The Health Consequences of Smoking,* Table 1, p. 367.
7. *Tobacco: Outlook and Situation Report,* Economic Research Service, United States Department of Agriculture, September 1985.

8. Lloyd D. Johnston, Patrick M. O'Malley, and Jerald G. Bachman, *Highlights from Drugs and American High School Students 1975-83* (Rockville, Md.: The National Institute on Drug Abuse, 1984), p. 12.

9. *1982 Worldwide Survey of Alcohol and Nonmedical Drug Use Among Military Personnel*, Table 7.17, p. 162.

10. Harris, "Cigarette Smoking among Successive Birth Cohorts," p. 475.

11. Nelson S. Hartunian, Charles N. Smart, and Mark S. Thompson, *The Incidence and Economic Costs of Major Health Impairments* (Lexington, Mass.: Lexington Books, 1981), p. 230, and Table 5-15, p. 231. Costs cited are in 1975 dollars; the index of medical care costs has more than doubled over the decade.

12. *Smoking and Health Reporter*, Center for Health and Safety Studies, Indiana University, Vol. 3, No. 1, October 1985, p. 8.

13. *New York State Journal of Medicine* 85, no. 7 (July 1985): 466.

14. Warren Breed and James R. De Foe, "Drinking and Smoking on Television, 1950-1982," *Journal of Health Policy* (June 1984): Table 1, p. 261.

CHAPTER 8

Public and Private Responsibilities in the Struggle against Poverty

Glenn C. Loury

A standard method employed by students of public opinion to discriminate between "conservatives" and "liberals" is to ask people about their attitudes toward the poor. Conservatives, conventional wisdom has it, think that poverty results from individuals' failings of character, that agitation for greater public assistance to the poor is but a thinly disguised argument for "soaking the rich," and that rational individual responses to transfer programs will probably only increase poverty. Liberals, the story goes, see poverty as linked to fundamental failings of the economic system—unemployment, discrimination—largely beyond the individual's control, insist that the more prosperous owe an obligation to their less fortunate fellow citizens, and minimize or ignore the effects of assistance on the behavior of the poor.

CAUSATION AND RESPONSIBILITY

At stake in this dispute are issues of *causation* and *responsibility.* What forces cause poverty? Who is responsible for the indigent? One's response to the latter question depends in part on the former. We are less likely to hold a victim of circumstance responsible for his condition than one whose willful acts have brought on his misery. People whose mental illness compels them to commit criminal acts typically are not punished, but treated. Hungry children are to be fed, not questioned as to their parents' attitudes toward work. This response is all the stronger if the circumstance that victimizes the individual involves patent injustice. The exploited, the discriminated against, the oppressed tend to be seen as worthy recipients of assistance, even when their need results most directly from their own behavior. Some argue that these people's behavior has been caused by their oppression. The fact of unjust victimization thus seems to indemnify the victim against being held responsible for subsequent acts—indeed against the very possibility of being regarded as a responsible moral agent.[1]

In considering the appropriate roles of public and private action regarding the problem of poverty, it may make sense to think in terms of causation and responsibility. We may ask then: Under what circumstances and for what reasons might the public sector undertake to redistribute income, or otherwise expend funds raised through coercive taxation, with the intent of reducing poverty? This is, of course, a very old query, ordinarily the province of political philosophers, approached in terms of the various conceptions of distributive justice. I will not attempt here to contribute to this rich and diverse philosophical literature; I can hardly hope to resolve the debate among such noted minds as Harvard's own John Rawls and Robert Nozick on this external question.[2]

In the next section I will address a more limited version of this question, offering arguments that an economist might make, largely on efficiency grounds, for such a public undertaking. Like most economic arguments aimed at rationalizing public action, these revolve around the presence of market failure. Whatever one's notions about distributive justice, it can be argued that the avoidance of inefficient economic outcomes provides a legitimate basis for public action.

But what of private responsibilities? Are there not circumstances in which the burden of responding to the problem of poverty most properly rests in private hands (including, importantly, the hands of the poor themselves)? We certainly expect (and through the law attempt to compel) parents to provide for their children to the extent they can. In his widely noted Godkin Lectures presented at the Kennedy School in the spring of 1985, Senator Daniel Patrick Moynihan focused public attention on the extent to which the problem of poverty has become a problem of women and their children with insufficient resources to live decently.[3] Over the last half-century, Moynihan declared, we have reversed the traditional relationship between poverty and age, so that now it is the young who are most likely to be living "below the line" rather than the aged, who are protected by extensive public systems of income and health provision.

Who is to be held accountable here? What are the public and private responsibilities? Unlike the case of the elderly, the circumstances of children are largely determined by the behavior of their parents. In seeking to limit the poverty of children, therefore, we must consider how the private actions of our agents—their custodial parents— promote or impede the betterment of the children's condition. Some fathers, as I discuss below, are getting quite a free ride.[4] Without doubt, some of these poor children are suffering because of their parents' dereliction of responsibility. Who, if anyone, can or should make these (sometimes teenage) parents behave more responsibly?

This is no idle question. We devolve on these young parents enormous responsibilities for which they are often unprepared. Consider the case of a pregnant minor trying to decide whether she should abort, put her child up for adoption, or bring the baby home to a possibly (though by no means necessarily) chaotic environment. It is her decision alone, but it is a fateful one for which she is probably not fully prepared. We do not permit this very same minor to decide legally about alcohol consumption; we strictly ration her access to an automobile, prohibit her from participation in our civic life through voting, and legally (though, obviously, not very effectively) prohibit her from consenting to sexual intercourse with an adult male. Yet we leave (by default?) the awesome choices about pregnancy entirely in her inexperienced hands. There seems to be an accountability gap here.

ECONOMIC ARGUMENTS FOR A PUBLIC ROLE

An individual is poor if he or she lives in a household with total income below the level society deems minimally necessary for a household of that size. That minimal level varies with the number of members of the household. The income of the household is the sum of the earnings of its members plus the (public and private) transfer payments received by members. The extent of poverty will thus depend on the income available to individuals and on individuals' decisions regarding household formation.

The economic theory of earnings determination is only one component of a full theory of the prevalence of poverty. Demographic factors are also of preeminent importance. (Thus, trends in the earnings of individuals and in the incidence of poverty need not move hand in hand.) Assuming competitive labor markets and a full-employment economy, modern economic theory provides an explanation of individuals' earnings potential based on their productivity in the market, which in turn, depends on the innate aptitudes and acquired skills of the individual workers. Actual earnings depend additionally on the individuals' preferences regarding occupations, risk bearing, and the enjoyment of leisure. A worker's acquired skills, or human capital, reflect the past productivity-enhancing investments undertaken on his behalf by himself, his family, or his employers. By "innate aptitudes" I mean that constellation of factors determining the worker's physical and mental abilities that are fixed, whether because of biological or irreversible environmental influences, and lie beyond the individual's control.[5]

The assumption of competitive labor markets and a full-employment economy is, of course, unrealistic. Some workers' low earnings result from correctable impediments to the free flow of labor among alternative employments (e.g., discrimination due to race or sex that is not competed away by the free entry of nondiscriminating employers who bid up the wages of equally productive but underpaid female or minority workers, or labor market segmentation that restricts, geographically or occupationally, certain categories of labor to a narrow range of employments, resulting in noncompeting groups of workers, some of whose earnings are depressed thereby).[6] Such conditions create a compelling argument for public action in the face of poverty. Moreover, failures of the macroeconomy—a protracted depression/recession due to insufficient aggregate demand not correctable through fiscal and monetary policy, for example—provide another rationale for public action aimed at restoring full employment and in consequence reducing the prevalence of poverty.

The "Public Good" Argument

Even when the conditions of competition and full employment are met, economic arguments may be adduced for some public responsibility in fighting poverty. The most direct of these rests on the public-goods character of the income distribution. If the members of a society care about some features of the overall distribution of income in society (like the number of persons living below the poverty line), and not just about their direct personal consumption, then the collective action of government can generally improve on the outcome of private transfers among persons. This is because the distribution of income, regarded as a "consumption good" affecting the welfare of members of the society, has the properties of a pure public good. As in the case of national defense, the typical textbook example of a public good, each member of the society "consumes" exactly the same "amount" of it, and their consumption does not alter what others consume. Since an individual's private investment in altering the distribution of income (by reducing poverty through charity and philanthropy, for example) produces benefits for every consumer who would like fewer people to be poor, standard arguments regarding the efficiency of the provision of public goods imply that the outcome of *laissez faire* can be uniformly improved upon through state action.

Thus, for example, if every member of society is averse to seeing starving children on the streets, people with resources will spend some of their income to reduce starvation, even without any government action. But in deciding how much to spend, they will not consider the benefits such private expenditures generate for all the other members. The aggregate expenditure on feeding the starving will therefore fall short of the efficient level; state intervention can produce a more efficient outcome (neglecting the efficiency loss due to the government's use of distorting taxation to raise revenues for such public expenditure).

Capital Market Failure

Another argument for public involvement in fighting poverty is based on capital market failure.[7] If, as in the human capital framework sketched above, individuals' earnings are partially the result of investments in training, education, migration, health care, and other productivity-enhancing activities, then unequal access to funds for undertaking such investments will generate inefficiency that can be corrected through public action. Imagine two individuals of identical innate aptitudes, though born to different economic circumstances. Early investments in nutrition, education within the home, and the like will vary for these two individuals because of the varying resources available to their families. Parents, who control the family resources, are presumably motivated to forgo some personal gratification so as to invest in their offspring because of the parents' natural concern for the well-being of their progeny. But because the parents' incomes differ, unless they have access to a competitive capital market on which they may borrow to finance productivity-enhancing expenditures for their children, the amount of investment actually made will vary positively with the family's private resources.

If the "production function" linking parental investments to later life earnings for the offspring exhibits diminishing returns to such investments, then two sets of parents making different income-constrained investment decisions face divergent expected marginal returns (in terms of the incremental impact of human capital expenditures on their offsprings' expected life earnings). Under these assumptions the poorer parents, investing less, will anticipate a higher marginal return, while the richer parents, investing more in their child, will anticipate a lower marginal benefit from additional expenditures of this kind. If the richer parents could be induced to transfer a small amount of their human capital investment to the poorer family's child, then the offspring of both families could, through subsequent interfamily income transfer in the opposite direction, have greater incomes in the future.

This is what a perfect capital market for investments in the young would accomplish. With such a market, the wealthier parents would find it advantageous to transfer resources to their child through a direct bequest rather than through investment in the child's human capital whenever the loan rate exceeded the expected marginal benefit from human capital investment, while the poorer parents would borrow to finance additional expenditures on their child's human capital whenever the expected marginal return from such investment exceeded the loan rate. In equilibrium both families would be investing in their offspring to the point where their expected marginal returns were equal to the opportunity cost of such investment (namely the loan rate) and hence equal to each other.

The point here is that efficient resource allocation for the development of human productivity requires that the children of low-income families not be restricted by limited parental resources in their access to training.[8] While devices certainly exist in our society for overcoming this problem (e.g., means-tested public subsidy for loans to finance college education), they are probably far from adequate, especially at overcoming the limiting consequences of extreme poverty for the future productivity of the young. Early childhood investments in nutrition, preschool education, or even prenatal medical care are fundamentally income constrained. Nor should we expect a competitive market to eliminate the difference among families in expected rates of return to such investments in children, as in the example just discussed. Parents are generally unable to bind their children legally to honor debts incurred in the children's behalf. Laws against slavery prevent the lenders in a human capital loan market from attaching the (human) assets of those on whose behalf such borrowing is undertaken, should the latter default on this obligation. (Indeed, default has been a pervasive problem in government-guaranteed educational loan programs.) Since the ability to make use of human capital investments is unknown even to the borrowing parents, genuine bankruptcies would occur as children mature to learn they are not as able as their parents gambled they would be. Thus, the direct public provision of skill-enhancing services to the children of poor families, financed through general taxation, can be rationalized as an effort to reduce the efficiency loss associated with the inadequate development of poor children's productive potential that could be expected under *laissez faire*.

Social Insurance

A final economic argument for public sector involvement in reduction of poverty has to do with the fact that individuals face income risks that are theoretically insurable but for which private insurance is not generally available.[9] This is the obvious rationale for unemployment insurance, which aims to pool individuals' risks of temporary joblessness. The moral hazard problems (deriving from the fact that income depends on effort as well as luck) ensure that private markets will fail to bring about complete risk spreading. Yet one can imagine that efficiency gains would be produced by a social compact through which individuals commit themselves, through the agency of their government, to assist extreme economic "losers" at the expense of economic "winners" on an ongoing basis.

Consider the intergenerational version of this argument in which the risks to be insured concern the lifetime incomes of the members of a given generation. Suppose that parents are uncertain of their offspring's future ability and luck and hence cannot tell where they will end up in the income distribution of the next generation.[10] By establishing a tradition of assistance to the poor (insurance for extreme economic losers), by committing future generations through current action to a somewhat egalitarian distributive policy, a society can reduce the risks of this sort faced by its current members. Their knowledge that income will be redistributed in the next generation allows parents to regard their offspring's random income as less risky, and thus to experience a higher level of welfare.[11]

SOME CONCEPTUAL PROBLEMS
IN MEASURING POVERTY

The notion of poverty involves an inherently arbitrary distinction. The condition is discrete—either one is poor or one is not—while its underlying determinant (household income) is continuous (suggesting the value of other indicia like the poverty gap, which measures the difference between the poor household's income and the relevant poverty line). This conceptual discreteness invites politicians and citizens to think of "the poor" as a distinct set of people typified by the characteristics of the "average poor person," even though the facts suggest this categorization is inaccurate.[12]

Moreover, the decision about where to draw the line can interact with this inherent labeling tendency to affect policy. A low official line will tend to identify as poor the very worst-off of individuals and magnify the visibility of nonworking people—hard-core unemployed, female family heads, the so-called underclass. With a higher line, many more working people would be categorized as poor, creating a very different perception in the public mind about precisely who the poor are. Similarly, defining household income to include the value of in-kind transfers (without any change in the official poverty line) would significantly change the characteristics of the typical poor person. In a political context in which the poor are conceived as a collectivity, such changes in definition are likely to influence the formulation of policy.

Relative Deprivation and Permanent Poverty

Though poverty is defined by an absolute criterion—whether household income is above or below the relevant line—it has operated in practice as a relative concept. Historically, the concept of need involves some variant of the notion of relative deprivation. By implication, even the best-functioning economic system may not be able to eliminate such poverty in the long run. For if poverty is the condition of having, say, one-half the average standard of living, then the poor shall indeed always be with us. So long as there is substantial variation in individuals' earning capacities and economic good fortune, in the absence of massive egalitarian redistribution, which would surely threaten the underlying productive capacity of the society, there will be relative deprivation.[13]

In this sense, it is impossible for the private sector, however productive, to eliminate poverty. The "fault" here lies not in our mode of production, but in our conception of need. In his essay "Can American Capitalism End Poverty?," Stanley Lebergott compares the standard of living of the contemporary poor with that of the typical worker of an earlier generation. In 1900, 15 percent of U.S. families had flush toilets (compared with 86 percent of poor Americans by 1970), 3 percent had electricity (compared with 99 percent of the poor by 1970), 18 percent had (ice) refrigeration (compared with 99 percent of the poor by 1970), 48 percent lived one or fewer to a room (compared with 96 percent of the poor by 1970), and so on.[14] None of this discussion is intended to deny the "ancient, decisive, and ubiquitous presence of envy," though it surely follows that if long-term economic development leads to real wage growth and if workers choose to spend that growing income on new and better products, then the economic system, *because* of its success, must continue to generate poverty!

Household (De)composition

By defining poverty in terms of household income relative to household needs, we make the incidence of poverty (and therefore the degree of public concern over poverty, the extent of political pressure to solve the problem, and so on) dependent on private decisions about living arrangements, which may or may not warrant public concern. Here we meet again the question of responsibility, though in practice this question is usually resolved implicitly, without deliberation. Under this definition, poverty may be increased in various ways without changing any individual's income—for example, by (1) allowing (or encouraging) older people to live apart from their children, (2) permitting young adults to set up independent households before marrying or establishing a career, or (3) having unwed teenage mothers live with their babies apart from their parents.

The household dissolutions that follow from these decisions may or may not be a good thing. (Since they are voluntary, they must be perceived as welfare enhancing for at least one of the parties to the original household.) Moreover, the trend toward smaller households generated by decisions such as these also reflects changing social mores, whose legitimacy would be defended by many. Indeed, it is possible that rising living standards could contribute indirectly to an increase in poverty through the effect of greater affluence on living arrangements. If households use some of their increased wealth to finance the greater acquisition of privacy (through the setting up of additional, independent households), the result could be to increase the number of people formally classified as poor.

As Mary Jo Bane has observed, these private decisions about living arrangements affect the extent of poverty in two ways. First, a trend toward more independent households implies that, within a certain range of incomes, the loss of economies of scale in household production (reflected in the fact that the poverty line, regarded as a function of household size, does not grow proportionately with the increasing number of household members) will lead to an increase in poverty. And second, the manner in which the income of household members is divided after a household split (due, say, to divorce) can generate poverty even though the total income of members of the original household is sufficient for both new households to live above their respective poverty lines.[15]

To posit a social obligation to address the poverty created by a young or elderly household member living apart from a family that could afford to support him as a member of the original household is implicitly to argue that society, and not the family, is responsible for the well-being of such persons. As has been widely noted, there is significant unexploited capacity to reduce poverty through the strict enforcement of court-ordered child support obligations on non-custodial parents.[16] Middle-class adult children, who may owe their economic security to past investments by their parents, could well be regarded as primarily responsible for the maintenance of their parents at a decent living standard in their old age. Such is our social custom, though not our law. Yet when we measure poverty in terms of the household (instead of a kin-based definition), we implicitly assign at least part of this responsibility otherwise.

POVERTY AND RACE

It is not obvious, as a theoretical matter, why the fact of racial heterogeneity in American society should affect an analysis of the roles of the public and private sectors in addressing the issue of poverty. Although poverty is far more prevalent among blacks than in the population at large, it has always been the case, and remains so today, that blacks constitute a minority of the poor. The practice of employment or other market discrimination against blacks, by lowering individual incomes in the group, has surely exacerbated poverty. The effort to remedy discrimination, however, is a public undertaking of inherent worth that is now far advanced (there is, of course, dispute about how far) and that in any event ought not to be construed as a poverty-fighting tool.[17]

The Weight of History

Even a cursory examination of the history of public antipoverty policy shows that the overrepresentation of blacks among the poor, and especially among the poorest of the poor, has played a crucial role in shaping the debate about causes and responsibility. The reasons for this seem to be historical. Particularly significant is the fact that the "War on Poverty" began just as the civil rights movement reached its peak. (It is interesting and instructive to speculate on how that program might have been different in the absence of this complex interaction.) The "blaming the victim" charge, so readily leveled at those who (like Senator Moynihan in 1965) were willing to consider the possibility that attitudes and behaviors among the poor "caused" some of their poverty, could quite easily become an accusation of racism. In fact, these two epithets often went hand in hand.[18]

Moreover, the obvious public responsibility to redress the historical injustices of slavery and Jim Crow exclusion, as a practical matter, became identified in the public mind with the need to do something about the poverty of black ghettos, especially as civil disturbances became more frequent there.[19] Often the most visible and effective advocates and spokesmen for the poor were also blacks who were veterans of the struggle for civil rights.[20] Discussions of poverty and of race have been inextricably linked in American public life for at least a generation.[21]

192 / THE MIND AND THE SPIRIT

Costly Consequences of the Race-Poverty Tangle

The linking of race and poverty has worked against clear thinking about the public and private responsibilities to deal with the problem of poverty. There are three main themes in this argument. First, a complex of racially based public policies—commonly referred to as "affirmative action," though I intend here much more than the preferential hiring policies government contractors are encouraged to follow—has developed and been sustained, in part, because of the continuing extent of poverty among blacks. Advocates of these policies have often linked the issues of race and poverty.[22] Clearly, political support for racially preferential policies rests in part on the conception that such redress is warranted by the extent of black poverty and the connection between current black economic status and the discrimination of the past (and present). Yet there is little evidence that poverty among blacks has been materially diminished by affirmative action.[23]

Second, and of much more importance, is the extent to which the overrepresentation of blacks among the poor has altered our public discourse about the nature of poverty. Ironically, two contradictory effects are at work here. Popular discussion of the problems of the so-called urban underclass—a population consisting largely of inner-city welfare families, drug addicts, hard-to-employ high school dropouts, and participants in the criminal labor market[24]—has often become identified with analysis of the problems of the poor. Yet, this underclass, even more disproportionately black than the set of people in poverty, appears to constitute a minority of the chronically poor and an even smaller fraction of those who experience poverty at some point during their lives.

For example, recent analysis of the longitudinal data of the Panel Study of Income Dynamics has shown that two-fifths of the persistently poor during the period 1969 to 1978 (defined as those having income, including transfer payments, below the poverty line in eight of the ten years) lived in households headed by a disabled person, that one-third were elderly or lived in a household headed by an elderly person, that two-thirds lived in the South, and that only one-fifth lived in large urban areas.[25] The inner-city underclass is a real and deeply troubling phenomenon; it constitutes the most important and intractable element of the problem of racial inequality in U.S. society; but it is not coincident with "the poor" and probably should be considered as distinct when thinking about policy questions. Yet because race and poverty are so closely linked in political advocacy and in the public imagination, and because poor inner-city blacks are such a large part of this underclass, the distinction is often not made.[26]

At the same time, at least until quite recently, the very fact that the underclass is so disproportionately black seems to have impeded a full analysis of the underlying behavioral basis of its problems. Since the difficult days of the mid-1960s, scholarly inquiry into this social phenomenon has been limited, and public discussion as to how it might be approached has been much impoverished.[27] The tendency has been to see the poverty of this population as inherently linked to racial disparities in opportunity, past and present, and to recommend as a solution the public policies that have evolved to deal with such disparities.[28]

Third, the close link between race and poverty has affected the ability (and willingness) of blacks to mobilize private resources to address behavioral problems internal to the group that cannot be effectively addressed through the public sector. Reducing poverty may require a change in the behavior of persons at high risk of becoming poor (e.g., avoidance of early unwed pregnancy, maintenance of steady employment in a low-wage job while gaining work experience and a stable employment record). If so, the public sector faces basic disadvantages in effecting such "changes of tastes." As suggested in Chapter 3 of this book, encouraging "good behavior" intrinsically requires discrimination among persons based on assessments that are difficult (legally and politically) for public agencies to make. This is particularly so when such distinctions are likely to have disparate impacts by race.[29] Yet, and especially in the current environment of upheaval in social policy, efforts to mobilize such private activity among blacks are seen as abetting the government's withdrawal from poverty reduction efforts.[30] This is a curious reversal of the usual "crowding out" argument concerning the effect of public action on the supply of private philanthropy. Here the notion seems to be that advocating greater private involvement makes the proposed reduction of public spending on these problems more politically palatable, even though the proposed private activities may be complementary to, rather than a substitute for, the public effort.

INFLUENCING BEHAVIOR: THE SPECIAL ROLE OF THE PRIVATE SECTOR

The formulation of public policy toward the poor requires some implicit or explicit conception of the causal mechanism at work. Disputes about policy often arise from divergent perceptions about the way the world works. In particular, much of the difference between liberal and conservative views of this problem stems from a dispute about the extent to which changes in individual behavior can be expected to diminish the prevalence of poverty. Debate over the "culture of poverty" thesis, initially advanced in the 1960s, exemplifies this point. This thesis holds that the poor have distinct values, aspirations, and psychological characteristics that inhibit achievement and produce behavior that increases the likelihood of poverty.[31]

If poverty and dependency are due to cultural and psychological factors characteristic of the poor, they cannot be remedied by simply giving people money. It would also be necessary to find some way to shape the tastes of poor people, to alter their values and aspirations. Such a shaping of values and aspirations is a highly difficult thing for public policy to achieve. The weak social structure, unstable family life, poor school performance, and involvement in illegal activities characteristic of poor communities have proven extremely resistant to the public interventions associated with the War on Poverty.[32] The mere provision of economic resources and opportunities to the poor has not been sufficient to eradicate these deficits.

This view, as a broad characterization of the poor, has been contested by those who argue that the values and aspirations of the poor cannot be understood without reference to their economic condition and that people's values and behavior would change in response to changes in economic circumstances. Some sociologists and psychologists have argued that the divergence of the attitudes and behaviors of the poor from those of middle-class Americans results from life circumstances, not from fundamentally different values.[33]

As discussed earlier (see note 12), the population of those who fall below the poverty line at some point during a given period of time is extremely heterogeneous; the majority will be poor for a relatively short time. One obviously cannot regard these people's poverty as due to their tastes. Yet it is also true that roughly half of the poor at a given moment are in the midst of a protracted spell of poverty. There is accumulating evidence that persons in this hard core of the poverty population are encumbered by a pattern of behavior, especially in adolescence, that, if unchanged, makes a permanent escape from poverty very unlikely.

This conclusion is supported by observation of the Harlem participants in Project Redirection, a two-year planned intervention with teenagers who had already borne one child out of wedlock aimed at preventing additional unwed pregnancies. Prevailing attitudes among these young women and their boyfriends were found to constitute a critical part of the teen pregnancy story. It was observed that "participants who lack self-esteem often find it difficult to resist pressure from boyfriends. . . . Participants tolerate [being beaten by their boyfriends or exploited economically] believing that because of their children, other men will not want them."[34] Moreover, concern about the issue of welfare dependency led to the following observation:

> Staff initially took an activist stance in their efforts to intercede with the welfare system on behalf of participants. This pattern changed, however, when [certain] behavior patterns emerged. . . . [Participants] were beginning to view getting their own welfare grants as the next stage in their careers. . . . [I] t became apparent that some participants' requests for separate grants and independent households were too often a sign of manipulation by boyfriends, in whose interest it was to have a girlfriend on welfare with an apartment of her own. . . . [S] taff realized that these attitudes and behaviors were . . . counterproductive to the . . . goal of promoting self-sufficiency.[35]

Project Redirection involved the use of "community women," older women who befriended and advised the teen mothers during the first year of the study. It is noteworthy that these community women " . . . have come out strongly against emancipated minor status for participants, feeling that it is better that teens remain under family guidance, no matter how difficult the family situation of conflict may be." Unfortunately, the project failed to reduce significantly the number of these teenaged mothers who gave birth to another child within the two years of participating in the program. Nor was it effective in altering participants' contraceptive practices. The researchers observed: "The major finding is that members of this target group hold a constellation of attitudes and values about boyfriends, sexual relationships, pregnancy and childbearing that are extremely resistant to change. Against the tenacity of these values, the presentation of factual information alone is inadequate to bring about substantial behavioral improvement."[36]

Behavioral problems of this sort probably cannot be solved by public action. The involvement of family members, religious institutions, and community-based organizations may be crucial to any effort to shape the values and attitudes of young people such as those participating in Project Redirection. Action from the public sector is encumbered by the diversity of views as to what constitutes appropriate values. The conflict over sex education curricula in the public schools provides a classic illustration of this point.[37]

The private sector has another decided advantage over the public sector in undertaking this task. Mutually concerned persons who trust one another enough to be able to exchange criticism constructively, establish codes of personal conduct, and enforce social sanctions against what is judged as undesirable behavior can create and enforce communal norms that lie beyond the capacity of the state to promulgate effectively. The coercive resources of the state, though great, are not particularly subtle. They are limited to the threat of incarceration and the denial of financial benefits. Yet within voluntary associations of individuals, precisely because they are voluntary and operate with the consent of those concerned, powerful mechanisms of persuasion are available. The teaching and enforcing of different values inherently requires judgments about and discriminations among individuals that it may be politically or even legally intolerable for a public entity to make, especially if such judgments have a racially discriminatory impact (see note 29, for example). The threat of ostracism, of the withdrawal of approval by those whose high regard is most avidly sought, can encourage individuals to conform to the expectations and opinions of significant others.

CONCLUSION

For many, a discussion of public and private responsibilities in the struggle against poverty means a discussion about the appropriate distribution of income, a discourse in the field of social justice. I hope to have shown here that such a view of the problem is too limited to provide a useful guide in this important debate. Of course there must be political debate about the extent to which the well-off are obliged to the less fortunate. But the problem of poverty is not simply equivalent to an absence of money among certain household heads. And finding the right public policies to deal with this problem requires more from us than a determination of our mutual obligations.

I have argued that there are reasons, based purely on efficiency grounds, that the public sector should be involved in providing benefits to the poor. One need not be a philosophical egalitarian to support such activity. I have also observed that, to the extent that long-term poverty reflects behavior (e.g., unwed child-bearing among adolescents) that can be modified only by changing people's basic values and aspirations, such transformations must take place primarily within the private sector. No degree of mutual social obligation, enforced through the taxation and transfer policies of the state, can substitute for what is to be had within freely entered associations of individuals. Such associations can establish and enforce for their members communal norms that work to reduce the prevalence of poverty-inducing behavior.

I have stressed the heterogeneity of the poverty population and the need to disaggregate it when thinking about policy in this area. It is particularly distressing to see the difficulties of the so-called under-class debated as if they were synonymous with the poverty problem. A similar confusion often arises when the problems of racial inequality and poverty are combined in public discourse. I have shown how failure to make these distinctions can inhibit clear thinking about the appropriate public and private roles.

Finally, there is the question of private responsibility within the family versus public responsibility to the indigent. The well-being of many of the poor, that is, poor children, depends on the proper discharge of familial responsibilities by their parents. So long as children remain in the custody of their parents, public efforts to assist them will be mediated by parental behavior. Putting more money in the hands of these parents may or may not be sufficient to affect the improvement in child welfare that justice would demand. Here we see a miniature version of the now much discussed public-private partnership at work.

My hope is that this discussion will encourage policy analysts to move beyond the fairness issue when debating what to do about poverty and to consider in more detail the matters of causation and responsibility analyzed here.

NOTES

1. The classic example of this excess is William Ryan, *Blaming the Victim* (New York: Pantheon Books, 1971). See also the extended discussion of the unwillingness of liberal social analysts to make demands of the poor in Lawrence M. Mead, *Beyond Entitlement: The Social Obligations of Citizenship* (New York: Free Press, 1986), chs. 8 and 9.

2. See John Rawls, *A Theory of Justice* (Cambridge, Mass.: Harvard University Press, 1971) and Robert Nozick, *Anarchy, State, and Utopia* (New York: Basic Books, 1974). In Chapter 4 in this volume Michael Walzer notes that it is not only considerations of distributive justice that come into play when considering the role of the state. Also important for a "theory of social assignments" — a theory seeking to explain what types of activities should be undertaken in the public or private sectors — is a consideration of how such assignments affect the energy and commitments citizens bring to the activity. Private philanthropy, for example, has virtues for a society beyond the reduction in income inequity its works might foster. Replacing the tradition of children caring for their elderly parents with publicly provided assistance to the elderly may advance the cause of justice, but at a cost.

3. Daniel P. Moynihan, *Family and Nation* (New York: Harcourt Brace Jovanovich, 1986).

4. For example, Martha S. Hill reports that child support was received by only 42 percent of the ever-married women living with a child under 21 years of age whose ex-husbands were not living in the household. Hill, "Child Support: What Absent Fathers Do and Could Provide" (Paper presented to the Population Association of America Meetings, Boston, March 1985).

5. A standard exposition of this theory may be found in Gary Becker, *Human Capital*, 2nd ed. (New York: National Bureau of Economic Research, 1975).

6. This argument is forcefully put forward in Lester Thurow, *Poverty and Discrimination* (Washington, D.C.: Brookings Institution, 1969).

7. This argument is developed rigorously in Glenn C. Loury, "Intergenerational Transfers and the Distribution of Earnings," *Econometrica* 49, no. 4 (July 1981): 843–67.

8. The late economist Arthur Okun once remarked, concerning the modern U.S. economy, that "the most important consequence [of an imperfect loan market] is the inadequate development of the human resources of the children of poor families — which I would judge one of the most serious inefficiencies of the American Economy today." Okun, *Equity and Efficiency: The Big Tradeoff* (Washington, D.C.: The Brookings Institution, 1975), pp. 80–81.

9. See the discussion of this problem in Richard Zeckhauser, "Risk Spreading and Distribution," in Harold M. Hochman and George E. Peterson, eds., *Redistribution Through Public Choice* (New York: Columbia University Press, 1974), pp. 206–28.

10. Note the similarity of this style of argumentation to that employed by Rawls in *A Theory of Justice*. In a manner analogous to Rawls's "veil of ignorance," parents' inability to predict their children's aptitudes and circumstances, together with intergenerational altruism and risk aversion

within the family, encourages current parents to consider the overall shape of the next generation's income profile in any discussion of permanent institutions of distribution.

11. There are at least two problems in this analysis that I am not addressing here. First, the question arises as to how the current generation of parents might sustain redistributive arrangements intended to operate among the next generation—the problem of "intergenerational commitment." Second, there is the "moral hazard" difficulty, which plagues all insurance schemes—the fact that the presence of risk-reducing institutions diminishes the risk-avoidance behavior of the individual (in this case, the effort expended to avoid the risk of a low income).

One possible argument regarding the problem of commitment is that in a steady state, each successive generation of individuals will face a future structurally similar to that of its predecessors and so will desire to ratify and pass on past institutional practice. As for moral hazard, it can be shown that a sufficiently modest program of redistribution will always generate insurance gains in excess of the efficiency costs associated with moral hazard. The intuitive reasoning is that the first-order effect of a "small amount" of taxation is zero, while the marginal effect of a "small amount" of insurance is strictly greater than zero. See the discussion in Glenn C. Loury, "Intergenerational Transfers and the Distribution of Earnings."

12. For example, Mary Jo Bane and David T. Ellwood have shown that while most of those experiencing a spell of poverty over a given period will be poor for a relatively short duration, roughly half of those who are poor at any given moment are in the midst of a protracted spell (eight years or more) of poverty. This implies a great deal of heterogeneity in the poverty population. Bane and Ellwood, "Slipping Into and Out of Poverty: The Dynamics of Spells," *The Journal of Human Resources* 21, no. 1 (Winter 1986): 1-23.

13. None of this denies the well-established relationship between the prevalence of poverty and the cyclical performance of the economy. See, for example, David Ellwood and Lawrence Summers, "Poverty in America: Is Welfare the Answer or the Problem?" (Paper presented at the conference "Poverty and Policy: Retrospect and Prospects," Williamsburg, Virg., December 1984); Sheldon Danziger and Peter Gottschalk, "Do Rising Tides Lift All Boats? The Impact of Secular and Cyclical Changes on Poverty" (Paper presented at the American Economic Association Meetings, New York, December 1985). I only suggest that in the long run the definition of *need* must be taken as endogenous, increasing with the general standard of living of the society. For a historical treatment of the evolution of the concept of need, see James T. Patterson, *America's Struggle Against Poverty: 1900-1980* (Cambridge, Mass.: Harvard University Press, 1981).

200 / THE MIND AND THE SPIRIT

14. See Stanley Lebergott, *The American Economy: Income, Wealth, and Want* (Princeton, N.J.: Princeton University Press, 1976).

15. See Mary Jo Bane, "Household Composition and Poverty" (Paper presented at the conference "Poverty and Policy: Retrospect and Prospects," Williamsburg, Virg., December 1984).

16. See Hill, "Child Support."

17. Enforcement of many public laws, such as those governing fair labor practices, could plausibly have the effect of reducing poverty, though such enforcement could not properly be construed primarily in these terms. Moreover, in the case of the minimum wage, there is evidence that the statute, intended to help the poor, has the effect of increasing the inequality of the distribution of family income. This was the finding of Linda Datcher and Glenn Loury, "The Effect of Minimum Wage Legislation on the Distribution of Family Earnings among Blacks and Whites, in *Report of the Minimum Wage Study Commission*, Vol. 7 (Washington, D.C.: U.S. Government Printing Office, 1986), pp. 125–46.

18. This becomes clear on reviewing the reaction to the publication in 1965 of the "Moynihan Report." This reaction is well summarized in Lee Rainwater and William Yancy, *The Moynihan Report and the Politics of Controversy* (Cambridge, Mass.: M.I.T. Press, 1967).

19. See the Kerner Commission, *Report of the National Advisory Commission on Civil Disorders* (Washington, D.C.: U.S. Government Printing Office, 1968).

20. At the end of his life Martin Luther King, Jr., was leading a Poor People's Campaign, calling attention to the problems of poor people of all races. Daniel P. Moynihan, *The Politics of Guaranteed Income* (New York: Random House, 1973) discusses the key role played by the largely black-led national Welfare Rights Organization in the political struggles surrounding President Nixon's proposed, though never enacted, Family Assistance Plan. The political career of Jesse Jackson provides a contemporary illustration of this relationship.

21. Indeed, Charles Murray, *Losing Ground: American Social Policy 1950–1980* (New York: Basic Books, 1984) speaks interchangeably about "young black men" and "the poor," taking the trends among the former as proxies for the effects of changes in social policy on the latter.

22. For example, writing in the *Washington Post* ("Goals Aren't Quotas," February 29, 1986), Derek Bok supported the legitimacy of affirmative action guidelines for federal contractors. Among the considerations he emphasized as bearing on the appropriateness of these guidelines was the extent of poverty in the black population: "[P]overty rates for minorities have risen in the 1980s. . . . In these circumstances . . . I, for one, will continue to set goals gladly, buoyed by the realization that they may at least make some contribution to diminishing [this] enormous problem."

23. See, for example, James Smith and Finis Welch, *Closing the Gap: Forty Years of Economic Progress for Blacks* (Santa Monica: The Rand Corporation, 1986).

24. The term *underclass* was popularized by Ken Auletta, whose description of the participants in an employment training program gained national attention. Auletta, *The Underclass* (New York: Random House, 1982).

25. See Mary Corcoran, Greg J. Duncan, Gerald Gurin, and Patricia Gurin, "Motivation, Culture and the Persistence of Poverty: Some Recent Evidence" (Survey Research Center, ISR, University of Michigan, 1985). (Photocopy.)

26. Recently several outstanding journalistic accounts of this "new urban poverty" problem have appeared, graphically underlining the special nature of the problems of the underclass. Most notable are the *Chicago Tribune* series "The American Millstone" (December 1985); the series of articles on teenage pregnancy by Leon Dash in the *Washington Post*, January 26–31, 1986; the editorial series "Wealth and Welfare" in the *Detroit News*, February 1986; and the Bill Moyers CBS television special "The Vanishing Black Family," originally broadcast January 26, 1986.

27. I have made this argument more fully in "The Moral Quandary of the Black Community," *The Public Interest* 79 (Spring 1985): 9–22. See also the discussion of the "Moynihan Controversy" in Rainwater and Yancy, *The Moynihan Report* and the reflections on the intellectual dialogue concerning the problems of the black poor offered in William Wilson, "Cycles of Deprivation and the Underclass Debate," *Social Service Review* (December 1985); 541–59. As Wilson put it, "The liberal perspective on the ghetto underclass has become less persuasive and convincing in public discourse principally because many of those who represented traditional liberal views on social issues have been reluctant to discuss openly or, in some instances, even acknowledge the sharp increase in social pathologies in ghetto communities" (p. 54).

28. For further discussion of this problem in public discourse about the formulation of policy toward the black poor, see my articles in *The New Republic*, "A New American Dilemma" (December 31, 1984): 14–18) and "Beyond Civil Rights" (October 7, 1985): 22–25).

29. For example, school districts with racially disproportionate student suspension rates have had to face racial discrimination charges and investigation by the Office of Civil Rights of the U.S. Department of Education (with the threat of loss of federal funding). See Jeremy Rabkin, "Office for Civil Rights," in J. Q. Wilson, ed., *The Politics of Regulation* (New York: Basic Books, 1981), pp. 304–53.

30. This argument is implicit in Roger Wilkins's criticism of those advocating greater self-help among black Americans. Wilkins, "Not by Bootstraps

Alone: Why the Black Neocons Are Wrong," *The Village Voice*, February 4, 1986.

31. A good summary of the debate over the "culture of poverty" thesis may be found in Corcoran et al., "Motivation, Culture and the Persistence of Poverty."

32. This case is convincingly made by Murray in *Losing Ground.*

33. For a critical view see Ryan, *Blaming the Victim* and Corcoran et al., "Motivation, Culture and the Persistence of Poverty." Qualified support for the "culture" thesis, with respect to the inner-city black poor, can be found in Wilson, "Cycles of Deprivation and the Underclass Debate." James Q. Wilson, "The Rediscovery of Character: Private Virtue and Public Policy," *The Public Interest* 81 (Fall 1985): 3–16, makes the argument that, in a broad range of policy areas, analysts have come to place increasing weight on the importance of promoting good "character" in the citizenry. Gertrude Himmelfarb, *The Idea of Poverty: England in the Early Industrial Age* (New York: Alfred Knopf, 1984), shows that the question of promoting "virtuous behavior" among the poor is very old, running throughout the intellectual debates in nineteenth-century Britain concerning policy toward the indigent.

34. See Alvia Branch, James Riccio, and Janet Quint, *Building Self-Sufficiency in Pregnant and Parenting Teens* (New York: Manpower Demonstration Research Corporation, April 1984), p. 39.

35. Ibid., p. 60.

36. Ibid., p. 103.

37. The debate over sex education in New York City during 1984 is instructive in this regard. When local clergy objected to a planned curriculum that was devoid of judgment regarding the relative merits of intact versus single-parent family structures, the *New York Times* observed that one could not teach the preferability of intact families to the great number of students who did not enjoy such backgrounds. At issue here is whether the high incidence of out-of-wedlock births in New York City requires public neutrality concerning the propriety of early unwed pregnancy or implies the need for a concerted effort to reaffirm values to children unlikely to have the judgment confirmed in their private lives.

CHAPTER 9

American Education: Public and Private Responsibilities

Diane Ravitch

In his elegant history of Harvard College, Samuel Eliot Morison noted that the college

> was established at a place which had been a wilderness eight years before, in a colony whose history was less than ten years old, and by a community of less than ten thousand people. The impulse and support came from no church, government, or individual in the Old World, but from an isolated people hemmed in between the forest and the ocean, who had barely secured the necessities of existence.[1]

Among the Puritan leaders was a significant number of university graduates, who well understood the importance of education in perpetuating their ideals and culture. In 1636, the same year that the college was created, the Boston Latin School was launched, as was a school in Charlestown. By 1647 the General Court of the Bay Colony directed every town of 50 or more families to maintain a teacher at public expense and every town of 100 or more families to provide a grammar school where young men might prepare for the university. Thus, the first generation of Puritans left a legacy of excellence in higher education and of communal responsibility for the education of youth.

Morison also wrote that " ... the two cardinal principles of English puritanism which most profoundly affected the social development of New England and the United States were not religious tenets, but educational ideals: a learned clergy and a lettered people."[2] The rationale for these educational ideals, however, was decidedly religious. Harvard College was established, in the words of *New England's First Fruits*, "to advance *Learning* and perpetuate it to Posterity; dreading to leave an illiterate Ministry to the Churches, when our present Ministers shall lie in the Dust." And the law of 1647 justified the need for publicly supported schools because "It [is] one chief project of that old deluder, Satan, to keep men from the knowledge of the Scriptures" and also so that "Learning may not be buried in the graves of our fore-fathers in Church and Commonwealth."[3]

Over the years, while the educational ideals of the founders became secularized, the religious zeal that inspired them was never entirely extinguished. Those who campaigned to open schools and colleges never ceased to remind potential supporters of the necessity to perpetuate learning in order to safeguard the future of the new society. Many institutions of higher learning were founded by religious denominations, intending (like the Puritans) to train right-thinking ministers; the first colleges for women were established to prepare missionaries and Christian teachers. Even the early public schools were justified by religious motives, and their texts contained heavy doses of religious materials. Most, if not all, common school reformers came to their tasks as secular missionaries, apostles of literacy and civilization. Repeatedly, when social and economic problems have riven American society, reformers have looked to the schools and to higher education to provide the means of salvation and regeneration.

As the public school took root in New England, other regions developed different patterns of schooling. In the cities of the Middle Atlantic states, free schools were initially provided by philanthropists for children whose parents were too poor to afford church schools. These early nineteenth-century "public" schools, free schools maintained by private funds, were stigmatized as pauper schools. In the South the schooling of children was primarily the responsibility of parents, not the entire community, and the South lagged far behind the rest of the nation in developing public schools. In the Midwest and West public schools tended to follow the New England model, not for religious reasons but because the tax-supported public school best fit the relatively homogeneous social structure of the frontier community.

In time, of course, the New England tradition of public schooling came to be seen as the American model. By the mid-nineteenth century, the philanthropic societies that ran free schools in New York, Philadelphia, and other cities were replaced by publicly controlled school committees; and after the Civil War, the Reconstruction state legislatures in the South laid the foundation for state-supported education. However, the dominance of the New England model was never total. To the present day, private philanthropies continue to provide education and social services for needy children; parents, dissatisfied with public schools, continue to bear the cost of educating their children in private schools; denominational agencies maintain numerous schools outside the public domain. Nationally, nearly 13 percent of all children attend nonpublic schools; in some cities, the proportion is as high as one-third.

Significant though these private alternatives were and still are, most children for the past century have attended their local public school, which in theory serves the children of the entire community. To be sure, there have been obvious omissions in the application of the model. Some states continued to charge fees until well into the nineteenth century; some children could attend for only a few years before they went to work in factories or on farms; the schools in big cities were sometimes (though not always) a reflection of ethnically and racially homogeneous neighborhoods rather than a common meeting place for the children of rich and poor. The most glaring flaw in the common school ideal was the treatment of black children, who usually were excluded from "white" public schools and segregated in "colored" schools, not only in the South but in other parts of the nation as well.

Just as the Puritans had worried about what might happen to their settlement "when our present Ministers shall lie in the Dust" and taxed themselves for schoolmasters so that "Learning may not be buried in the graves of our fore-fathers . . . ," school reformers throughout American history have turned to education as a means of protecting the community against the perils of the present and the future. As massive immigration changed the nation's population, threatening the hegemony of white Anglo-Saxon Protestants, the schools were expected to provide the cultural glue to bind the nation together and make a polyglot population into one people with a common language, common heroes, and a common heritage. When urbanization produced slums, schools were expected to provide the skills and opportunity to enable poor children to rise above their parents' social origins. When demands for racial equality became insistent, the schools became the setting for a reconstruction of relations between the races and of the place of blacks in American society. The expectation that education was an effective agency of social reform was customarily limited to the public elementary and secondary schools; however, by the mid-twentieth century, the rising tide of egalitarianism finally reached higher education, when admission to college was transformed into a right available to all, not a privilege for the rich and unusually talented.

Because they have been central to so many diverse aspirations and crises, the public schools have often been the object of quasi-religious rhetoric. In the latter half of the nineteenth century, the public schools were hailed by school superintendents and politicians as "the bulwark of our republic," the "foundation-stone of democracy," and the like. Whatever their defects, there were many Americans who believed that the American experiment in democratic self-government could not succeed without the mass education provided by the public schools. Until the mid-twentieth century, the critics of the public schools were friendly critics who questioned not their value but their quality and despaired because of the inadequacies of teachers, facilities, methods, and resources.

For most of the nineteenth century, reformers struggled to establish free public schooling supported by taxes, controlled by public authorities, and separated from sectarian influence. The triumph of public over sectarian schools was abetted by intense anti-Catholic sentiment, which encouraged the belief that nonpublic schools were somehow not the American way: If they were sectarian, they were divisive, and if they were nonsectarian, then they were elitist. By the end of the nineteenth century, the battle to establish the preeminence of public schooling was all but over, and the public school movement concentrated its energies on two additional goals: the provision of public secondary school for an ever-increasing proportion of the adolescent population, and the professionalization of those who worked in schools. The evolution of these trends has left American education with unresolved problems.

In the mid-nineteenth century, students who wanted more than a common school education enrolled in a private academy; at their peak, in 1850, there were some 6,000 academies, with an enrollment of about 260,000. By 1890, the enrollment in public high schools had overtaken the private academies, and they continued to grow in the following decades. The widespread adoption of compulsory education laws and the closing of the labor market to adolescents brought high school enrollment up to 7,000,000 by 1940; in that year, about 50 percent of the nation's youth graduated from high school, a level of mass education unmatched in the world at that time. The rise in high school graduation rates continued until the late 1960s, when it leveled off at 75 percent.[4]

Growth of high school enrollments and professionalization of education coincided and perhaps interacted to stimulate one another. In the early twentieth century, the new profession began to sense its own identity and unique mission; it led the campaign to expand enrollment, on grounds that universal secondary education would enhance American democracy. Expanding enrollments enhanced the complexity of school administration, contributing to the belief that special studies were needed to work in education. Leaders of the new profession believed that those who intended to teach or administer needed special training, much like other professions. But while professions such as law and medicine established their programs of training at the graduate level, education remained essentially an undergraduate study, perhaps reflecting the low wages and status of teachers. In colleges and universities, the field of education became a separate program with its own department or undergraduate division or, in a few instances, graduate school. The physical separation between the professors of education and the professors of arts and sciences isolated the education profession in its own academic enclave, with its own psychologists, sociologists, philosophers, historians, and pedagogues. Many, though not all, came to see themselves as champions of public education rather than as critics or neutral scholars, a view that contributed to the pedagogical faculty's low status within the academic world. The nation's nonpublic schools were for the most part by-passed by the leaders of the new profession, who were devoted on principle to public education; depending on state legislation, many private schools continued to hire their teachers and administrators from graduates of liberal arts colleges rather than from the ranks of those who had studied pedagogy and administration in order to be properly credentialed as professionals.

By the 1930s the new profession had evolved its own philosophy, which treated as inseparable the prospects of the public school and the fate of democratic society. This outlook commanded the allegiance of most of those within the profession. Some educators, however, were scornful of the profession's pretensions. Robert Hutchins, for example, complained of the philosophical vacuity of the profession and described its *idée fixe* as "more"—more students, more buildings, more courses, more money. Pedagogically, the profession embraced curricular diversity as an article of faith. At professional meetings, in journals, and in pedagogical textbooks it was constantly reiterated that the broadest possible curriculum was needed in order to draw all the community's children into the high school. Diversity meant incorporation into the regular curriculum of every imaginable vocational, avocational, and recreational study. Like vendors in a crowded marketplace spreading their multitudinous wares to entice buyers, the leaders of the profession seemed willing to adopt anything that might "hold" students for a longer period of time, even if it meant ceding academic time to organized sports or to job training.

In addition to reconstructing the curriculum as a means of appealing to student interests, the profession conceived of the role of the school as a vast occupational machine, meeting the needs of the economy by preparing the young to take their places in society as adults; this was the *social function* of the school. Those who saw the school in sociological terms argued that the great majority of students needed above all to learn about the world of work or domesticity and had little need for the traditional academic curriculum. Seen in this light, vocational and commercial studies actually had more social value than did the academic curriculum. Something resembling a democratic banner could be raised high by those who crusaded to make the curriculum more useful to future occupations, more relevant to current interests, and more concerned with immediate need than the old, traditional studies like history, foreign languages, and literature.

With the champions of relevance in the ascendancy by the 1930s and 1940s, the academic subjects were recast: history became social studies, de-emphasizing the past and instead stressing current events and community studies; English became language arts, reducing the academic grip of literature and replacing it with almost anything that could be read or written or spoken or heard. These developments flowed from the belief that for most young people, the traditional academic curriculum was irrelevant. Students were divided at some point in their school life into "tracks," academic, vocational, or general. The academic curriculum was considered appropriate only for the minority who intended to go to college. Most were placed either in a vocational or nonacademic general track. The practice of tracking in public schools was justified as the best way to meet the needs of students.

Since high school enrollment grew so rapidly during most of the twentieth century, the profession felt that its faith in a pluralistic curriculum had been vindicated. Of course, it was impossible to know whether enrollment increased because the curriculum was broadened, the job market for adolescents disappeared, employers favored high school graduates, the social life of adolescents shifted to the public high school, or for some other reason. Nonetheless, the profession held fast to the view that the granting of equal status to nonacademic courses in the curriculum had democratized the school, a view that implied that the academic curriculum was by its nature elitist and therefore undemocratic.

Following the Russians launch of *Sputnik* in 1958 there was intense criticism of the U.S. public schools' curriculum. Critics complained that the schools had paid too little attention to academic studies, that enrollments in mathematics, science, and foreign languages were too low, that standards in academic subjects were inadequate, and that the nation was ignoring science and technology at its peril. Within the profession there was a defensive reaction, which translated into the retort that the Russians were first into space because *their* German scientists had beaten *our* German scientists. But this response was insufficient to stem public discontent; enrollments in science, mathematics, and foreign languages *were* low, and Congress enacted a program of financial assistance to stimulate the study of those subjects in the schools. Until the mid-1960s, when the memory of *Sputnik* faded, there was an upturn in enrollments and test scores in the "hard" subjects, though most high school students continued to be enrolled in a nonacademic track.

Higher education was not immune from many of the same trends. Most leaders of American higher education thought that higher education should be more broadly available, that there should be public assistance for able but needy students, and that expanded enrollments would generally benefit American society. But few went so far as to argue that most colleges should open their doors to anyone who wanted to attend. In the absence of federal aid to college students, demand was naturally limited by cost.

The expansion of higher education was not a function of the attitudes of its leaders. Enrollments in higher education doubled every fifteen years or so between 1870 and 1970.[5] Possibly the most important breakthrough in popularizing higher education was the G.I. Bill of Rights, which brought a new population to American college campuses and broadened the popular view of who should attend college. The G.I. bill brought more than two million young men (and some women) to American campuses, many of humble origins. With veterans crowding the campuses, a popular movie of the late 1940s showed a presidential candidate promising to send every man, woman, and child in the nation to Harvard. A professor at Harvard quipped that the answer to this new rage for credentials was to endow every American at birth with a college diploma, so that only those truly interested in learning would actually go to college.

The jokes reflected reality, but they did not deter the growing number who wanted a college education. More and more students sought higher education—because a parent had gone to college, or because their parents had *not* gone to college, or because they needed a college education for the career they wanted to pursue, or because a college education seemed to be the best way to get ahead. The steady rise in the high school graduation rate combined with the maturing of the postwar baby-boom generation to produce record levels of growth in higher education in the 1960s. By 1970, 8 million students were enrolled in higher education; and by the early 1980s, enrollment reached a peak of 12.4 million.[6]

In the United States today, a greater percentage of the population is engaged in postsecondary education than in any other nation in the world. With the aging of the postwar baby-boom generation, many institutions of higher education realized that they had to recruit new students or face the prospect of closing. Except for a small minority of campuses where the number of applicants continued to outnumber those admitted, most colleges and universities were accepting all or almost all of their applicants by the late 1970s. First marginal and then well-established institutions discovered that they had to learn to think like a business and to hire a director of marketing to guide their pursuit of new students. Women made great strides during this period, in part because of the effectiveness of the women's movement but also because colleges and universities were eager to maintain their enrollments; during the decade of the 1970s, the proportion of women in higher education grew from 40 to 52 percent. Similarly, enrollments of racial minorities quadrupled in the fifteen years from 1965 to 1980, bringing them nearly in line with their proportion in the population (blacks, for example, were 9.9 percent of the students in postsecondary academic programs in 1982).[7]

Since the youth market apparently was already well saturated, most institutions turned to adults to fill the growing gap between their applications and the places available. By 1980 nearly 40 percent of all postsecondary students were over the age of twenty-five, and government analysts projected that the proportion of older students might rise to nearly 50 percent by 1990. Clearly, there is a new student body in higher education, more reflective of the entire population. Furthermore, the nature of the institutions these students attend has changed significantly. In 1950 half of the nation's students were in private institutions and half were in public institutions. By the early 1980s less than 25 percent attended private colleges and universities. Rapid expansion also meant a dramatic increase in the size of the average institution. In 1948 there were only ten universities with an enrollment larger than 20,000; by 1979 there were ninety-eight campuses of that size, attended by nearly one-quarter of all students. About half of all students attend institutions that enroll more than 10,000.[8]

This extended period of growth has brought mixed blessings to higher education. On the one hand, the United States has developed a somewhat anarchic system that provides the widest access to higher education that the world has ever known. Public higher education is available at low cost to almost everyone who wants it, for a wide variety of academic, vocational, and technical purposes. But on the other, the rise of sprawling megaversities has created its own set of problems. By necessity, these are large, impersonal, and bureaucratic institutions. On many campuses a significant number of the students commute or attend part-time. Because so many courses of necessity enroll several hundred students, it is often difficult for students to have personal contact with professors. On a large and complex campus, where there is little sense of shared purpose, it is equally difficult for students or faculty to feel themselves part of a learning community.

Although the absolute number of students enrolled in private institutions grew from 1.1 million in 1950 to 2.7 million in 1980, public institutions during the same period increased their enrollment from 1.1 million to 9.5 million, in large measure because of their low, heavily subsidized tuition rates.[9] With its power to tax, the public sector has emerged as the dominant provider of higher education. The risk to private institutions is obvious. Lacking the heavy state and federal subsidies available to their public competitors, private institutions are expensive, dependent on tuition, and likely to suffer disproportionately if government aid to students is reduced. Reduction of financial aid will drive large numbers of students from relatively costly private colleges to relatively inexpensive public institutions. In that event, many small private colleges would be compelled to close. Among them would be many that provide excellent education, small classes, and the human scale that creates a sense of purpose in learning. The diminution of the number of these colleges would be a loss to American higher education.

The curricular consequences of giantism in higher education have been striking. With notable exceptions (mainly in the private sector), higher education tries to give prospective consumers whatever they want. While the causes differ, higher education has found itself in a curricular dilemma not unlike that of the secondary schools, where the guiding principle has also been to give the students what they want. At both levels consumerism and vocationalism have been triumphant, and at both levels the traditional arts and sciences have suffered in the competition with more practical subjects. The circumstances are quite different, however. In the public schools, consumerism has prevailed because of a widespread belief that students will stay in school longer if they can study what interests them at the moment. In higher education, if an institution fails to offer a vocational or technical course for which there is a demand, another institution in the community will fill the vacuum, and prospective students will go where they can buy what they need. This trend of selective shopping has been accelerated by the increase in the number of part-time, commuting, adult students who shop for degree programs or course offerings the way they would shop for any other service, without regard to sports teams, extracurricular activities, ambiance, dormitory life, or other social factors that might appeal to residential students of traditional college age. Consumerism and vocationalism have been especially pronounced in public colleges and universities. Public institutions must strive to meet the needs of the local community and must also maintain the enrollment levels necessary to sustain public funding. In contrast, private institutions can rarely afford to inaugurate costly vocational programs or to follow the shifts of the employment market in any other than a tentative way. Their restrained budgets have limited the ability of private institutions to follow the consumerist philosophy as aggressively as most public institutions.

Thus, in the 350 years since the founding of Harvard College in 1636, the educational landscape has changed as much as the wilderness in which the new institution was planted. Now Harvard University is but one among more than 3,000 institutions of higher learning in the United States. While Harvard may still seek "to advance *Learning* and perpetuate it to Posterity," many of Harvard's fellow institutions have a definition of learning that would furrow the brows of Harvard's founding fathers. Virtually no activity or occupation was too mundane or too humble to be offered by colleges in the 1980s, whether it was a course called "Fun with Jello" at a community college in the West, or a degree program in "Professional Golf Management" at a college in the Midwest where students prepare for a career running a golf course.

Both the public schools and higher education have come under intense scrutiny because the services they provide are integrally linked to the public interest. It is widely recognized that education directly and indirectly affects the economy, the political climate, the society, and the culture; for these reasons, the policy cannot afford to ignore serious lapses in the provision of education, whether in the public or the private sector. This is why the state requires compulsory education and retains the right to monitor nonpublic institutions; the services they offer are as basic to the health of society as police protection and hospitals.

As the decade of the 1980s began, public officials reflected widespread concern about the quality of education provided in their states. Are the taxpayers getting their money's worth, they asked? Are we producing the educated workforce we need to compete in the world economy? Do our people have the literacy required to satisfy the needs of employers? Some echoes of doubt and uncertainty about the future that moved the Puritans to found educational institutions can be heard in contemporary complaints about the inadequacies of our present systems. Even when expressed in the most materialistic, Babbitt-like of terms, there is an underlying fear that we have failed to prepare for hard times ahead or even for the blandishments of fat times, and it is to our educational agencies that we must turn to secure the future.

Much of the concern was expressed in the outpouring of critical reports by commissions, task forces, and study groups in the early 1980s. The first wave of reports examined the secondary schools and found them wanting. The most prominent of the high school reports was the National Commission on Excellence in Education's *A Nation at Risk*, which captured the attention of the mass media on its appearance in 1983. It pointed to unacceptably high rates of functional illiteracy among 17-year-old youths (13 percent for the age group as a whole, 40 percent for blacks of that age);[10] to the fall of standardized test scores since the mid-1960s; to the fall of enrollments and test scores in mathematics and the sciences; to the proliferation of nonacademic electives in the secondary curriculum; and to the adoption of goals so broad and so diffuse in the high school that the academic curriculum often seemed lost or neglected. The commission recommended that all states and school districts adopt a core academic curriculum for all students, whether they were college-bound or not.[11] In most states, this meant an increase in the number of years of required mathematics and science. Other reports released almost simultaneously reiterated some version of this proposal, and most states (following the advice of their own commissions) increased academic requirements for graduation.

A second group of reports appeared soon afterward, scrutinizing the condition of higher education. All expressed a vague sense of unease, based on the overwhelming trend toward vocationalism and specialization in higher education, but their complaints and remedies were far less specific than those directed to the schools. One reason for this was the different kind of information available for the two different levels. Researchers who studied the secondary schools had ample data about performance and course enrollments. (However, this data was often so superficial as to be of questionable validity; for example, it was often impossible to know what students enrolled in generic courses in English and social studies were doing, since both have become such broad, all-inclusive fields.) Those who examined higher education, however, had almost no assessments of performance comparing fields or institutions, and course enrollment data were often unobtainable. Although there was a wealth of information about the students, faculties, and financing of higher education, there had been little systematic examination of the nature or quality of the education offered, other than statistics on major fields of study. Unlike the schools, which have long been closely regulated by the state and have been the subject of data collection by the federal government, higher education has a tradition of relative independence, even when it is publicly funded. In colleges and universities, most curricular decisions are made by the faculty, not the state legislature or the state education department.

The common theme of the major reports on higher education was a call for the restoration of liberal education in the curriculum. A study sponsored by the National Institute of Education, *Involvement in Learning*, recommended that all bachelor's degree recipients should have at least two full years of liberal education in order to counterbalance a trend toward narrow specialization. The study noted regretfully that the proportion of bachelor's degrees awarded in arts and sciences had fallen from 49 percent in 1971 to 36 percent in 1982; at the same time, there were sharp increases in degrees granted in professional and vocational fields.[12]

The report from the Association of American Colleges echoed similar concerns, lashing out even more forcefully at what it called "the debasement of baccalaureate education." Again the curriculum was the focus of criticism. "As for what passes as a college curriculum," the report observed, "almost anything goes. We have reached a point at which we are more confident about the length of a college education than its content and purpose." Its remedy was a "minimum required curriculum" based not on specific subjects but on essential modes of inquiry.[13]

A third report, by William J. Bennett, chairman of the National Endowment for the Humanities, proposed a revival of emphasis on the humanities in higher education. The humanities, he warned, were in danger of becoming marginal in colleges and universities. He pointed out that the number of majors in subjects like history, English, philosophy, and modern languages had dropped sharply in the previous decade, and that students could receive a bachelor's degree from most American colleges and universities without studying European history, American history, or American literature. He urged that "study of the humanities and Western civilization must take its place at the heart of the college curriculum."[14] Although he did not mention it in his report, only 7 percent of the bachelor's degrees awarded in 1980 were received by majors in the arts and letters (a decline of approximately 50 percent since 1970).[15]

The common thread connecting the critiques of both secondary schools and higher education was a plea for general education, for unspecialized literacy as the best preparation for career decisions instead of the highly specific career education that had become the rule. In response to this near-unanimous rhetorical barrage, legislators and state education officials clumsily translated the clamor for liberal education into such simple-minded remedies as an increase in requirements for high school graduation in certain subjects, especially mathematics and science, or into requirements that students pass basic competency tests before advancing to the next grade. Such bureaucratic and legislative responses tended to trivialize and demean the widespread yearning for a renaissance of literacy. At their best, the critics of the schools and higher education hoped for a society in which all students received an education of the highest quality; where the mysteries of science, literature, numeracy, culture, aesthetics, the past, the political and economic systems of our own and other societies were unfolded for all students; where the object of learning was to gain the skills and motivation to continue learning for the rest of one's life. This ideal was expressed simply and directly by Mortimer J. Adler in *The Paideia Proposal*, which was at once the most sensible and yet the most radical reform program for the schools. Adler proposed an end to tracking, explaining:

> We should have a one-track system of schooling, not a system with two or more tracks, only one of which goes straight ahead while the others shunt the young off onto sidetracks not headed toward the goals our society opens to all. The innermost meaning of social equality is *substantially the same quality of life for all*. That calls for: *the same quality of schooling for all.*[16]

The tide running against liberal education was so powerful that it was possible that efforts to revive it were nothing more than rhetoric, doomed to fail in a society where schooling had become nearly synonymous with preparation for jobs and careers. Was it too late to convince campus administrators worried about institutional survival, school superintendents worried about dropout rates, and parents worried about their children's ability to succeed in life that a liberal education was a sound investment? That history and literature, taught with imagination and verve, could be as relevant and riveting as vocational and technical courses? Selective universities and small liberal-arts colleges, like outstanding public and private schools, had never doubted the validity of an education grounded in history, literature, mathematics, the sciences, art, and music; but by the 1980s that vision of an educated public, a "lettered people" (as Morison put it), had become dim, and the prospects for its revival uncertain.

Proposals to provide liberal education for all students invariably aroused contentious debates about the supposed conflict between "excellence" and "equality." Those who championed a liberal rather than utilitarian education as the foundation for studies in the schools were accused of trying to foist elitist education on the common schools, which (it was charged) would cause high school dropout rates to rise beyond the current national rate of 25 percent. Critics of "excellence" insisted that only the talented minority could profit by study of the arts and sciences; from this perspective, the purpose of the schools was to hold students as long as possible, socializing them for work and civic duty without risking an encounter with studies that had no immediate meaning for them and that might even alienate them from school (thus making it impossible to socialize them). The advocates of liberal education for all contended that the concept of equality was not served by a system of educational triage and that the problem of education in a democratic society was not whom to educate but how to educate everyone.

The problem is far more compelling at the precollegiate level than it is in higher education. After all, if all high school graduates had a solid foundation in the major disciplines, then their choices in college or university would matter less. After studying American and European history in high school, they should be free to choose more of the same or the history of other regions; if they studied little or no American and European history in high school, then its absence in the postsecondary years is worrisome. The same is true in other areas of the curriculum, like science; the student who never studies science beyond general science in the ninth grade lacks a basic vocabulary for understanding the major technological issues of the contemporary world. If colleges and universities are to be free to shape their curricula as they wish or to meet the demands of student-consumers, then it is imperative that these institutions are able to assume that their students have already received a firm grounding in the basic arts and sciences.

The future of public education is jeopardized by the popular perception that there has been a marked decline in the quality of education and pervasive doubts about the capacity of the schools to improve. At the receiving end of mandates from courts, federal agencies, state agencies, and legislatures, public education has been saddled with bureaucratic procedures that impair its capacity to respond flexibly and imaginatively to new problems and that dampen the morale of even the most heroic teachers. For the first time in at least a century, substantial numbers of people began to look at the public schools as a public utility to be judged by the quality of their services rather than as a sacrosanct pillar of the republic. The nineteenth-century rhetoric about the role of the public school as a safeguard of our democratic way of life was seldom heard in the policy debates of the 1980s. The focus instead was either on reviving the quality of public education or on finding constitutionally acceptable ways to finance nonpublic schools, on grounds that they would provide better education than the public schools did.

Amid the criticism of the 1980s, it was easy to forget that the American educational system with its pluralistic blend of public and private schools had worked well, as national systems go. Writing in 1958, as the post-*Sputnik* criticism of the schools neared a crescendo, Henry Steele Commager pointed out that since our schools

> are commonly blamed for the failings or inadequacies of society, perhaps it is not unfair to give them some credit for the larger successes and achievements. After all, the products of the American educational system succeeded in a great many things which involve intelligence and judgment. They established a nation and held it together, expanding thirteen to fifty states with less difficulty than England had with Ireland alone in the same period. They made democracy work reasonably well and did not gratify the expectations of those who were so sure that a majority would inevitably exercise tyranny over minorities. They elected mediocre Presidents, but never a wicked or a dangerous one. They never yielded to a military dictator. They settled all their problems, but one, by compromise and concession (and perhaps that one, slavery, could not be solved by compromise). They adjusted themselves speedily to their responsibilities as a world power. These are not accomplishments that can be confidently traced to the educational system, but it would be absurd to deny that the schools contributed to them.[17]

Many of the historic accomplishments of this nation would be inconceivable without a strong educational system. The schools surely can take credit, at least in part, for the fact that the United States has consistently maintained a degree of political rights and civil liberties equalled by few other societies, that our scientific and technological achievements have made possible an extraordinarily high standard of living, and that the many divergent ethnic groups that make up this nation have eventually learned to speak the same language and to cooperate within a common political system.

In *Nations and Nationalism* Ernest Gellner observes that modern society depends on education because education makes it possible for strangers to communicate with one another in an explicit and standardized language and to shift activities or occupations with minimal training. In the modern state, writes Gellner,

The employability, dignity, security and self-respect of individuals, typically, and for the majority of men now hinges on their *education*; and the limits of the culture within which they were educated are also the limits of the world within which they can, morally and professionally, breathe. A man's education is by far his most precious investment, and in effect confers his identity on him. . . . The obverse of the fact that a school-transmitted culture, not a folk-transmitted one, alone confers his usability and dignity and self-respect on industrial man, is the fact that nothing else can do it for him to any comparable extent [emphasis mine] .[18]

Our educational system has been essential to our social and economic progress. Over time we have demonstrated, at all levels of schooling, the value of a pluralistic system, one that is neither entirely public nor entirely private. Had the system been entirely private, it would not have been institutionally capable of responding to the just demands of the civil rights movement of the 1960s; the dependence of most schools, colleges, and universities on public support provided a lever for eliminating racial segregation and other discriminatory practices. But a system that was without a vigorous private sector would suffer in different, and no less important, ways. Private schools, both religious and nonsectarian, have been free to be idiosyncratic and to pursue educational ideals of their own choosing, sometimes based on religious conviction, sometimes based on pedagogical principles; idiosyncrasy in the private sector has provided a wide umbrella, covering academic traditionalism at one pole and anarchic progressivism at the other. Private institutions of higher education have proven their distinctive value, whether as international beacons of academic excellence—like Harvard, Stanford, and M.I.T.—or as bastions of excellence on a human scale—like Reed, Amherst, and Wellesley, where the liberal arts and sciences continue to be the heart of the curriculum.

In both public and private institutions, what matters most is the quality of education. The ability of any institution to provide good education depends on the seriousness of purpose of those who educate the young and not-so-young, their readiness to define and defend their educational ideals, their capacity to blend their ideals and their practices, and their willingness to attend to the details and arrangements of their institutions without becoming enslaved by the bureaucratic process. As we have seen in other fields, institutional forms come and go, depending on whether they meet genuine needs.

The relevance of educational institutions has always depended on social and economic factors, not on the quality of rhetoric propounded by boosters. As the world changes, as the international economy becomes increasingly competitive, as international tensions require greater depths of knowledge and diplomacy, as science and technology transform the terms of our daily lives, we will need as never before a well-educated citizenry. If the schools as we now know them cannot provide the education that is needed, they will be changed or other forms will arise to take their place.

NOTES

1. Samuel Eliot Morison, *The Founding of Harvard College* (Cambridge, Mass.: Harvard University Press, 1985), p. 148.
2. Ibid., p. 45.
3. Ibid., pp. 160, 158.
4. I. L. Kandel, *A History of Secondary Education* (Boston: Houghton Mifflin, 1930), pp. 294–422; The Report of the Harvard Committee, *General Education in a Free Society* (Cambridge, Mass.: Harvard University Press, 1945), p. 7; U.S. Department of Education, National Center for Education Statistics, *The Condition of Education* (Washington, D.C.: Government Printing Office, 1982), pp. 18–19.
5. Ben J. Wattenberg, ed., *The Statistical History of the United States: From Colonial Times to the Present* (New York: Basic Books, 1976), pp. 382–83.
6. U.S. Department of Education, National Center for Education Statistics, *The Condition of Education* (Washington, D.C.: Government Printing Office, 1985), p. 94.
7. Ibid., pp. 94, 90.
8. Ibid., p. 94; U.S. Department of Education, National Center for Education Statistics, *The Condition of Education* (Washington, D.C.: Government Printing Office, 1981), p. 17.
9. Wattenberg, *The Statistical History of the United States*, pp. 382–83; U.S. Department of Education, National Center for Education Statistics, *The Condition of Education* 1982, p. 138.
10. National Commission on Excellence in Education, *A Nation at Risk* (Washington, D.C.: Government Printing Office, 1983), p. 8.
11. Ibid., pp. 24–27.
12. U.S. Department of Education, National Institute of Education, *Involvement in Learning: Realizing the Potential of American Higher Education* (Washington, D.C.: Government Printing Office, 1984), p. 9.
13. Association of American Colleges, *Integrity in the College Curriculum: A Report to the Academic Community* (Washington, D.C.: Association of American Colleges, 1985), pp. 2–3, 15.

14. William H. Bennett, *To Reclaim a Legacy* (Washington, D.C.: National Endowment for the Humanities, 1984), p. 2.

15. National Endowment for the Humanities, "A Statistical Overview of Undergraduate Education in the Humanities," study prepared for the Chairman's Study Group on the State of Learning in the Humanities in Higher Education by the National Endowment for the Humanities Office in Program and Policy Studies, April 17, 1984, p. 2. (Unpublished.)

16. Mortimer J. Adler, *The Paideia Proposal: An Educational Manifesto* (New York: Macmillan, 1982), pp. 5-6.

17. Henry Steele Commager, *The Commonwealth of Learning* (New York: Harper & Row, 1968), p. 6.

18. Ernest Gellner, *Nations and Nationalism* (Ithaca, N.Y.: Cornell University Press, 1983), p. 36.

CHAPTER 10

Profits and Prophecy:
A Partial View of American Science
near the Millennium

Gerald M. Edelman

I t is curiosity that drives scientific effort, not profit, but in a modern age it is profit that makes science possible. In these days of particle accelerators of ten-mile diameter and large genetic engineering establishments, economies of scale operate with a vengeance. The past may have seen a gentleman of both cerebral and fiscal endowments peer at stars or animalcules while savoring the delicious rewards of the natural philosopher, but now he would need twenty well-trained postdoctoral associates to carry out his studies. What consequences does this change in scale have for the progress of science in America? Does the promised increase in technological progress prefigure a return to public belief in the general idea of progress? What are the roles of the private and public sectors in the provision of moral and financial support to an enlarging scientific enterprise?

In this chapter I shall consider how notions of profit can intrude upon the scientific stance in basic research, which is that of prediction (or prophecy), and how that intrusion might alter private and public judgments of science. Then I shall describe a scientific prophecy that if realized may revolutionize ideology to the same extent as Darwinism did in the last century. These ambitious tasks are well set in the American frame—since World War II the United States has been dominant in scientific technology and in the last two decades dominant in brain science, the main source of my prophecy. Although I shall speak in the international and ecumenical spirit that

224 / THE MIND AND THE SPIRIT

is central to modern science, I shall also speak personally as an American scientist reporting subjectively on the changes wrought by altered attitudes in this country toward profit and prophecy in science.

PROPHECY AS THE ORIGIN OF PROFITS

As the great physical chemist Jacobus Hendricus van't Hoff pointed out, science is imagination in the service of the verifiable truth and as such it is eminently practical.[1] Outside of the delights of recognition[2] afforded by its predictions, science has two main social effects: (1) its prophecies (predictions) can be turned to use (profits) and (2) it can change human ideology, largely by challenging beliefs established by nonscientific means. With few exceptions, the first effect is welcomed, but the second, which is almost always the result of a large overturn in scientific theory, is usually received with mixed feelings.

The source of both effects is the same: empirical science itself. The stance of the empirical scientist is that of the detached observer or experimenter exercising imagination in the service of the verifiable truth. Clearly, this detachment implies a certain frame of mind: No nonscientific ideology may intervene on judgment, and no immediate practical ends should constrict the imaginative view. If it is carried out at all effectively in this fashion, science must inevitably make progress in both methodology and aim.

Scientific predictions and prophecies based on such progress can in some cases be converted to enormous profits. But it is not so well grasped by the general public that the technological pursuits yielding such profits are only rarely convertible into new scientific prophecies. The course of basic inquiry that leads to good scientific prediction requires an attitude toward time and money that differs greatly from that which must be adopted during the course of technological development. Applied research and development are much more expensive than basic research, and they are carried out over short schedules of time, under high-pressure conditions, using well-understood scientific principles. Although basic research is much cheaper, it requires unconstrained time insofar as its major heuristic search is for new principles or a deep revision of old ones. Once understood, these principles may of course be used for new applications.

A remarkably tortuous and unimaginable course must usually be taken before a basic scientific prophecy can be turned to profit. To illustrate this, I shall briefly discuss two profitable areas of modern biology—molecular genetics and immunology. Although I must take some liberties with detail because this is not a technical article, in its essentials this account is correct. These examples will show that while the use to which a scientific principle is put can be prophesied loosely by qualified scientists, the prophecy cannot be realized as profit until a complex course of inquiry that is full of surprise is nearly completed.

This may seem obvious, but it is repeatedly forgotten by scientific administrators in the public sector, driven as they are by needs for definition, regulation, timeliness, and practicality. Influenced by such needs, their decisions often alter the climate required to undertake a basic inquiry, and the consequences of these decisions can discourage the development of individuals more suited to that climate. The result is somewhat paradoxical because a continued growth of basic science is not only essential to applied science but it costs far less money.

Unlike applied science, basic science will not yield simply to will or to money, although both are useful. My two examples illustrate this nicely. Genetics (the science concerned with the principles of heredity) was founded in 1865 by Gregor Mendel, an obscure Austrian monk. His discoveries indicated that there were units of inheritance (now called genes) that were particulate, that is, genes were donated to progeny by each member of a mating pair and they segregated and assorted more or less independently in the offspring. This momentous discovery was forgotten and was re-established in 1901 by Hugo De Vries and others. The reasons for the failure to recognize Mendel's discovery have been analyzed elsewhere.[3] The main point I want to emphasize here is twofold. First, Mendel's discovery and the subsequent rediscovery of the gene provided the basis for an extraordinary liaison with Darwin's theory of evolution, the so-called *modern synthesis*.[4] Two large generalizations—that evolution occurred by natural selection and that heredity occurred through particulate means—were thereby joined and together provided the central theoretical basis of biology. Both generalizations and their adjunct predictions and prophecies were of course based on large bodies of empirical evidence. Second, the subsequent establishment of different genes as varieties of a chemical known as deoxyribonucleic acid or DNA made possible the development of molecular genetics and genetic engineering.

Before describing genetic engineering, it is important to note that, like Mendel's, the second great discovery (that of DNA as the genetic material) did not at first receive appropriate notice.[5] Yet this basic discovery by Avery and his colleagues at the Rockefeller Institute[6] made the Mendelian heritage potentially profitable to a degree that still cannot be fully calculated. Of course, animal and plant breeders used Mendelian principles, but with Avery's discoveries and the subsequent demonstration of the structure of DNA by James Watson and Francis Crick,[7] the possibility of introducing chosen genes *directly* from one organism to another was on the brink of becoming a reality.

It is revealing to reflect upon how long and what means it took to discover, undiscover, and rediscover these great advances. They occurred in peaks of insight over 100 years; they required great bodies of workers in different countries; and their historical course could not have been predicted. Furthermore, it took time to appreciate their significance. Even the scientific community in possession of expertise (or at least exposed to the necessary principles) lapsed in its recognition of these ideas or, rather, took time to see what they meant. And the individuals concerned, Mendel, a retiring monk raising flowers, and Avery, a reclusive medical researcher studying pneumonia, were hardly driven by the direct hope of profit from their predictions.

What is the outcome for profit? It is still too early to make a precise assessment, but the outlook appears remarkable. Genes (or pieces of DNA) specify the structure of the intricate molecules known as proteins that control all basic biological processes. The fact that we can introduce the DNA of humans or other species into fast-growing bacteria and produce large quantities of these proteins (hormones, drugs, and so on) opens up whole vistas for the treatment of disease. Moreover, the possibility of diagnosing and altering genetic disorders emerges. A recent example is the location on the human chromosome of the gene for a heritable human disorder, called Huntington's disease, that leads inevitably to motor discoordination and death.[8] The advent of molecular genetics makes is possible for individuals who carry that gene to know in advance of marriage whether the disorder will show up in progeny.

Prophecy in another basic scientific field has also led to large profit. Immunology arose as a branch of medicine in the late nineteenth century, a time when the principles of bacteriology and infectious disease were first emerging from the work of Louis Pasteur and Robert Koch. It was observed by various investigators that the blood (or its fluid component, the serum) of a person could prevent the growth of particular bacterium if the person from whom the blood was taken had been infected previously by that agent.

Of course, it had been known since ancient times that survivors of a disease were often immune to it, and the notion was put into practice more than a century before by Edward Jenner, who infected people with cowpox (vaccination) in order to protect them from smallpox. But it took prophecy based on the search for the recognizing principle in the blood to turn immunology into a full-fledged science. At the turn of the century, von Behring showed that the blood contained substances named antibodies that were not only responsible for the recognition of foreign intruders but also for facilitating their destruction by special cells of the organism. It was realized that these substances or agents of defense were remarkably specific—particular antibodies recognized one infectious agent by binding to it but usually not to others.

A profound extension of this idea of specificity came when Karl Landsteiner (whose discovery of blood groups made transfusion possible) showed at the Rockefeller Institute that practically *any* organic chemical that could be made by a chemist could be specifically recognized by antibodies if that chemical were first linked to a protein and injected into a laboratory animal. This discovery allied immunology with chemistry and opened up a vast area of exploration. But the chemical nature of antibodies was still obscure, and its determination seemed hopelessly difficult because there appeared to be so many different kinds, each of different specificity. Indeed, the body was able through these antibody molecules to recognize *self* from *not-self*, to use a felicitous distinction coined by Sir MacFarlane Burnet.[9] To account for their capabilities of recognition, another great scientist, Linus Pauling, made a prophecy about the key issue of specificity in 1941 that has since turned out to be wrong. He suggested that the not-self foreign molecules (or antigens, as they were called) acted as templates around which nascent antibodies folded. The impressed shape of the antigen remained in the antibody molecules (think of cookies and a cookie-cutter) and served as

228 / THE MIND AND THE SPIRIT

the vehicle by which given antibodies recognized their specific antigens upon a second encounter.

While reading a book on immunology in 1956, I was struck by the fact that much attention was paid to antigens but not to antibodies, the molecules that were obviously the central clue to the mystery of immunity. I resolved to study the molecular structure of antibodies, and eventually I came to the Rockefeller University to do so, innocent of how difficult a task I had set for myself. At that time (1957) in London, the late Rodney Porter also became curious about the structure of antibodies; each of us was ignorant of the other's existence.

The obstacle to be overcome was twofold: (1) the large size of antibodies as molecules (about thirty times larger than insulin, the chemical structure of which had just been worked out in a *tour de force* by Porter's professor, Frederick Sanger); (2) the immense heterogeneity of the antibody molecules even in one individual's blood—no two kinds were identical. Since antibodies recognized different antigens by their shape and there were so many shapes, this heterogeneity was no surprise. But in order to study structure, chemists need to have pure substances (that is, every one of the molecules must be alike in shape).

To solve this first problem, Porter and I independently set out to break the antibody in smaller pieces, and each of us succeeded by different chemical means. In the course of work on the pieces I made (which turned out to be the natural chains of the antibody molecule), I noted that one of the chains was the same as a protein excreted in the urine of patients with a cancer of certain blood cells that make antibodies. This cancer, called multiple myeloma, invades bones and produces huge amounts of a pure protein in the blood. This protein looked in every respect like an antibody except that we could not know what it would recognize inasmuch as it did not arise by previous immunization with a foreign antigen. This discovery and those of Porter made it possible to determine the entire structure of a pure antibody protein, a task accomplished with my colleagues at the Rockefeller Institute in 1967. By looking at molecules from cancers of different individuals, each of whom made one pure antibody protein, the chemical basis of how antibodies of different specificity differed in their shape became clear.

As it turned out, one antibody-producing cell made one kind of antibody only, a finding that corresponded with a theory proposed by Sir MacFarlane Burnet.[10] In this theory, Burnet suggested that animals with backbones already had a huge number of different antibodies, each with a different shape, *before* ever seeing the foreign antigens. Encounter with a particular antigen *selected* the antibodies that fit best, and the binding of the antigen by antibodies on a selected cell resulted in the manufacture by that cell of more antibodies with the appropriate specificity.

The two developments above-described, the determination of the structure of antibodies and Burnet's so-called clonal selection theory, revolutionized and rationalized immunology as a science. Moreover, they allied it to molecular genetics and genetic engineering.

At this point, the field was ripe for profit. Antibodies were chemicals that could recognize other chemicals in terms of their shape. Suppose you could make one kind of antibody in a test tube of just the specificity you needed? Cesar Milstein and George Kohler attacked this question at Cambridge University, using the knowledge that one cell made one kind of antibody and that some cancer cells were "immortal," that is, could keep on dividing in a dish outside of the animal. These scientists immunized mice with a chosen antigen, took cells making one kind of antibody, and fused them with a multiple myeloma (or cancer) cell, which was *not* making antibody. The hybrid cell (called a hybridoma) kept making antibodies of that kind more or less indefinitely: Like one of its parents, it was immortal in that it produced progeny cells asexually, and like the other, it was specific in that it made just one kind of antibody.

As a result of this development, it became possible to make antibodies in the test tube that were specific in binding whatever antigen one might choose: viruses, bacteria, blood proteins, and the like. Today an industry in which these so-called monoclonal antibodies are made is being applied to medical diagnosis and treatment, and the chemical tricks learned from the work on the structure of antibodies are being applied to modifying them in order to treat disease.

This time everyone was recognized—all the above-mentioned individuals were awarded the Nobel Prize. But none was motivated by profit, and none took out patents on his work. All were supported by government funds and to a lesser extent by local institutional means. My own work on antibodies was largely supported by a grant from the U.S. Public Health Service for the study of the emission of light by molecules (fluorescence), a grant that was not even aimed at studying antibodies. Including salaries, the budget of my laboratory from 1960 to 1967 did not exceed $250,000 per year. My colleagues at the Rockefeller University knew vaguely about my work but respectfully left it and me alone.

Things are different now. It is inconceivable that I would now be allowed to study the structure of a molecule while supported by a proposal to analyze fluorescence spectra. Instead, the present policy guiding application for government grants is that you deliver the goods you promised, that you not apply for two grants that have overlapping subject matter (without running risks of slashes in their budgets), and, above all, that you stick to the name of your subject. A switch of subject matter is a costly proposition for the imaginative researcher and is promptly punished; to avoid punishment, the scientist must stop working to write an appropriately named, lengthy, and specifically detailed grant proposal.

We will explore this regrettable change in a later section. At this point, I want to summarize the general characteristics guiding the pursuit of profits and prophecy in science and contrast the climates that they seem to require. It is my thesis that the separation of these climates is essential for the maintenance of growth in each arena.

The gross characteristics of each are shown in the table below. Without denying invention, we may say that profit in applied science is based largely on the known, is secure in principle, has a short time scale for success, is task oriented, and is fractionated into narrow channels by specialists taking up defined tasks. It is costly, for a large number of people are involved. The pursuit of profit is logically acceptable in the sense that the principles on which it is based are

Characteristics of Applied and Basic Research.

	Applied Science	*Basic Science*
Scientific Principle	Understood	Object of search
Time Scale	Short to medium range (1–5 yrs.)	Long range (5–100 yrs.)
Cost	Great	Relatively small
Workers	Highly specialized; large numbers	Cross-disciplinary; smaller numbers
Strategy	Recombinational; inventive	Recategorical; imaginative

and must be known before it can proceed. The key strategy of profit is recombinational—it takes one known thing and combines it in an efficient manner with another.[11]

Prophecy in predictive basic science is based upon a search into the unknown, and it is fundamentally insecure. Basic science must not keep its eye on the clock, for results may take a long time to arise (each of the sagas I have recounted involved blocks of time amounting to about one-third of each single individual's life). In basic science, the task falls upon fewer people to make the key moves, and, in general, it is relatively cheap (I exclude atom smashing, for now). It often seems bizarre and unconventional for it requires strange forays into unlikely areas, ideas that are departures from received notions, and the stubborn persistence of single-minded scholars willing to face intractable (and apparently impractical) issues. The basic strategy of prophecy is recategorical—it challenges the accepted names of things or how they are coordinated or linked.

Three observations are worth making. First, the kinds of individuals carrying out these essential scientific activities of profit and prophecy are generally different from one another, although very occasionally an individual can traverse from one arena to the other. Second, the mores and the support structure likely to yield success for each activity are often extremely different. Third, it is easier to assess the profit side, even from a scientific viewpoint, than it is to assess the prophecy side.

Despite these distinctions, much current scientific research at the basic level is governed by styles more suited to research at the applied level. This has had mixed consequences that are not easy to assess; my view is that it represents a turn for the worse, and I shall touch upon a few current practices to support that judgment.

THE SWING TOWARD PROFIT IN SCIENCE

Thus far my account has given concrete examples only from biology. To a physicist acquainted with government interests in the military uses of nuclear power and lasers, these examples may seem quaint, for even at their most ambitious scale, genetic engineering facilities can hardly compare in cost with accelerators or super colliders having radii of miles. In this arena, one is speaking of power in big terms: power as a subject central to physics as well as political power exercised by nations as they vie in defense capability or by different states as they bid for the billions of dollars that might be brought in by having a super collider sited on their land.

Regardless of such differences of scale, both biology and physics in this country have encountered similar changes, changes that govern which individuals pursue which subject and what they will find when they get there. I can speak reliably only about my own experience and shall attempt to synthesize the responses of my colleagues to changes in research sociology that have occurred in the last decade. The anecdotal nature of this account may vitiate it to some degree; nonetheless, I believe that it is symptomatic of sociological changes in the support of American science.

It is obvious that the scale of an individual research operation is now much grander than it used to be. If the annual budget of my laboratory in the days of antibody structure determination was at most $250,000, it is now well in excess of $1 million. The reasons have largely to do with inflation and mounting salary requirements of trained personnel in an urban setting, with the labor-intensive quality of the new technology, and with the material costs of that technology. Moreover, much of the activity in modern biology is dedicated to a vast information-gathering effort: There are at least 200,000 human genes, and the structure of each is in principle determinable. Typical of most scientific effort, however, the search at any one time is usually focused upon just a few examples by a number of laboratories, and there is fierce competition to make the first breakthrough.

A combination of these factors with changes in the structure of government funding has altered the atmosphere required for prophecy as well as made that atmosphere more similar to that of applied research institutions in industry. The basic-scientific entrepreneur has emerged as a definite type: a shrewd individual, knowledgeable but not necessarily skilled in his or her subject area, capable of enlisting support either from the government system or from business (with rights of first refusal guaranteed to the donor of research funds), capable of managing up to 100 workers, active and visible on international scenes, and an author of many papers each with many coauthors. Despite these activities, he mixes freely with the more old-fashioned types, and the telephone is one of his main scientific instruments.

A different but related development is the emergence of what I call the premature professor, a young person out of Ph.D. training for three or so years, who is searching for an assistant professorial appointment and for a sizeable grant that he will exercise by fulfilling exactly what he promised to do in his grant application. While he generally will aim to emulate the basic-science entrepreneur, at least he is in his laboratory fulfilling the promises of his specialist proposal. His starting budget (for a biology laboratory) can be as much as $150,000 to $200,000 per year. He is generally highly skilled and active but in no way inclined to dream obsessively on a scientific question. His goals are to achieve specialist recognition and a stable career. In general, if one such individual can be found in a university in a particular area such as immunology, there are ten similar individuals to be found elsewhere, all fairly accomplished. The premature professor does not cross subject boundaries readily or often. His concern (as it must be, given the nature of the stringent system for reviewing his grant proposals) is apparent productivity—not one paper of depth to be recognized as a breakthrough ten years hence but ten papers a year. Speed, certainty, and increasing laboratory size are all reasonable intermediate-range goals for the premature professor. These goals are set before his emergence, and it is probably the case that most such young people have few alternatives but to pursue them for survival's sake.

What is gained and what is lost from the evolution of such scientists? Clearly, much has been gained in the areas of methodological improvement and sheer accumulation of fact. The rate of emergence of new facts and of small answers is greatly increased, as any one perusing the key specialist journals may witness. Science in this mode has achieved statistical success—there are more facts, established more quickly and more quickly perceived. In this respect, basic research reflects (with some social lag) what has already occurred in other parts of our society. On the average, assessable performance has improved while individual depth of performance (if it is assessable at all) is not as great. There is a tighter governance of money spent and greater accountability. Regulatory provisions of funding agencies pervade, at the level of both the individual and his home institution.

It is more difficult to determine what has been lost because of these changes in the practice of basic science, for several reasons: depth of performance is a qualitative matter affecting individuals, and very little time has passed. To see whether the number of fundamental discoveries will be compromised by such changes, we may have to wait thirty-five years or at least one-third of a lifetime. What is clear, at least in my experience, is that the complaints and the fears of the individual scientists have changed, and my impression is that the shift indicates loss. Where the prevailing complaints were previously against the difficulty of the material (i.e., the impenetrability of a scientific question) or against the unfeeling bureaucracy of university administrations, they now tend to be against the tendentiousness of peer group review or the failure to get *more* money.

Only government support can handle the increased scale of most modern scientific efforts, however valiantly even rich private foundations try to lend their help. The change wrought by economies of scale is clear: With the loss of private support as a major means, there is loss of a characteristically American pluralism, a source of diversity that handled in a nonuniform way the mismatch between intent and accomplishment that must occur in basic science. While this nongovernmental support system was nonuniform in its standards and it was never enough, it did a creditable job in handling a diversity of research approaches.

With increasing growth and inflation, even government support now threatens to be curtailed, and at this point business has stepped in with an eye to profit. In biology this has meant that certain scientists have received large guaranteed sums for basic research in exchange for rights of first refusal should something practical emerge. By and large this is a reasonably loose-end, liberal arrangement, but it is not without the implication of a defined target that goes against the grain of basic research. Nonetheless, a number of universities under monetary pressure, as well as individual researchers seeking relief from the tense bureaucracy of federal funding, have chosen this route.

The present picture is a shifting and eclectic one composed of mixtures of new and old customs. It is not easy to predict how much gain will accrue to basic science in America. But if there is any generality in my two anecdotes about the style of fundamental biological research, we can see sufficiently well to issue some warnings. First, the support of fact-gathering and methodologically oriented research driven by industry support with short-term goals may select competitively against individuals and climates that allow the pursuit of deep questions. Certainly the atmospheres of many biological laboratories are at present not those of dreaming, of refining questions, or even of questioning old answers. Instead, the rewards are for action and for getting answers fast.

My second warning is explicit: Universities or institutes will lose sight of long-range goals and individuals of great creative gifts. Imaginative persons who do not enjoy engaging in endless competition will be selected against; individuals with managerial skills will be selected for. Over some intermediate range of time, research styles of proven value may be lost and a tradition broken. That tradition might be summarized in the words of an accomplished scientist and mathematician, the late Mark Kac: "Universities should be that part of our society dedicated to fifty years hence." [12] If things go on as they are in basic science laboratories, the goals set will be at best for five years hence, the maximal period of a government grant.

A third warning has to do with the individual discontent engendered by the paradigm of statistical success. In the aggregate, there seems to be more output of significant scientific facts, but there is less contentment with the individual circumstances effected by unending competition and the need to manipulate the support system. This situation does not differ from other situations and arenas of society in which the paradigm of statistical success applies. In medicine, diagnosis rates are on the average better than twenty years ago, but the independent role of the individual physician (and I might add, the individual patient) is reduced. In basic research, the effect of the statistical paradigm will be to select against the most imaginative long-range projects. Lest this seem a small price to pay, let me suggest that it has not been assessed whether the present apparent success of the statistical paradigm does not largely feed off the achievement of its more inefficient precursors. If this is true in science, the maintenance of the sizeable competitive establishments and the competitive exclusion of dreamers may result in future impoverishment.

My fourth warning is against satisfaction with the merely combinatorial aspects of contemporary research efforts as distinguished from the recategorical aspects of truly profound basic research (Table 10-1). I call this satisfaction the *Magister Ludi* effect, after Hesse's utopian (or cacatopian) novel *Das Glasperlenspiel*. [13] The *Magister Ludi*, or Master of the Games, could recombine knowledge but not create it. The fact is that the number of possible recombinations of current knowledge is effectively endless. As in a modern urban environment in which the recombination of just six or seven technological inventions can fill everyday life with an overwhelming density of tasks, so in science one may get on forever with endless fretwork. But the key goal of basic research is to develop new insights, new questions, and new categories. Although some recombination is required, a visit to uncharted jungle suburbs is mandatory. The inculcation of the questioning view—Why should we stay here? Why not overthrow the subject?—is under threat. Few scholar scientists are left, and if their absolute number was always small, then their relative number is today sharply diminished. People must be reminded that knowledge is neither static nor just recombinatorial. It is dynamic and context dependent, and new discoveries are needed for the tasks of refurbishing and reshaping the meaning of old knowledge.

These qualitative and subjective remarks would be worthless if they did not generate more than a querulous account by one individual of the consequences of the present system of research sponsorship in America. I shall propose three positive suggestions. The first focuses on the practical dilemmas of funding a search into the unknown, an activity that I call the capitalism of curiosity. The second is a proposal that the most important defense to be taken by science against its own large movements is moratorium—the creation of small places or scientific monasteries conserving old styles of inquiry. The third is nothing less than a millennial prophecy—that, despite its present difficulties, American science (and science in general) will see another conceptual revolution before the turn of the century. That revolution is in the field of neurobiology, or brain science, and the message is optimistic: Both science and society are likely to be transformed for the better as a result.

THE CAPITALISM OF CURIOSITY

Basic research is necessarily an inefficient process. It is not subject to ordinary rules of management and stewardship. Instead, it develops rich and unpredictable stores of facts and ideas that comprise a kind of research capital, which can be spent later for practical ends such as the cure of disease. But, as with other capital, attempts to spend it before it is accumulated can be hazardous. Although many people think that the line from curiosity to application is a straight one, my anecdotes have shown that this is not the case. The fact is that research capitalism or the capitalism of curiosity follows a quirky and difficult route in no way subject to the ordinary rules of good business practice.

One reason for this is that basic research is a reflection of a kind of play. This characteristic tends to be obscured by the technical and planning aspects of research that scientists must place among their major concerns. Nonetheless, I believe that the spirit of play underlies most basic research efforts.[14] Beyond a certain point you can't make play efficient without ruining it. If that is true, the imposing question becomes: Why pay scientists to play? My reply is that there is no other way to assure that proper climate in which fundamental discoveries about our world can be made.

The task of basic research is to discover and describe significant new features of that world under the guidance of a surmise, hypothesis, or theory. This is frequently misunderstood. Often I've had graduate students ask in the middle of an experiment, "Why are we doing this? Can't we just go to the library and look it up?" That this question would come from students of science might seem astonishing, but it indicates a point of view that is common enough, even in specialized precincts. The answer is, one cannot look it up—one guesses and one tries. The question reflects misconceptions about the scientific method: Whatever it is, this method is not a formula to calculate discoveries. It is a means to tidy up one's fumbling and guesses after one has finally found some apparently coordinated facts or clues to the solution of a problem.

In basic research we often do not know the connection between the results of our studies and their practical applications. But, as we have seen, there is one reassuring historical point: Almost always, apparently inefficient basic research pays off handsomely, efficiently, and in unpredictable ways. It is obvious that a new vaccine that prevents the spread of a major incapacitating illness is a vital development in both humane and economic terms. Not so obvious are the humane and economic benefits of a basic discovery that organizes a field, opens new vistas, or makes development of a vaccine possible. What is the calculable dollar-and-cents value of the structure of DNA?

I am always embarrassed when reporters ask me to explain the practical benefits of my own work on antibody structure. That work has cured no disease, but it has helped to reorganize our thinking about the causes, diagnosis, and therapy of diseases. For example, now that we know the structure of the antibody molecule, it can be cut up in various ways and its properties altered in order to treat people more efficiently, in ways that the body itself has not yet managed to contrive through evolution. In other words, this kind of knowledge is basic research capital that is ready to be invested in useful and humane projects. For the most part, the accumulation of such research capital does not proceed in a straight line nor does it begin with a narrow result in mind.

Given that there is a necessary inefficiency in accumulating research capital, we may ask how such inefficiency can be supported by real capital. The present means relies upon a system of peer-group review, calling upon scientists both to determine the merits of other scientists' proposals and to criticize their proposed budgets. Such reviewers interact with a trained bureaucracy in institutions such as the National Institutes of Health (NIH) and the National Science Foundation (NSF). This system has many merits, but it may be in need of broader insights. One is that more recognition must be given to the fact that the capitalism of curiosity is a curious form of capitalism indeed—one that lacks the usual buffers of space, time, or money that a capitalist or a businessperson would employ to put funds to the best use.

Certainly, there are features of research funding that no sane capitalist would tolerate in his or her business. Basic research funds usually are given as grants in fixed periods after proposals have been reviewed by scientific peers and agency officials, and in the case of government agencies, only after the funds have been appropriated by the Congress. The plans proposed by large agencies often fail to recognize sufficiently that a substantial amount of basic research capital must be accumulated before societal application is possible. In the absence of this capital, direct, mission-oriented pushes or large task forces almost always fail. They are not even justifiable as propaganda to persuade senators who vote on the budget, for such drives most certainly will lead to disappointment and skepticism. Government funds usually must be given according to strict budgets for defined periods of time, and this is all well and good. But a close scrutiny of the creative process indicates that if there are any untoward developments in a project or if it needs to change during the research period, the basic scientist has recourse to only one method—reapplication for funding over time periods that usually are too long to be beneficial or to meet the immediate economic crisis. Even if an official at an institution such as the NIH has understood what the problem is, he or she will have a very hard time rustling up sufficient contingency funds to tide the researcher over. The need for accountability, the political process, and large increases in the number of applications all in some sense conflict with the needs of the established researcher.

As salaries and fringe benefits increase over the time period of a grant, the total proportion of the budget that they occupy becomes huge, and the unencumbered funds available to the researcher represent a diminishing and sometimes minuscule part of the budget. Project costs and demands cannot realistically be budgeted ahead. On the other side, one must consider the labor-intensive and distracting task of grant renewal as well as delays in the grant decisionmaking process. If a scientist has three or four grants supported by different agencies with different starting and ending periods and one grant ends, a remarkable juggling act is essential to keep a constant flow of money into the laboratory. This requires the cooperation of officials in the various agencies as well as that of officials in a home institution such as a university. Although a grant may be awarded in principle, a grant-decision delay means that the money simply is not there, and some way of buffering the absence of that money must be provided.

In addition, there are other long-range needs that create additional major stresses for institutions. One of these is the increasing cost of setting up researchers in a new research venture—beginning assistant professors, for example. Everybody in the research enterprise knows that young brains are the ones that we can count on for new developments and imagination in a variety of fields. But it no longer is possible to have every kind of field represented in every good institution. There must be some fractionation of fields, a circumstance that can influence both grant-making decisions and local administrative support.

In the face of these difficulties, one is tempted to ask, "Given such short- and long-range needs, would a businessperson run a company without some form of buffering provided by equity, investment capital, and bank loans?" I think it unlikely and would therefore suggest that perhaps the time has come to consider the idea of a research bank, a storehouse in which government funds are placed to buffer the various situations and contingencies that arise during a research project. Such a bank could serve to meet a number of contingencies that confront the researcher in the course of basic research. Of course, this proposal for a research bank is not sufficiently detailed, and there is a conceptual problem: Basic research provides no direct profit and no obvious tangible product. Nonetheless, science has an invisible product with enormous implications for our economy. Indeed, some economists have estimated that over 30 percent of the economic development in this country since World War II can be related in a more or less direct way to the basic research accomplished in that period.

The idea of a research bank may not be practical in reality because of the political difficulties that it might engender. Moreover, private support provided by local institutions already serves many of the functions of a research bank. Good research institutions have traditionally provided some buffers, but it is a hard tradition to maintain in the face of mounting costs. It is time to reinstate the support of excellent local institutions at the basic level by private sources and foundations without concern for some of the notions of democracy that must be heeded in disbursing government funds. This will require an aggressive campaign to educate the public and to assure private foundations that no pretext of practicality or democracy is required. Presenting university needs as equivalent to those of a research bank may make attractive good sense to businesspeople.

THE SCIENTIFIC MONASTERY

Robert Nisbet has pointed out that in history the ruling mode is religious, political, revolutionary, or monastic.[15] So far, I have suggested that basic research originates in imagination and curiosity, that it cannot be predicted, that it takes a long time, and that its major progress usually centers on the work of a few individuals trained in a certain "tradition." At the same time, exploiting the practical benefits of this research in applied work requires prediction from known principle, short-term rewards, a large number of people, and much money. As progress has occurred, these two modes have become mixed and this has generated many ambiguities about the magnitude, style, criteria of success, and sources of support in the scientific enterprise.

We now face a new dilemma—basic research is beginning to cost more money. If the original view ruling basic research was quasi-religious (the university as a place for fifty years hence with the researcher-professor as the inculcator of a tradition, guiding searches for the right question), the current ruling view is political. That is to say, many or most of the discussions among scientists now concern who gives the money, who gets it, and how it is to be spent. Is there an alternative to this view?

Science, by its very nature, cannot adopt a revolutionary mode in the sphere of politics. And it is not likely that the present administrators of big science or of business-supported science will change their criteria, for much that is being done is good for the country, for technology, for business, and for science. If we accept these conclusions, how do we preserve what we also know to be good in the scientific tradition about sources of individual creation and the teaching of styles related to deep questions? I submit here the suggestion of the scientific monastery, a small, privately supported institution for refining questions. Science, of course, is the art of the soluble,[16] an exercise in answers. But the answers come from framing the right question in a nourishing and supportive environment.

As director of the Neurosciences Institute (NSI) an institution dedicated to providing such an environment, I may be accused of special pleading by describing its activities. Rather, I hope that it may be taken as a sign of special fervor if I describe the activities of this institution as one kind (not the only imaginable kind) of scientific monastery. In its heyday (and to a certain extent at present), the Institute for Advanced Study in Princeton was another kind. The Neurosciences Institute is part of the Neurosciences Research Program (NRP), a voluntary association of scholars in the brain sciences begun in 1962 at the Massachusetts Institute of Technology. At any one time, the NRP is composed of thirty-two to thirty-six scientists who are centrally interested in brain science. Their original purpose was to develop increased communication across the boundaries of the ten or so subdisciplines in neuroscience by arranging for frequent meetings of small groups and an occasional grand summary across all fields. The Neurosciences Institute was founded in 1982 to help an individual basic scientist refine a main question of interest in his field and to formulate experimental or theoretical problems that might require meeting with specialists even from remote fields.

The NSI is housed at the Rockefeller University but is separate from it and supported by a not-for-profit foundation, the Neurosciences Research Foundation. The rules of the NSI are few: There is no tenure; people may come or go on any schedule that pleases them or their home institutions; no more than twelve people may be at the NSI at one time; and no formal scientific meetings are allowed. Instead, each fellow may arrange a conference of up to eight people around any issue. Fellows are allowed to appoint one junior fellow without further review (a junior fellow being one with assistant professorial or postdoctoral rank); the chosen junior fellow may come to the NSI at the same or a different time as the designator. Junior fellows are also appointed independently by NRP associates. In its three years of active existence, the NSI has been host to more than 500 scientists from 130 institutions and 17 countries.

One of the most successful enterprises of the NSI is the so-called Summer Atelier run entirely by junior fellows. Each summer these fellows invite up to twenty people (from different countries and in whatever field they deem suitable) to join them for up to five weeks to consider the refinement of questions of mutual interest. Several scientific collaborations have arisen from these encounters; young scientists in these collaborations may use the resources of the NSI throughout the year without elaborate application procedures. These resources include a large computer, a specialized library, a staff organization trained to expedite conferences, an editorial staff, and, above all, interesting people. Nearly all fellows and junior fellows report alleviation from bureaucratic despotism as well as a burst of creative activity during their stay. There is ample evidence that a mutual scholarly reinforcement takes place at the NSI. At the same time, there is no competition with home institutions: Individuals return to these institutions to carry out the research planned at the NSI.

In a field such as neuroscience that consists of many subdisciplines, it is perhaps particularly easy to justify the existence of an NSI. Nonetheless, one may envision many fields in which a similar institution might be useful to help counteract the competitive, specialized, relatively bureaucratic tendencies of present large-scale research. Such institutions must, of course, be privately supported by enlightened individuals or by foundations, for they could hardly deliver the kind of product demanded perforce by federal agencies. Nonetheless, they are places for restoring belief in the obligate refinement of scientific questions and in pluralistic modes of behavior, of support, and of scientific exchange.

In this sense, such scientific monasteries are a return to the style of small science based on the individual without taking an adversarial stance against the necessary or inevitable trends of big science. In other words, while institutes such as NSI are not practical, they are useful in sustaining the tradition of the imaginative individual scientific scholar in parallel with big science. At their budget levels ($0.5 to $1 million a year), they are the least costly alternative to the large political modes of carrying on specialist science. In dealing with problems of scale by self-selection and mutual education, they bring historically proven advantages to bear upon the problem of preserving and encouraging imagination in basic science. In this sense, they *are* practical.

THE OBSERVER OBSERVED:
A MILLENNIAL PROPHECY

It is time to return in this essay to the true end of science: to enlarge our view of ourselves and of nature. Science is embedded in a particular society at a given time in history, and to some extent it is subject to the beliefs, trends, and values of that society, even to its whims. A review of the history of the support of American science from the beginning of World War II to the present would amply sustain that statement. At the same time, however, science alters the acceptance of ideology (at least by contradiction of promulgated false beliefs). While it would be absurd to think that science can predict historical events, scientific descriptions and products set important boundary conditions determining the frames within which events unfold and beliefs are shared. The development of automation, nuclear power, computer technology, and aeronautics and the exploration of outer space have altered the pattern of our lives. The very interdependence of such systems has put us at hazard: In a psychic equivalent of Malthus' law, if the fraction of psychotics or fanatics in a society has grown no greater, the possibility that one or a few might cause irreparable damage has grown exponentially. At the same time, the advances of biology and of medical research have brought extraordinary benefits to humankind, without national restrictions.

Science, above all science in America, represents the very best principles of internationalism. This internationalism is, of course, obligatory in the pursuit of basic science, but even in the applied sphere, the United States has been generous in opening opportunities for others, whether it be the support of physicists during the 1930s by the Rockefeller Foundation or the export of medical advances by that and other institutions in the 1950s.

Internationalism in science is one of the most impressive realizations of the idea of progress. This idea, which sweeps through Western history over twenty-six centuries from Hesiod through St. Augustine and from the Reformation through the post-Newtonian age, has two main ingredients, as Nisbet has pointed out.[17] The first is the gradual but unmistakable increase in human knowledge. The second is the continued improvement of the moral state of humanity. Both of these elements can be discerned in a series of developments stemming from medical research, from the humane pragmatism of pre-scientific medicine to the diagnostic and therapeutic triumphs of modern scientific medicine.

As we approach the millennium, can we say that this progressivism will continue without limit or that the successful practical applications of scientific medicine will reinforce the general belief in the idea of progress? This is by no means guaranteed. At the present moment we see an increasing bureaucratization of our technology and a waning of public confidence in science. Even the flow of practical advances of medicine to needy countries in the best spirit of internationalism will not, I believe, bring about a reversal in this trend. The reason is that, as important as practical medical scientific change is to individuals and countries, it has no direct effect on human belief.

There is in the offing, however, another development in basic medical research that promises to bring about as momentous a revolution in the understanding of our nature as has been achieved in the Copernician, Darwinian, and Einsteinian revolutions.[18] I refer to the rapidly increasing understanding of the biological bases of the workings of the human brain. This is, simply put, like no other scientific adventure yet embarked upon.

Let me defend this view with a few summary statements. First, the brain is a special organ—it is at the center of human nature and human concern, and to understand it as we understand a kidney would therefore not merely imply another technological triumph but rather an epistemological revolution. Second, the brain is not like its works or products. There is, for example, no evidence whatsoever that the biological operation of the brain will be adequately described by the principles of physics alone as a logic machine by analogy to a computer.[19] Third, these two statements are presently not generally recognized as having major revolutionary implications for science or society. Instead, the prevailing view of science is based on the traditions of physics, that is, on simple systems used by societies for the transmission of power. From the viewpoint of basic biology however, it appears that the operation of the brain resembles complex systems more akin to those of evolution, that is, the operations of the brain are exercises in variation and selection.[20] While we are far from understanding fully the mechanisms of these operations, progress is rapid, and by the millennium I believe we can expect a revolution.

What is it we will know when we understand the mechanisms of brain operation as well as we currently understand those of the kidney or other organs? I suspect that we will regard the possessors of human brains once more as precious sources of individuality and variability and not as computerlike entities to be made more efficient. I believe that we will also have a richer understanding of the Lamarckian principles of social transmission that, in a species like ours, complement the Darwinian principles of genetic transmission.[21]

Most important of all, we may expect these developments to give a great boost to the idea of progress. The idea of progress is, after all, an idea concerning the workings of the human mind, and that mind arises in the workings of the brain. It has only barely been envisioned what life will be like when we have an understanding of the material basis of what it is to be a human being. Recent advances have already made it conceivable that we will soon understand the molecular bases of anatomy, which in turn will engender a great increase in understanding higher brain functions and physiology of the brain. It is, of course, more adventurous to predict that all of this will have a *positive* effect on the idea of progress. If we admit, however, that the brain is at least the necessary base of human definition, knowledge of the brain is sacred knowledge. And without implying mysticism, it is the notion of the sacred that has driven the idea of progress in society.[22]

Progress is not just power, it is insight. And we are on the threshold in medical research of the largest single insight imaginable into our own nature. It will be tragic if we shrink from it or fail to support it. To do as we have always done to support medical research in America will not be enough. It is now necessary to consider how support should be given in order to safeguard the entire scientific enterprise as well as the public interest. I believe that the questions raised here about our current modes of support are worthy of continuing debate and that simple practicality and progressivism are not sufficient to the case posed by the exploration of the brain. The engagement of public and private sectors in the United States in the support of brain science will require new modes of support and great imagination. The scientific exploration of the material basis of inner space has begun, and in it lies a new hope for our view of ourselves and of our future.

NOTES

1. J. H. van't Hoff, *Imagination in Science*, Molecular Biology, Biophysics and Biochemistry Series, vol. 1 (New York: Springer Verlag, 1967).

2. G. M. Edelman, "The Shock of Molecular Recognition," in E. E. Smith and D. W. Ribbons, eds., *Approaches to Immunology*, Miami Winter Symposium, vol. 9 (New York: Academic Press, 1975), pp. 1–21.

3. R. A. Brink and E. P. Styles, eds., *Heritage from Mendel: Proceedings of the Mendel Centennial Symposium* sponsored by the Genetic Society of America (Madison: University of Wisconsin Press, 1965); E. Mayr and W. Provine, *The Evolutionary Synthesis: Perspectives on the Unification of Biology* (Cambridge, Mass.: Harvard University Press, 1980).

4. Mayr and Provine, *The Evolutionary Synthesis*.

5. R. J. Dubos, *The Professor, The Institute, and DNA* (New York: Rockefeller University Press, 1976); M. McCarty, *The Transforming Principle: Discovering That Genes Are Made of DNA* (New York: W. W. Norton and Co., 1985).

6. McCarty, *The Transforming Principle*.

7. H. F. Judson, *The Eighth Day of Creation* (New York: Simon & Schuster, 1980).

8. J. F. Gusella, N. S. Wexler, P. M. Conneally, and D. Housman, "A DNA Polymorphism for Huntington's Disease Marks the Future," *Archives of Neurology* 42 (1985): 20–24.

9. M. Burnet, *The Clonal Selection Theory of Acquired Immunity* (Nashville, Tenn.: Vanderbilt University Press, 1959).

10. Burnet, *The Clonal Selection Theory*.

11. I am grateful to Professor Harvey Brooks for several constructive criticisms of this view and of these distinctions. While generally supporting my main thesis and extending its sweep from the vantage point of his larger experience in both industry and university life, Brooks has pointed out that my distinctions between basic and applied research are perhaps too sharp. He notes that applied research and development often can have the tortuous and serendipitous character I attribute to basic research. Moreover, he

indicates that fructifying and indeed revolutionary developments have come from the areas of applied and developmental research, and he points to the genealogy of the Josephson effect in physics as a good recent example.

My response is to agree that the distinctions I have made hold only modally. The fact is that technology not only helps basic science in an essential fashion but can occasionally lead to new arenas for basic research. It remains to be seen, however, whether even the enlightened styles of an IBM or of Bell Telephone Laboratories would result in such a grand tradition of very great and overarching discoveries as has the pursuit over the years of the styles of the university. My main point is that, in general, social stresses are such that the modes of each of these support environments create different intellectual environments over the long run. It is this social fact that draws my attention, not any need to make snobbish or absolute distinctions between basic and applied research.

In an ironic and well-posed example supporting my thesis of the threat to the university mode, Brooks observes that in several recent experiences he has had on review committees, the consensus was that "several candidates of close to Nobel Prize stature had eventually to be winnowed out by [a] search committee." This was "because it was predicted that their achievements would be considerably more modest in the less supportive environment of the university than they had been in the industrial laboratory from which they came." I take this to be a dire sign of decline in the mores of university support rather than proof that a universal mode of basic research support could come from industry. Nonetheless, as Brooks has so clearly delineated, at least in the recent short run, enlightened industry can provide a superb climate for certain kinds of basic research.

12. M. Kac, *Enigmas of Chance: An Autobiography* (New York: Harper & Row, 1985).

13. H. Hesse, *Magister Ludi: The Glass Bead Game* (New York: Bantam Books, 1970).

14. Kac, *Enigmas of Chance*.

15. R. Nisbet, *The Social Philosophers* (New York: Washington Square Press, 1983).

16. P. B. Medawar, *Pluto's Republic: Incorporating "The Art of the Soluble" and "Induction and Intuition in Scientific Thought"* (New York: Oxford University Press, 1982).

17. R. Nisbet, *History of the Idea of Progress* (New York: Basic Books, 1979).

18. I. B. Cohen, *Revolution in Science* (Cambridge, Mass.: Harvard University Press, 1985).

19. G. M. Edelman, "Neural Darwinism: Population Thinking and Higher Brain Functions," in Michael Shafto, ed., *Proceedings of Nobel Conference XX: How We Know: The Inner Frontiers of Cognitive Science* (San Francisco: Harper & Row, 1985), pp. 1–30.

20. Edelman, "Neural Darwinism"; G. M. Edelman, "Through a Computer Darkly: Group Selection and Higher Brain Function," *Bulletin of the American Academy of Arts and Sciences* 36 (October 1982): 18–49.
21. R. Boyd and P. J. Richerson, *Culture and the Evolutionary Process* (Chicago: Chicago University Press, 1985).
22. Nisbet, *History of the Idea of Progress.*

PART IV

THE CORPORATION
AND THE ECONOMY

CHAPTER 11

Tender Offers and
Corporate Governance

Robert C. Clark

C*orporate governance* is a somewhat ambiguous term. Sometimes the phrase is used as a shorthand for discussions about proposals to change the residual goal of the managers of for-profit business corporations (from profit maximization to something else) or about proposals to expand the formal voice, at the board level, of nonshareholder groups affected by corporate activities. Such proposals are considered in a large and increasingly unreceptive literature.[1] Interest in these ideas comes in waves, the most recent of which seems now to have crested.

Another, more enduring focus of concern about the governance of corporations is the search for optimal controls on managerial discretion. This is the core problem attacked by the American Law Institute's ongoing Corporate Governance Project. The major task in this area of law is to work out the right balance between the efficiency-motivated grant of broad powers to corporate managers (often symbolized by the judge-made "business judgment rule") and the imposition of controls to reduce the use of such powers for personal rather than corporate ends (often symbolized by the judicially created "fiduciary duties of care and loyalty"). Economically minded writers now often formulate this very old problem as one of reducing agency costs. Whatever the formulation, the problem is persistent, and the way it is handled significantly influences the functioning of our economic system.

Recent writers on corporate law generally agree that there are two fundamental kinds of controls available to limit managerial discretion to engage in negligent or disloyal behavior. Market controls include the kinds of discipline emanating from competitive product markets, labor markets (especially as they involve executives), and capital markets. Legal controls include the derivative lawsuit and the various legal doctrines concerning fraud and self-dealing that are enforceable by its use. Other legal rules are intertwined with the various markets and help define their scope and operation.

Various forms of capital market discipline have been noted, such as the monitoring and implicit pricing of managerial conduct that occurs when companies sell new securities to the public. But the hostile tender offer is generally thought to be the most potent. Indeed, many writers assume that the hostile tender offer is the most powerful of all market and legal controls over managerial discretion. Tender offers therefore have a key place in contemporary theorizing about corporate governance. The facts that hostile tender offers are dramatic, newsworthy, and interesting events and that there have been many of them in recent years only reinforce this position of intellectual centrality.

There has been much debate about the true motives and effects of hostile takeovers and about the equally important phenomenon of elaborate and costly defensive tactics. Before examining these topics, I shall pause to examine how the policy issues might be framed in terms of the allocation of responsibilities between the public and private sectors. The final section of this chapter summarizes my argument and offers a policy proposal.

PRIVATE AND PUBLIC RESPONSIBILITIES

Assume that investors and managers have the primary responsibility for worrying about the problem of agency costs. Since the costs fall mainly on them, they have an incentive to work out the optimal way of encouraging managerial business judgment while efficiently controlling managerial tendencies toward slack and self-dealing. But because information may be distributed asymmetrically, because bargaining around present legal rules may be costly, because externalities may be generated, and for other reasons, the stance of the legal system toward their efforts cannot be a matter of indifference.[2]

As for tender offers in particular, three points should be made about the government's potential role.

First, classic public utility-type regulation would not be appropriate. There is no sound basis for government to prohibit all hostile takeovers, or subsidize them, or to make routine judgments about which takeovers are meritorious and should be allowed and which are socially bad and should be prohibited. The review of theories and evidence in the following section should support this view.

On the other hand, there is no sense in talking about a complete absence of governmental intervention in the takeover process. The role of legal doctrines in setting up the rules of the road is both crucial and unavoidable. In many contexts it is not very consequential whether we acknowledge that basic legal rules provide a necessary substratum or background to private activities in markets. But the role of the legal substratum in governing tender offers is much deeper and more important than, say, the role of basic contract and property law in governing ordinary contractual relationships among businesses. In the latter context, business custom can supply expectations and a sense of right and wrong, market forces do most of the enforcement of these widely appreciated norms, and the parties can readily "contract around" many legal rules that are not to their liking (for example, a default rule as to whether a party breaking a contract is liable to the other for so-called consequential damages). But the market for corporate control is significantly different in all three respects. The legal rules of the road are *deeply constitutive* of this market: They have a great influence rather than a peripheral bearing on what is likely to happen.

For example, the very possibility of hostile takeovers depends on basic design principles governing the relationship among corporations, directors, and shareholders—in particular, on the principle (which does not apply to business forms like the partnership) that a shareholder can sell all his rights, including voting rights, in one bundle. More obviously, the rules governing which defensive tactics are permissible, and under what conditions, have a great bearing on whether hostile tender offers can succeed. Variations in these rules can seriously affect the rate and cost of takeover attempts. Defining the rules thus should be a matter of great concern to policymakers. We cannot rely on private bargaining and innovations to correct any flaws in the starting rules created by the legal system.

A third point is that private parties in the takeover context have great incentives, and some ability, not only to strike Pareto-superior deals with each other but also to establish or change the legal rules to their own benefit. For example, under pressure from lobbying groups representing managements of potential targets, many state legislatures have adopted anti-takeover statutes. Precisely because the legal rules are so deeply constitutive of private sector possibilities in the takeover area, yet are subject to the uneven influence of various groups of private parties, critical re-examination of the legal rules and rulemaking institutions is clearly warranted. Conversely, there is no reason to presume that the private sector practices and patterns of the moment are efficient.

My principal objective will be to inquire whether the public sector, acting mainly through the courts, has responded well to tender offers and, more important, to defensive tactics used in fighting them. My proposed answer is that the public sector has done better than one might have thought, but not as well as it might.

THEORIES OF TENDER OFFERS

Why are tender offers made? What side effects do they have? Our answers to these questions will influence our view of what kinds of regulation of tender offers, and of managerial responses to them, are appropriated.

Explanations of Tender Offers

There are at least five common explanations as to why corporations make tender offers. The first is that the acquirer wants to capture the target company's potential value, which has not been realized in current performance. As commentators since Manne's[3] seminal work have put it, tender offerors are crucial forces in the "market for corporate control": They monitor the performance of other companies and act as vehicles for disciplining suboptimal performance. Lawmakers who accept this explanation ought to regard tender offers as good things, both for shareholders and for society.

In an ideal application of this model, the offeror spends significant effort in monitoring the performance of another company and its management. The acquiring firm discovers a potential for increasing the value of the target company by improving operating efficiency and actually brings about that improvement. The gains of this sort are larger than the losses to some affected parties (for example, the target's top managers). These gains are shared with the stockholders of the target. Certain empirical studies, discussed below, suggest that this model is a good characterization of many real takeover attempts.

The second explanation of tender offers is that they are motivated by many of the same, basically good, business reasons that prompt firms to embark on friendly acquisitions like mergers. The reasons for takeovers are the same as the reasons for corporate combinations generally. They include expectations of economies of scale in operations, management, or finance; synergistic gains from combining two complementary lines of business; elimination of the sometimes high costs of coordinating activities by contracting with another firm instead of subjecting both activities to a common boss; and so on.

But why would an acquiring company motivated solely by such reasons resort to a hostile tender offer rather than a friendly merger, which is usually much less costly? An acquirer foreseeing only conventional merger gains would take its case to the target's managers, show them that a merger would benefit both companies and their managers and shareholders, and negotiate a deal that would distribute these advantages. Notice that this problem does not embarrass the first explanation of tender offers: If the target gains value after acquisition because its original management is suboptimal and must be replaced, then obviously there is less likelihood that the acquirer can carry out a friendly merger.

This is not to say that conventional business reasons for combination play no part in the motivations behind an attempted takeover. Also, some tender offers may occur when efforts to negotiate a conventionally motivated friendly merger have failed. If target managers insist on getting an extremely large share of the expected gains, the acquirer may think it cheaper to incur the usually higher transaction costs of a tender offer.

The third explanation is that the tender offeror is trying to monopolize trade or commerce or to embark on some other anticompetitive course of conduct. If this model describes most tender offers, then policymakers ought to be alarmed.

The monopoly benefits explanation is not plausible, however. Most tender offers do not appear to present serious anticompetitive risks. They usually do not involve a horizontal combination of two firms operating principally in a single, dangerously concentrated market. Frequently, offerors propose vertical and conglomerate acquisitions. Especially in the past, courts and commentators have envisioned numerous conceivable anticompetitive risks that could be created by such acquisitions, but much informed current commentary regards these risks as greatly exaggerated.[4] Moreover, because tender offers are visible, controversial, and subject to the waiting period requirements of the Hart-Scott-Rodino Antitrust Improvements Act,[5] as well as to suits by the Justice Department, the Federal Trade Commission, and various private parties, rational tender offerors are unlikely to think they could get away with a significantly anticompetitive acquisition. Yet many tender offers are made. This suggests that many of them are not motivated by anticompetitive desires. Finally, one can ask, as in the case of the second explanation, why monopolistic acquirers would not prefer a friendly merger to a tender offer.

The fourth explanation for tender offers is that they yield benefits to bidding company managers. Perhaps they expect to acquire greater power and prestige as bosses of bigger companies. Perhaps these managers expect to get greater executive compensation, another alleged correlate of company size. Or, since so much of their personal wealth is tied up with the fortunes of their company—they own substantial stock, stock options, and the like—they may be trying to diversify their portfolios of investment assets. (Ordinary passive investors, by contrast, can diversify more cheaply and in a more fine-tuned way by investing in a mix of securities. They do not need managers to diversify for them at the company level by making conglomerate acquisitions.) Or managers may launch takeovers simply because they like a good fight. A takeover battle is more exciting than the painstaking job of actually running a company.

If managerial benefits are the sole motive and effect of hostile takeovers, then takeovers are bound to be bad for shareholders. By hypothesis, the bidding company managers will be indifferent to the hard task of identifying and making just those acquisitions that present the best opportunities for increasing shareholder wealth. They will make acquisitions when no synergistic gains or gains from better management can be expected, or even when declines in efficiency, or synergistic losses, are likely to occur.

How great would the impact on the wealth of the bidding company shareholders be if this theory is correct? The answer depends in part on whether bidding company managers motivated solely by personal benefits would make, on average, neutral acquisitions—business combinations that result neither in gains nor in losses to real efficiency—or would be driven by their unquenchable thirst for targets to make bad acquisitions—those having a detrimental effect on efficiency. Our guess about this might depend on which of the varieties of the managerial benefits theory we have in mind. Even if the managers made only neutral acquisitions, their own shareholders' wealth would decrease because of two factors: (1) the very considerable costs of the acquisition transactions themselves—for example, investment bankers' fees, lawyers' fees, and the loss of top management's services during the busy acquisition period; and (2) the premiums paid to target company shareholders. If the managers made bad acquisitions, the shareholders would also suffer (3) losses from a drop in business efficiency.

Probably no well-informed observer thinks that managerial benefits are the *sole* motive and effect of hostile takeovers. And few would contend that benefits to managers are completely irrelevant. The point of considering the explanation in its pure form is to draw out its implications more clearly. As we saw, this hypothesis strongly implies that shareholder wealth will suffer if acquisitions are motivated by managerial benefits. If we find empirically that on average shareholders are not hurt by hostile takeovers or that they are greatly benefited by them, then we would have to conclude that managerial benefits cannot be a predominant factor in explaining takeovers, however intuitively appealing that hypothesis may be.

The fifth explanation of tender offers is that acquirers want to loot target companies. An extreme example is the raider who wants to get control of the target in order to rip off its accumulated cash, strip it of inventory easily converted into cash, and liquidate the remaining carcass for the acquirer's own benefit. In practice, offerors are often accused of planning to liquidate the target company if they get control of it rather than maintain it as a going concern.

Almost by definition—a *proper* definition, that is—looting-oriented takeovers are bad. But the important issue is whether bust-up takeovers can sensibly be characterized as looting. Suppose an offeror plans to sell off the target's assets piecemeal, dissolve the corporate entity, and pay out the proceeds in a final liquidating distribution. This will be a positively good thing for any remaining (now minority) shareholders of the target if two conditions are satisfied: (1) the distribution is paid to shareholders on a pro rata basis and (2) the business of the corporation had a liquidating value that was higher than its going concern value—it was actually worth more dead than alive. Satisfaction of the first condition is a legal requirement. It is in the self-interest of the offeror to determine whether the second condition is met before it causes a liquidation. As major owner of the target, the offeror wants to liquidate if and only if doing so is the economically sensible course of action.

Other aspects of tender offers are sometimes alleged as bases for regulation. Often the arguments are casual and anecdotal. For example, managers of potential targets sometimes contend that hostile takeovers destroy jobs or injure local communities. They invoke the specter that the bidder will close or relocate plants. Several points about this argument are worth noting. First, there seems to be no good systematic evidence showing that bidding firms, as a class, are very likely to do such things. Second, plants are most often closed and employees laid off by companies in trouble, quite apart from any recent shift in the ownership of their shares. (Since only a small percentage of companies are subject to takeovers, the great majority of plant closings are probably done by firms that have not been subjected to a takeover bid.) If further legal regulation concerning these problems is appropriate, then surely the rational approach is to deal with them directly rather than by making takeovers difficult. Third, plants are usually closed because they are losing money—they are less efficient than competing plants elsewhere. For the longer-run good of the economy, they should be closed. Abrupt plant closings may indeed cause losses for employees and local communities, and these may well be legitimate cause for governmental reaction. But the better response would appear to be some form of transition assistance, not a flat prohibition on closings. And preventing takeovers as an indirect way of pursuing that flawed second strategy is doubly irrational.

A similar argument is that takeovers contribute to the supposedly dangerous increase in the amount of leverage in the American economy, because so many of them are financed heavily by borrowing. But the process of leveraging up results mainly from the tax law's differential treatment of debt and equity, and it expresses itself in many forms other than debt financing of takeovers. Hampering takeovers would be an inappropriate, and probably ineffective, way of dealing with the basic problem. A more generally applicable reform of the basic tax law pattern is needed.

Evidence about the Theories

Which of these five explanations of tender offers is most accurate? One approach to answering this question is to look at stock prices. Is the total value of the acquiring and target companies, as measured by the stock market, greater (on average) after a successful hostile takeover than it was before it? If yes, and if we trust the collective judgment of players in the market, then we must discard the last two explanations. And if we could then rule out the third, or monopoly benefits, explanation on other grounds, we might conclude that hostile takeovers are, on average, value-creating transactions. But if total value does not increase after a takeover, we are left with a choice between the fourth and fifth explanations. We might conclude that hostile takeovers are, on average, value-destroying transactions.

Using market prices is not a simple matter, of course. Many difficult issues must be resolved to do the job right. For example, the researcher must choose between the completion date and the announcement date of acquisitions, select an appropriate time period before and after the chosen date, factor out portions of price changes that simply reflect changes in the market (or the industry) as a whole, and, ideally, adjust for changes in risk level caused by takeovers. Statistics reported in the popular press or assembled by practicing lawyers sometimes fail miserably to take adequate account of these problems. Economists have done better. Some have used the technique of measuring cumulative average residuals (CARS) before and after the announcement of takeover bids. Roughly speaking, CARS measure "abnormal" returns or losses—those not due simply to fluctuations in the market as a whole, to changes in risk level, or to other factors in the economists' capital asset pricing model but to the market's reaction to the specific takeover bid. Using this technique, economists have compared successful and unsuccessful takeovers, takeovers in different time periods, and hostile takeovers versus friendly acquisitions.

The results of this substantial body of research are hard to summarize quickly, but the gist of them can be indicated here. Jensen and Ruback reviewed CARS studies of mergers and tender offers using announcement dates as reference points.[6] For target firms, abnormal *positive* returns are found to be 29 percent for successful takeovers, over the month or two surrounding the announcement.[7] Targets of *un*successful takeovers maintain high returns, provided they receive a new offer within two years.[8] Do the bidding firms' shareholders lose what the target companies' shareholders gain? No. For the bidding company shareholders, abnormal *positive* returns are found to be 4 percent for successful takeovers.[9] But in the case of unsuccessful takeover attempts, bidders have a negative abnormal return of 1 percent.[10]

To summarize, in percentage terms shareholders of target firms gain *substantially* from takeover attempts, and shareholders of bidding firms gain, though by more modest amounts, when attempts are successful. The results are impressive, and they strongly suggest that takeovers are perceived by the stock market as *value-creating* transactions.

Proponents of curbs on takeovers have attacked the CARS studies, sometimes vehemently. One common objection is that the financial performance of acquired targets, as measured by accounting data before and after the acquisition, would be a more relevant test of the real effects of takeovers. Unfortunately, this method of research has severe drawbacks. Real operating gains or losses after an acquisition may take years to materialize, and it is hard to sort out the effects of the acquisition from numerous other factors, including management's reallocations of personnel, functions, and costs.

The most serious attack on the CARS studies focuses on their underlying assumptions and relevance to policymaking. Why should we take the stock market's reactions to business combinations as indicators of whether they are "really" good or bad? Does the fact that the market *thinks* a transaction creates value mean that, in some basic economic sense, the transaction *does* increase value?

In technical terms, the question resolves to whether the stock market is allocatively efficient as well as speculatively efficient. A great amount of research supports the notion that the organized stock markets are efficient in the sense that investors without access to inside information can expect only a competitive return on their investments. But conceivably the market might not be efficient in an allocative sense. If all investors valued stocks on the basis of "irrational" factors rather than by considering information about the actual and expected economic performance of issuing companies, stock prices would tell us little about which companies were really creating value and generating high earnings and dividends. (Such a market could still be an efficient game for the investors in that few players could systematically get the jump on everyone else.) A stock market with these characteristics would have a bad effect on the real economy.[11]

The extent to which the market is allocatively efficient is a lively topic of debate among contemporary economists.[12] Resolution of the debate is not expected soon. But most economists seem to think that the stock market is allocatively efficient to a significant extent. Even if it is not, the implications for policy about takeovers are not at all clear. True, the CARS studies could not then be interpreted as showing that takeovers create "real" efficiency in business operations. But neither could they—or any other systematic evidence now in print—be interpreted to show that takeovers produce a bad effect on real efficiency. The rational policymaker who did not trust the market would simply have to be agnostic as to the real effects of takeovers on business operations. This agnosticism might lead to a neutral set of legal rules, such as the Williams Act supposedly embodies. Or it might lead to restraints on costly defensive tactics, since the empirical evidence does at least suggest that *shareholders* benefit from takeovers.

Possible Implications

Substantial evidence indicates that shareholders benefit from takeovers and that defensive tactics may harm them. Though the policy implications of this evidence are not entirely clear, some commentators have seen a need to extend regulation of the tactics of *offerors*; partial bids and two-tiered pricing have seemed especially troublesome.[13] But the evidence casts a sharper and darker shadow over *targets* that employ takeover defenses.

DEFENSES TO TAKEOVER ATTEMPTS

In this section I describe some representative ways companies have tried to defend themselves against takeover, review how the courts have responded to their tactics, and assess the courts' handiwork.

Tactics

The active repertoire of resistance tactics to takeovers has evolved continuously since passage of the Williams Act in 1968, and it shows no sign of ceasing to develop. I have given a fuller catalog and description of current tactics elsewhere.[14] Here I shall deal selectively with a few key defenses that, at least on initial analysis, seem to create very different risks of harm to the target corporation's shareholders.

Asset-light Defenses. Some kinds of defenses present little obvious risk that defending managers will waste a very substantial portion of their firm's assets or value. (Of course, if successful they may deprive the shareholders of an important opportunity, which may or may not be presented again.) One approach might be labeled propaganda. The target managers, using company funds, issue press releases, take out newspaper advertisements, and otherwise communicate arguments to the shareholders as to why they should not tender. Unless they involve misrepresentation or material omissions, these actions are legally unproblematic. One could even argue that the managers have a positive duty to express their views to the shareholders. The main problem is practical. Alongside a premium bid, propaganda has a hollow sound.

A second category consists of defensive lawsuits. Management causes the target company to sue the offeror, alleging violations of federal securities laws, antitrust laws, and other protean bodies of law. The federal courts seem to have become somewhat cynical about claims of this kind.[15] Consequently, target managers can rarely hope for a final victory on the merits in such litigation. They can hope that it will buy valuable time.

Asset-heavy Defenses. Other defenses involve the commitment of much larger chunks of the company's resources. One type is the defensive merger or acquisition. The target tries to arrange hasty acquisitions of companies that, if acquired, will create an antitrust problem for the offeror (because, for example, the acquired company is a direct competitor of the offeror in a concentrated market). This tactic poses an obvious risk that the target managers will waste corporate assets—by making a poor acquisition at an excessive price—in their desperate scramble to preserve their control and their jobs. (A more benign variation, from the shareholders' viewpoint, is target management's search for a "white knight"—a rival bidder that will save them from the first offeror by offering a more attractive deal.)

A second kind of asset-heavy tactic, the lockup, can be illustrated by a simple example. Suppose Targg, the target company, has a valuable asset, such as a remarkably productive oil field, that is a critical attribute of Targg in the eyes of potential acquirers but that does not constitute substantially all the assets of the target within the meaning of the relevant corporation statute. Under the typical statute, the board of directors is therefore able, without seeking shareholder approval, to sell the asset or grant an option to buy it. Locking up that asset can thwart a takeover.

Omen, a hostile bidder, makes a tender offer to buy all of Targg's stock at $50 per share. Targg's managers solicit Gunn, a white knight that implicitly promises to treat them better after a takeover. Gunn makes an offer at $55, which Omen quickly matches. To make sure that Gunn wins the bidding war, Targg's directors vote to grant Gunn, for a fixed consideration, an option to buy the oil field for $100 million. Thereafter, Gunn has a crushing advantage. If Omen were to raise its bid price high enough—say, to $100—to win the bidding contest, Gunn would still be able to buy the oil field at the same fixed price. Omen could find that it had paid far too much for what was left of Targg. This would not happen to Gunn.

The lockup strategy depends on the ability of the target management to sell a major interest in the company to the favored bidder without getting the approval of the majority of the shareholders. During a bidding war, of course, the shareholders would not approve any such deal but would prefer a free and unhampered auction for their shares. The strategy poses an obvious danger to shareholders: In their haste to retain control, target managers will not sell or option the "crown jewels" at the best price. They will put a cap on the bidding process, and the assets may not move to the bidder that values them most highly.

A third type of asset-heavy tactic is to pay greenmail. The target company pays a substantial premium to buy back the shares already obtained by the hostile would-be acquirer, with the understanding that the takeover attempt will be aborted. Other shareholders are likely to be outraged by this tactic. Not only do they lose a chance to sell at a premium but they may also find that their shares' value has been diluted by the exorbitant payment to the greenmailer.

Shareholder-protecting Defenses. An interesting special class of tactics is designed, if target management's rhetoric is to be believed, to furnish equal treatment or other protections to some or all of their shareholders. The most glamorous examples are certain types of "poison pill" plans. As originally conceived, the plans were directed at two-tier takeover attempts in which the acquirer first makes a tender offer not for all shares but for a controlling interest, with the intent or possibility of later freezing out the remaining shareholders, perhaps at a lower price.

The target's poison pill plan might consist of distributing, as a dividend to its common stockholders, newly created preferred stock possessing special, very generous conversion or redemption rights that are triggered only after a hostile bidder has acquired a substantial stake, say 40 percent, in the target's equity. These rights presumably protect those shareholders who do not sell all their shares to the hostile bidder from being frozen out at a low price. Not coincidentally, they also encourage shareholders not to tender in the first place. Note too that if the special rights are redemption rights, the plan may be a scorched earth tactic: The bidder gets control of the target only to find it suddenly obligated to pay out vast sums to the right holders.

Another type of poison pill was the subject of a major recent court opinion (the *Household International* case, discussed below). It involves giving the target's common shareholders, as a dividend on their shares, rights, or warrants, instead of preferred stock. The governing document provides that the rights can be detached and sold separately from the common on which they are issued when a person or group acquires 20 percent of the target's common or when a tender offer for 30 percent of the common is announced. The holder of a right is entitled to buy new preferred stock on certain terms or, in the event of a merger of which the target is not the survivor, $200 worth of the *acquiring* company's equity for $100. Thus, an offeror making a classic two-tiered offer might find the interests of its own shareholders being *substantially* diluted.

Case Law

Case law involving challenges to defensive (and offensive) tactics in takeover struggles is in a state of rapid development. It is important to distinguish actions brought under provisions of the federal securities laws from those invoking principles of state law, such as the fiduciary duties of care and loyalty.

Federal Law. The case law on defensive tactics under the securities laws indicates that challengers will often have a tough time. At bottom, the philosophy of the securities laws is to ensure full and honest disclosure to investors, not (for the most part) to impose substantive rules of conduct. Consider this paradigmatic issue: If a target's directors cause it to grant lockup options on its crown jewel or on a substantial block of authorized common shares to one of two rival bidders (a white knight), and this helps defeat the original bidder's offer, does such conduct constitute illegal manipulation within the meaning of Section 14(e) of the Exchange Act? Though the Sixth Circuit answered yes,[16] the Second Circuit later took the opposite view in *Data Probe Acquisition Corp. v. Datatab, Inc.*[17]

In the former case, the fact that the lockups made it virtually impossible for the hostile bidder to win was thought to have artificially affected market prices—to wit, the prices the bidders were willing to offer—in a way characteristic of manipulative schemes. In the latter case, Judge Winter reasoned that manipulation under 14(e) involves not only artificially affecting the price of a security, but doing so in a way that misleads other investors into misinterpreting market activity and acting on their misinterpretation to their detriment. More generally, Section 14(e) is basically just an antifraud statute, but the real gist of the plaintiff's objections to the lockup scheme was that the target's managers breached their fiduciary duties—a state law claim.

Subsequently, the *Data Probe* viewpoint was adopted by the Supreme Court in *Schreiber v. Burlington Northern, Inc.,*[18] which held that manipulation or nondisclosure is a necessary element of a Section 14(e) violation. The case rejected the broader conception of manipulation urged by some commentators.[19] In a similar vein are holdings that a two-tiered offer does not by itself constitute a violation of Section 14(e),[20] nor does a poison pill plan.[21] A related set of questions arises under Rule 10b-5, the most widely used of the Securities Exchange Act's antifraud rules. For example, an overt greenmail attempt is not by itself a manipulative or deceptive device prohibited by that rule;[22] the very frankness of the greenmailer, who after all has an interest in sending his message clearly, negates such a conclusion.

State Law. At least five types of rules could be adopted to govern the behavior of target company directors and officers who cause their company to take defensive measures against a takeover attempt. They are set out below in order of decreasing severity.

The first is a rule of pure passivity: Apart from arguing their case to the shareholders (the propaganda tactic), target managers should refrain from other defensive tactics.[23] They should simply let the shareholders decide whether they want to sell their shares to the tender offeror. This rule is based on the belief that defensive tactics raise the cost of takeovers and reduce their frequency and therefore decrease shareholder welfare in the long run. It can also be based on a perception of the severe conflict of interest faced by managers who use corporate resources for defensive purposes and a doubt that the legal system can regularly sort out good defensive maneuvers from bad ones in real cases.

A second rule is one of modified passivity: Target managers would be allowed only to engage in propaganda and in the solicitation of rival bids.[24] Proponents of this view usually tend to support legislation that requires tender offers to be kept open for some minimum time period. The idea behind the second rule is to allow auctions to flourish. Supposedly, target shareholders will be better off if their managers and the legal system combine to encourage competitive bidding for their shares. At the same time, this rule would strictly prohibit target managers from engaging in defensive tactics that are likely to waste corporate resources and hurt shareholders.

A third approach is differential regulation: Different categories of defenses would be governed by different rules.[25] For example, greenmail might be flatly prohibited; defensive lawsuits would be allowed and shielded by the business judgment rule; poison pill plans would be regulated so that "backloaded" plans were illegal but plans merely assuring equal treatment of shareholders in different stages of an acquisition were proper; and so on. The idea behind this approach is that some types of defenses pose a much greater risk to shareholder welfare than others and that regulators can distinguish between types where a strict preventive rule is desirable and types where other considerations justify a more permissive rule. Note that this approach calls for rather definite rules, even though types of takeover defenses are continually being created and are always evolving. Therefore, as I argue below, it ought to be administered by a rulemaking regulatory agency such as the SEC rather than embodied in a detailed statute or developed by the courts.

A fourth rule is a primary purpose test: If a defensive tactic were challenged by target company shareholders in a derivative lawsuit, the target's managers would have the burden of proving that the tactic was engaged in for the primary purpose of implementing a bona fide corporate business purpose rather than the self-regarding purpose of preserving their own control. This rule recognizes that managers are fiduciaries and that defensive tactics usually involve them in a conflict of interest. It reflects a typical judicial response to such a situation. It is quite analogous, for example, to the usual rule about challenges to transactions between a corporation and its directors and/or officers: The fiduciary has the burden of proving that the transaction was entirely fair to the corporation.

A fifth rule is the business judgment rule: The decision to commit corporate resources to a takeover defense would be a matter within the normal business discretion of the target's directors and officers and could not be successfully challenged unless the plaintiff could prove some serious failure on the defendants' part—such as gross negligence or palpable overreaching. Since target managers usually go through the forms of carefulness—they hire expensive counsel and investment bankers, hold many meetings, and leave a justificatory paper trail—and since they can and do allege the corporate good as a basis for their defensive maneuvers, this rule makes it impossible to attack any but the most outrageous defensive maneuvers.

Who supports which of the five approaches? A number of respected scholars in the law and economics tradition argue about whether the first or second rule is the better one. But courts seem to hover between the fourth and fifth approaches. Something like the third approach has been urged by the SEC's Advisory Committee,[26] by trade associations and other interest groups, and by the more middle-of-the-road commentators. Some practitioners have argued for a version of the fifth approach that amounts to almost total deference to management.

Now for some case law. Federal courts, acting on their pendent jurisdiction over state law claims in cases also alleging violations of the federal securities laws, have rendered a fair number of decisions on substantive challenges to defensive maneuvers.[27] A noteworthy example, because it represents a low-water mark in the protection of investor interests, is *Panter v. Marshall Field & Co.*[28] For several years the target had responded to unwanted acquisition attempts by making defensive acquisitions that created antitrust problems for the prospective acquirers. It appears to have paid dearly for some very poor retail stores. After a lucrative tender offer was withdrawn because of this tactic, angry Field shareholders sued the company and its directors. The Seventh Circuit Court of Appeals opined that the relevant state law, that of Delaware, would analyze claims such as those made by the plaintiffs under the business judgment rule. Thus, instead of requiring the directors to prove a compelling business purpose for their defensive tactics, the court required the plaintiffs to prove that impermissible motives predominated and found they had not met that burden. In a stinging dissent that questioned every aspect of the rationale and application of the majority's rule, Judge Cudahy charged the majority with moving "one giant step closer to shredding whatever constraints still remain upon the ability of corporate directors to place self-interest before shareholder interest in resisting a hostile tender offer for control of the corporation."[29]

A question raised by such decisions was whether the federal courts correctly stated and applied state law. For example, would the Delaware Supreme Court apply the business judgment rule to a target board's adoption of takeover defenses, so long as the board consisted of a majority of nonmanagement directors? After years of suspense the emerging answer appears to be yes, *but* that court has added some important guidelines as to how the rule should be applied in the takeover context.

Let's look at some of the Delaware Supreme Court decisions. *Cheff v. Mathes*[30] was decided in 1964, before the rise of modern-style takeover bids. The directors of a company were sued for causing it to buy out an insurgent shareholder (who was attempting a takeover) at a premium price (greenmail, in modern jargon). The court said that several directors faced a conflict of interest and had the burden of proving that a legitimate corporate business purpose lay behind their action rather than a mere desire to retain control. (It found, however, that they had met that burden, for it credited their argument that they were simply trying to prevent control from passing into the hands of someone who could change business practices in a way that would damage the corporation.)

In 1984 the Delaware Supreme Court decided *Pogostin v. Rice*[31] in which it held that the business judgment rule, including the standards by which director conduct is judged, is applicable in the context of a takeover.[32] The holding suggests that the adoption of defenses is not a conflict of interest transaction and that plaintiffs have a tough burden of proof.

In 1985 the same court decided *Unocal Corp. v. Mesa Petroleum Co.*[33] wherein it purported to reaffirm and apply the principles of *both* of the cases just mentioned, despite the tension between them. The target company (Unocal) had made a defensive repurchase offer to its shareholders but excluded the hostile bidder (Mesa) from tendering its own Unocal shares. In an opinion that is a monument to slippery jurisprudence, the court found the exclusion to be proper. It announced a variety of principles; I shall try to sort out the main ones in the discussion of the next Delaware case. Among the particular points established, the court affirmed that a Delaware corporation is not absolutely forbidden from buying some shareholders' stock without giving the others an equal opportunity to sell. Indeed, *Cheff* had already established this much. But there, ironically, the court *sanctioned* the payment of greenmail, and here it found Unocal's exclusion of Mesa partly justified as a device to thwart a bidder who *might* soon demand greenmail!

In the same year, the same court decided another case involving a modern-style defensive tactic. *Moran v. Household International, Inc.*[34] involved a poison pill rights plan similar to the one described above. The plan was challenged by John Moran, the largest shareholder and a director who voted against its adoption. The Delaware Supreme Court upheld the plan. The court first held that the board's adoption of the rights plan was within the scope of its authority. It bolstered this conclusion by stating that the plan did not, at least in theory, usurp the shareholders' right to receive tender offers. The court noted that would-be offerors could avoid the lethal aspects of the poison pill by several methods, such as making a tender offer with a condition that the board redeem the rights or acquiring 50 percent of the shares and causing Household to self-tender for the rights.

More importantly, the court reaffirmed the *Unocal* decision and the applicability of the business judgment rule to takeover defenses. Its restatement indicates, however, that the rule is subject to three important guidelines, or subrules, in the takeover context.

First, the target directors have the initial burden of showing a reasonable belief that a takeover would threaten corporate policy and welfare. Among the sorts of beliefs that, if reasonably held, will apparently qualify for this purpose are a belief (as in *Cheff*) that the offeror will change business practices in a way that will be disastrous for the company; a belief (as in *Household* itself) that the most likely offerors will resort to coercive takeover tactics," such as a two-tier pricing, that can be countered by the particular defensive measure in question; and a belief that the offeror will use "junk bond" financing and then break up the target to pay for the enormous debt burden thereby acquired.

Second, the defensive action taken by the board must be reasonable in relation to the threat posed to corporate welfare. The court thought the rights plan in *Household* was not unreasonable because it did not absolutely preclude a takeover bid. Presumably, then, a defensive tactic that *did* foreclose all genuine bidding for the target's shares would be subject to attack. Likewise vulnerable would be a defensive tactic that demonstrably wasted corporate assets.

Third, the presence and the informed activity of independent directors will help the board to meet the burden of making the two initial showings just described. Once these showings are made, the burden of proof shifts to the plaintiffs and is difficult to meet.

At least one other court has flatly refused to follow the Delaware Supreme Court's approach.[35] What the majority rule(s) will be in the state courts has yet to be determined.

Even more recently courts in Delaware and elsewhere have invalidated lockups.[36] Arguably, these results are consistent with previous case law on the ground that lockups tend to have a significantly greater chilling effect on further bidding for shares. But if anything is not arguable, it is that the decisions to date are flabby and can be manipulated by advocates into many shapes.

Assessment

Some general observations on the judicial decisions about takeover defenses may be ventured. On the one hand, courts have recently been tougher on lockups than some practitioners had expected; it is not true that anything goes but outright lying and stealing. Moreover, the courts' general statements of guiding principles often seem sensible and reasonable, if not precise or consistent. On the other hand, the Delaware Supreme Court's opinions, taken as a totality, are messy, confusing, and vague. They invite further costly litigation. In practical operation, the standards are also too lenient. Many a harmful practice can pass muster because of (1) the courts' willful naivete about the supposed independence of outside directors and their supposed ability and incentive to defend shareholder interests and (2) the courts' willful credulity with respect to the "business" purposes asserted to underlie defensive tactics. It is hard not to conclude that courts either dislike tender offers (perhaps because they hold to a value-decreasing explanation of them) or do not appreciate the general case for skepticism about takeover defenses.

The general case against allowing managers to engage in takeover defensive tactics can be put in several ways. One is a traditional legal argument. Directors and officers of a corporation whose shares are subject to a hostile takeover bid face a serious conflict of interest. Indeed, we could well conclude that *in no other context is the conflict of interest as serious as in the takeover situation.* Often, the managers' jobs are at stake. The temptation to find that what is best for oneself is also best for the corporation and shareholders (for example, to assert that the company's stock is undervalued and that shareholders will eventually do better if the pending offer fails), the temptation to spend corporate resources extravagantly in the attempt to fend off the raider (it's always easier to spend other people's money), and the temptation to sacrifice the shareholders' interests (as by paying exorbitant amounts of greenmail), must be overwhelming. No human being can be expected to resist such temptations. Nor does it matter much if a majority of the board consists of outside directors. They still have a social bond with the inside directors and officers, not with the diffuse public shareholders, and they may care about the status and perquisites that go along with being a director.

A second line of argument is cast in economic terms. Defensive tactics raise the cost of effecting a takeover, sometimes significantly so. If the law permits them and allows the average level of takeover costs to rise, there will be fewer takeover attempts. With a lower probability of facing a takeover attempt and possible ouster, managers will feel less pressure to perform as well as they can. There will be more managerial discretion and slack, since the market price of a company's shares will have to fall further below its potential value before the gap triggers a takeover attempt. Managers will have much more discretion that is unpoliced by market forces. Companies will be run much less efficiently. In the aggregate, shareholder welfare and general economic efficiency will be sharply reduced.

An important point about this argument is that *it holds true even though, after a particular tender offer has been made, the shareholders of that particular company might get a higher price for their shares than the original tender offer price if their managers are allowed to engage in some sorts of defensive tactics—such as those that force the offeror to raise its bid.* The fact is that this can and does happen, but shareholders are not necessarily better off *in the aggregate* if such defensive tactics are allowed. Quite the reverse is likely to be true. Shareholders as a group may be better off in the long run if the cost of takeovers is kept low and the number of takeovers high. Rational shareholders who realize this should desire legal rules that uniformly ban defensive tactics that have the overall effect of raising costs and reducing the frequency of takeovers. Over the course of their investing careers, they will be better off with such rules.

What are the arguments for permitting defensive tactics? One is that they may allow the directors to protect the corporation against "raiders" who would not run the company as well as the incumbent ones. As discussed above, the empirical evidence does not suggest that most tender offerors fit into this category. Yet almost all hostile tender offers are met with defensive tactics.

Another argument is that defensive tactics may result in an eventual better price for shareholders. One might cite Jarrell's study of the effects of defensive litigation as evidence that this is a valuable characteristic of at least some defensive tactics.[37] But this argument, as we have just seen, neglects the systemic effect of such tactics: overall, they may reduce shareholder welfare. Jarrell's evidence is not inconsistent with this theoretically strong possibility.

It has been suggested that some tactics do not produce bad systemic effects. When target managers solicit rival bidders, for example, their activity does not consume much in the way of corporate resources, and it may lead to competitive bidding. Competitive bidding is usually thought to be good since it is likely to lead to resources being channeled into their most valuable uses.

There are complications, however. Some believe that first bidders incur special costs in identifying good targets and that rival bidders should not get a free ride on the first bidders' search efforts. Making rival bids too easy could discourage takeover attempts since few would want to take the risks of being first bidders. Moreover, it is practically difficult to allow target management to solicit rival bids that do not involve more questionable aspects like lockups, side payments to the target managers, and so on. Finally, one could argue that all that is required to generate an auction among rival bidders is a legal rule that, as the Williams Act now does, requires a tender offer to be kept open for a modest amount of time; letting target managers actively solicit or pick the rival bidders seems unnecessary.

There is a small amount of systematic empirical evidence on the effects of defensive maneuvers. Some work on defensive litigation has already been mentioned. A study of greenmail payments and standstill agreements found they were bad for nonparticipating share-holders.[38] Negative average returns were associated with these trans-actions. On the other hand, another study provided only weak pre-liminary support for the view that certain types of anti-takeover charter amendments drove down share prices.[39] The weak result might be explained by the fact that the amendments in question—staggered boards, supermajority merger approval provisions, and asso-ciated fair price provisions—do not preclude a successful takeover and may not significantly deter takeover attempts. A recent SEC study found that announcement of the adoption of poison pill plans caused share prices to drop.

Unfortunately, it is very difficult to devise a test to measure sys-temic effects. Arguments about some tactics (such as defensive litigation) must therefore be based more on theory than on hard evidence. By contrast, empirical evidence showing that certain other defensive tactics (such as greenmail) have negative near-term effects is fairly damning since there is little theoretical reason to expect posi-tive systemic effects that might offset the observed bad effects.[40]

A PROPOSAL

My argument has three main phases, two of which have already been developed.

First, the courts have not favored either of the polar positions about the proper legal treatment of takeover defenses—the recom-mendation of managerial passivity put forward by many economi-cally oriented academic commentators or the virtually complete laissez-faire approach urged by some heavily involved practitioners. Actual legal developments have been more complex and selective. The legal viability of a particular takeover defense depends on many facts and circumstances. It does appear that courts now view some *types* of defensive tactics with more suspicion than others, but this evolution toward general rules of thumb is a far cry from the univer-sal but fairly definite rules urged by commentators.

Second, while reassuringly moderate and sensible in some respects (and by comparison to what might have happened), the case law handling of tender offer defensive tactics has been slow, messy, vague, uncertain, and substantively unsatisfactory.

Third, serious consideration should be given to shifting more of the job of developing the law to the SEC. This approach might alleviate the faults just catalogued. The proposal is that the SEC be empowered to make substantive rules concerning tender offers and defenses to tender offers. It should do so pursuant to the statutory guideline that its rules be for the protection of investors and for the promotion of fair and efficient securities markets. Nothing would be said in the authorizing statute about the accommodation or protection of other interests. As with the present securities laws, such silence would not preclude other federal statutes aimed at protecting other kinds of interests, such as those of consumers and employees. (Antitrust rules about acquisitions are presumably already geared to the interests of consumers.)

There are two main reasons for choosing the SEC as the principal definer of rules about takeovers. First, the SEC is less likely than state legislatures and other federal agencies to be captured by the regulated groups. This point should be abundantly clear to anyone who has followed the first and now the second waves of state anti-takeover legislation. Moreover, the SEC has earned a uniquely high reputation for effective enforcement.[41]

Second, the SEC has several advantages over the courts. One is that it is generally more concerned with the welfare of investors. Courts tend to give relatively more weight to their desires to give "fair" treatment and lots of due process to defendant managers. This different bias stems from institutional differences and basic human psychology. The SEC acts in a rulemaking context, where the personal appeal of the abstractly conceived mass of investors may be as strong as or stronger than the personal appeal of managers in general. Courts in the typical lawsuit see the managers as flesh-and-blood individuals, whereas the shareholders whose interests are at stake are abstractions—only poorly, and often nonappealingly, represented by the particular plaintiff. The interests of vividly concrete human beings usually acquire psychological dominance over the interests of people who are present only abstractly.

Another advantage of the SEC over courts is that it is likelier to generate relatively more certain rules that will reduce, though not eliminate, expensive litigation. The experience under Rule 13e-3, the SEC's going-private rule, is instructive in this regard.

A final major advantage of the SEC is that it is a specialized agency whose concern is with the securities markets. Its staff is more likely to develop quickly a degree of sophistication and expertise in assessing developments in tender offer defenses, in understanding and evaluating econometric studies and the criticisms leveled against them, and in perceiving the often hidden import of corporate tactics and the reasons alleged for them. Experienced judges are not bad at seeing through hocus pocus and rationalizations, but in the corporate arena it often takes them time, and several repetitions of a pattern, before they do. Early experience under the Williams Act bears this out. Courts were initially willing to consider quite seriously target companies' requests that offerors allegedly violating timing and disclosure rules be subjected to harsh equitable remedies such as "sterilization" of voting rights or injunctions against further purchases, but they eventually came to be much more cynical about the likelihood of violations, the motivations of the target managers, and the value of harsh remedies.

Some objections to the proposal should now be considered. The most obvious is its current political infeasibility since the proposal involves giving more power, and a new kind of power, to a federal regulatory agency. Nevertheless, commentators have an obligation to present what they think are the best proposals. The idea ought to be planted now. If kept alive and developed, it may come to fruition in a different political climate. Meanwhile, even circulation and serious consideration of such a proposal may have a beneficial influence on the performance of state courts: They may try to do an especially good job in order to ward off the proposal.

Similarly, it can be objected that the proposal runs counter to the traditional division in the United States between federal and state concerns with respect to corporations. States define and enforce substantive rules of fiduciary conduct; the federal government concerns itself only with antifraud rules and mandatory disclosure requirements for corporations whose securities are publicly traded. But this jurisdictional split, peculiar to the United States, was never a good idea. Publicly held corporations whose securities are bought and sold by citizens of many states ought to be regulated at the federal level (whether by courts or by an agency), as to rules about both fraud and unfairness, and closely held firms ought to be regulated at the state level. There is little logic to a legal system that says that if managers of a public corporation injure investors by defrauding them, the remedy is a federal one, but if they injure them by an unfair self-dealing transaction, the remedy must only be found in state law. In many contexts, as tender offer litigation invoking the federal courts' pendent jurisdiction over state claims routinely illustrates, the two lines toward injury are intertwined, as well as being reasonably close substitutes.

Those who believe most strongly that a rule of pure passivity should be imposed on target company managers may argue that the SEC is overly concerned with equal treatment of investors. It might, for example, press for elimination of two-tiered pricing, which these commentators think is actually a good thing for investors in the long run. Without taking a position on the merits of such equal treatment rules, I would only observe that, even if the SEC does have such an inclination and it is a mistaken impulse, a rulemaking body could have many worse faults. This alleged fault is a natural and perhaps inevitable accompaniment of the SEC's overriding concern for investors. Its more-than-countervailing virtue is an instinct to suspect and resist practices that would chill genuine bidding for shares and to thwart new developments (such as nonvoting common shares) that would effectively reduce the real scope of the securities markets.

Another possible objection is that the SEC would be too slow and cumbersome in learning about and responding to new tactics and practices in the actively evolving world of the corporate takeover. By the time it adopted a sensible rule about lockups, for example, many abusive instances of the technique might have occurred. But the SEC's responsiveness, imperfect as it will inevitably be, must be compared with that of the courts. One might argue that courts should be favored because they can respond flexibly to the particular case being litigated before them. But they are likely to be much slower at producing useful doctrine, if only because it takes so long after a new tactic is invented before litigation is brought and pushed far enough to elicit a fairly definitive and widely applicable judicial opinion about it. (Although a few judicial opinions may emerge within months after a new tactic is first employed, the early decisions are not likely to give lawyers firm guidance about what is and is not permissible precisely because many judicial opinions are so carefully and "flexibly" oriented to the facts and circumstances of the particular case being decided. Courts often go out of their way to make it difficult for lawyers to generalize their holdings in a clear and precise way. Doing so preserves the courts' discretion to "do justice" as they see it in later cases that come before them.)

As suggested, my main purpose here has not been to prove the wisdom of my proposal to everyone's satisfaction, but simply to put it on the table and persuade others that it ought to be studied seriously.

NOTES

1. Robert C. Clark, "What Is the Proper Role of the Corporation?" in H. Brooks, L. Liebman, and C. Schelling, eds., *Public-Private Partnership: New Opportunities for Meeting Social Needs* (Cambridge, Mass.: Ballinger Publishing Co., 1984), pp. 195–220; Melvin A. Eisenberg, "Corporate Legitimacy, Conduct, and Governance—Two Models of the Corporation," *Creighton Law Review* 17 (1983): 1–19; Michael C. Jensen and William H. Meckling, "Rights and Production Functions: An Application to Labor-Managed Firms and Codetermination," *The Journal of Business* 52 (1979): 469–506; Oliver Williamson, "Corporate Governance," *Yale Law Journal* 93 (1984): 1197–1230.

2. Robert C. Clark, "Agency Costs versus Fiduciary Duties," in J. Pratt and R. Zeckhauser, eds., *Principals and Agents: The Structure of Business* (Boston: Harvard Business School Press, 1985), pp. 55–79.

3. Henry Manne, "Mergers and the Market for Corporate Control," *Journal of Political Economy* 73 (1965): 110.

4. See, for example, Phillip E. Areeda and Donald Turner, *Antitrust Law* (Boston: Little, Brown, 1978) pars. 701(c), 711(a) n. 3, 730; Robert H. Bork, *The Antitrust Paradox: A Policy at War with Itself* (New York: Basic Books, 1978), pp. 144–45, 250–60, 380–81; Richard Posner, *Antitrust Law: An Economic Perspective* (Chicago: University of Chicago Press, 1976), pp. 122–24, 182; Frederic M. Scherer, *Industrial Market Structure and Economic Performance*, 2d ed. (Boston: Houghton Mifflin, 1980), pp. 335–47.

5. 15 U.S.C. sec. 18a.

6. Michael C. Jensen and Richard Ruback, "The Market for Corporate Control: The Scientific Evidence," *Journal of Financial Economics* 11 (1983): 5.

7. By contrast, the abnormal positive returns found for mergers were only 16 percent. Why the difference? Perhaps because mergers involve only the prospect of ordinary synergies—the second type of explanation proposed earlier in this section—whereas hostile takeovers may produce *both* ordinary synergies and better management, alias "reduction of agency costs."

8. Again by contrast, abnormal returns to shareholders are lost in the case of mergers as soon as the failure of the proposed merger becomes known.

9. For mergers, the comparable figure is only 1.4 percent, and the results from study to study are less consistent than in the takeover case.

10. For mergers, the negative return figure is about 2.5 percent.

11. For example, the market might value Firm A's stock much higher than Firm B's, even though the latter had better future earnings prospects, with the unfortunate result that relatively inefficient A might have an easier time raising money to expand its lackluster operations.

12. Contrast Shiller, "Do Stock Prices Move Too Much to Be Justified by Subsequent Changes in Dividends?" *American Economic Review* 71 (June 1981): 421, with Leroy, "Efficiency and the Variability of Asset Prices," *American Economic Review* 74 (May 1984): 183. Roughly speaking, the Shiller paper explores the idea that, because over time the stock prices of public companies are very much more volatile than the companies' dividend payouts, the market must be responding to factors foreign to a rational capital asset pricing model; it may therefore be allocatively inefficient to a significant degree. Leroy criticizes this type of study and some of the conclusions sought to be based on it. (There are many debatable issues, of course. For example, a large part of the relative volatility of stock prices might be explained by fluctuations in the general level of interest rates. This phenomenon would not impugn the market's efficiency, because the usual capital asset pricing model depends on the risk-free rate of interest, which clearly does fluctuate greatly from time to time.)

13. Lucian Bebchuk, "Towards an Undistorted Choice and Equal Treatment in Corporate Takeovers," *Harvard Law Review* 98 (1985): 1693–1808; John C. Coffee, "Regulating the Market for Corporate Control: A Critical Assessment of the Tender Offer's Role in Corporate Governance," *Columbia Law Review* 84 (1984): 1145–1296.

14. Robert C. Clark, *Corporate Law* (Boston: Little, Brown and Co., forthcoming), ch. 13.

15. See, for example, Electronic Specialty Co. v. International Controls Corp., 409 F.2d 937 (2d Cir. 1969) (Friendly, J.) (arguing that, in view of the stressful, warlike nature of the takeover context, Congress intended to assure "basic honesty and fair dealing, not to impose an unrealistic requirement of laboratory conditions that might make the new statute a potent tool for incumbent management to protect its own interests against the desires and welfare of the stockholders."); Missouri Portland Cement Co. v. Cargill Inc., 498 F.2d 851 (2d Cir. 1974) (Friendly, J.) (warning against imposition of "a duty of self-flagellation" on offerors).

16. Mobil Corp. v. Marathon Oil Co., 669 F.2d 368 (6th Cir. 1981), cert. denied, 455 U.S. 982 (1982).

17. 722 F.2d 1 (2d Cir. 1983) (Winter, J.) cert. denied, 465 U.S. 1052 (1984).
18. 105 S.Ct. 2458 (1985).
19. Elliot J. Weiss, "Defensive Responses to Tender Offers and the Williams Act's Prohibition Against Manipulation," *Vanderbilt Law Review* 35 (1982): 1087–1129.
20. Radol v. Thomas, 534 F. Supp. 1302 (S.D. Ohio 1982), partial summary judgment granted to defendants in 556 F. Supp. 586 (S.D. Ohio 1983), aff'd, 772 F.2d 244 (6th Cir. 1985).
21. Gearhart Industries, Inc. v. Smith International, Inc., 741 F.2d 707 (5th Cir. 1984).
22. Dan River, Inc. v. Icahn, 701 F.2d 278, 284–5 (4th Cir. 1983).
23. Frank H. Easterbrook and Daniel R. Fischel, "The Proper Role of a Target's Management in Responding to a Tender Offer," *Harvard Law Review* 94 (1981): 1161–1204.
24. Lucian Bebchuk, "The Case for Facilitating Competing Tender Offers," *Harvard Law Review* 95 (1982): 1028–56; Ronald J. Gilson, "A Structural Approach to Corporations: The Case Against Defensive Tactics in Tender Offers," *Stanford Law Review* 33 (1981): 819–91. A debate between Bebchuk and Gilson and Easterbrook and Fischel appears in *Stanford Law Review* 35 (1982): 1, 23, 51.
25. Edward F. Greene and James J. Junewicz, "A Reappraisal of Current Regulation of Mergers and Acquisitions," *University of Pennsylvania Law Review* 132 (1984): 647–739; Coffee, "Regulating the Market for Corporate Control"; Louis Lowenstein, "Pruning Deadwood in Hostile Takeovers: A Proposal for Legislation," *Columbia Law Review* 83 (1983): 249–334.
26. SEC Advisory Committee on Tender Offers, Report of Recommendations (July 8, 1983).
27. See Arthur Fleischer, *Tender Offers: Defenses, Responses, and Planning*, 2d ed., 3 vols. (San Diego: Harcourt Brace Jovanovich, 1984), pp. 160–93; Martin Lipton and Erica Steinberger, *Takeovers and Freezeouts* sec. 6.01 (New York: Law Journal Seminars-Press, 1984).
28. 646 F.2d 271 (7th Cir.), cert. denied, 454 U.S. 1092 (1981).
29. 646 F.2d at 299.
30. 199 A.2d 548 (Del. Supr. 1964). See also Bennett v. Propp, 187 A.2d 405 (Del. Supr. 1962); Kors v. Carey, 158 A.2d 136 (Del. Ch. 1960).
31. 480 A.2d 619 (Del. Supr. 1984).
32. Id. at 627.
33. 493 A.2d 946 (Del. Supr. 1985).
34. 500 A.2d 1346 (Del. Supr. 1985), aff'g 490 A.2d 1059 (Del. Ch. 1985).
35. Minstar Acquiring Corp. v. AMF Inc., [1985] Fed. Sec. L. Rep. (CCH) par. 92,066 (S.D.N.Y. 1985) (opinion of Lowe, J.). The court stated its belief that the courts of New Jersey would not follow the *Unocal* opinion.

36. In MacAndrews & Forbes Holdings, Inc. v. Revlon, Inc., [1985] Fed. Sec. L. Rep. (CCH) par. 92,333 (Del. Ch. Oct. 23, 1985), aff'd.—A.2d—(Del. Supr. 1986), the Delaware courts decided that the business judgment rule does not protect a lockup extended to foreclose further bidding in an active bidding situation. In another case applying New York law, Hanson Trust PLC v. ML Acquisition Corp., Inc., 781 F.2d 264 (2d Cir. 1986), the court held that the plaintiffs had shown a likelihood of success on the merits of their claim that the directors did not exercise honest business judgment in granting a lockup option, and so reversed the lower court's denial of a preliminary injunction.

37. Gregg A. Jarrell, "The Wealth Effects of Litigation by Targets: Do Interests Diverge in a Merge?" *Journal of Law and Economics* 28 (1985): 151–77.

38. Larry Dann and Harry DeAngelo, "Standstill Agreements, Privately Negotiated Stock Repurchases, and the Market for Corporate Control," *Journal of Financial Economics* 11 (1983): 275.

39. Harry DeAngelo and Edward M. Rice, "Antitakeover Charter Amendments and Stockholder Wealth," *Journal of Financial Economics* 11 (1983): 329.

40. Even this can be doubted, of course. Macey and McChesney argue that greenmail may be a desirable way of compensating an investor-bidder who performs the valuable service of discovering the hidden value of a target and signaling, by its bid, that value to the market. Jonathan R. Macey and Fred S. McChesney, "A Theoretical Analysis of Corporate Greenmail," *Yale Law Journal* 95 (1985): 13–61.

41. Thomas K. McCraw, "With Consent of the Governed: SEC's Formative Years," *Journal of Policy Analysis and Management* 1 (1982): 346–70.

CHAPTER 12

Taxation of Corporations

Alvin C. Warren, Jr.

O ne of the major areas of contemporary interaction between the
public and private sectors is the federal income tax on corporations. This tax not only shifts significant resources from the private
to the public sector but it also has a profound impact on economic
activity within the private sector. In addition, the current U.S. income tax on corporations is conceptually inconsistent and fabulously
complex. To a large extent, these characteristics derive from the failure of the tax system to adopt a coherent position on such basic tax
policy issues as whether capital income should be taxed in general
and whether corporate income in particular should be subject to an
additional tax burden. This chapter will first describe the current
federal corporate income tax and the consider how corporations
should be taxed.

HOW IS CORPORATE INCOME TAXED?

The United States is often described as having a "classical" or "double" corporate tax system in which corporations are taxed on their
income as it is earned, with that income taxed again when distributed to shareholders as dividends. Such a regime regards the corporation as a distinct economic entity, with its own rights and its own
obligations to society, rather than as simply a conduit for the economic activity of individuals. A classical system is often criticized for

imposing a burden on capital income earned through corporate entities that is greater than the tax burden on capital income that does not flow through corporations.

This general description, while basically accurate, ignores the exceptions and inconsistencies that are responsible for the complexity of the current regime. Four areas in which current law deviates substantially from this general description will be examined here: (1) treatment of debt, (2) failure to tax all distributions to shareholders as ordinary income, (3) capital recovery provisions, and (4) instances in which the corporate income tax can be avoided by distributing assets to shareholders.

Debt Finance

To the extent corporate investments are financed by debt capital rather than equity capital, corporate income is not subject to double taxation because interest payments to debtholders are generally deductible by corporations. This difference in treatment apparently originated in an early thinking about the corporation as a separate entity that, like a human being, could make an investment with either borrowed funds or its own assets (i.e., those of the shareholders).

Whatever one thinks of this view of the corporation, the difference between debt and equity today is fragile, at best. At the extremes, the distinction is clear: Suppliers of capital who receive debt instruments obtain a fixed return on their investment and a senior claim on the assets of the corporation in the event of financial difficulty. Holders of common stock, on the other hand, receive a claim to the residual earnings of the corporation and a junior interest in the assets of the corporation in the event of financial difficulty. A variety of contractual arrangements can be made along this continuum, however, muddying the conceptual distinction between debt and equity. For example, preferred stock is often issued in a form that makes it virtually indistinguishable from subordinated debt, with both sets of claims involving a fixed return and bankruptcy rights that are junior to those of some suppliers of capital but senior to others.

Financial and economic discussions of the different treatment of corporate debt and equity have long focused on two questions — whether there is an optimal mix of debt and equity that can maximize a corporation's after-tax profitability and whether the tax system's preferential treatment of debt creates an undesirable incentive for corporate capital structures with fixed returns, which in turn increases the possibility of bankruptcy, with its attendant transactions costs.[1] There is a vast literature on these issues, neither of which is easily resolvable. The first is complicated by the fact that, unlike interest payments to debtholders, distributions of corporate earnings to shareholders are not always subject to the full burden of the shareholder income tax. The second issue involves difficult problems of disaggregating the tax effects on corporate debt from a very complex set of relevant economic factors.

Legal analysts have focused on the difficulty of applying the debt-equity distinction in practice. Until 1969 application of the distinction was left to the courts, resulting in a throng of judicial decisions that were difficult, if not impossible, to reconcile. Unable to resolve the matter satisfactorily with legislation, Congress in 1969 authorized the Treasury Department to issue regulations specifying the difference between debt and equity for tax purposes, based on the following factors: whether there is a written unconditional promise to repay the principal on demand or on a specified date and to pay a fixed rate of interest in the interim; whether there is subordination to any indebtedness of the corporation; the ratio of the corporation's debt to equity; whether there is convertibility into stock of the corporation; and the relationship between holdings of stock in the corporation and holdings of the interest in question. In the early 1980s, after more than a decade, the Treasury Department issued lengthy proposed regulations based on these factors. These regulations were then substantially revised and finally completely withdrawn in 1983, in part because under the Treasury's own proposals, interests that the government clearly considered debt might be treated as equity. The Treasury has no plans to reissue regulations in the foreseeable future.

The result is a corporate income tax that treats returns to suppliers of capital very differently depending on the type of claim issued in return for their capital, with the categories of claim themselves somewhat indeterminate. Although the ultimate economic effect of this differential is difficult to identify, the difference pervades corporate financial planning. For example, the current wave of leveraged buyouts of public corporations (in which management typically purchases outstanding shares with borrowed funds) is at least partially attributable to the tax benefits of a highly leveraged capital structure. On the other hand, corporate loans to other corporations are often structured as purchases of stock because intercorporate dividend receipts are largely untaxed, while intercorporate interest receipts are fully taxed.

Shareholder Taxation of Corporate Distributions

Whatever treatment is accorded suppliers of capital who receive debt claims against the corporation, a basic tenet of the classical (double) tax system is that shareholders will be taxed in full—as having received what the Internal Revenue Code calls ordinary income—on distributions of corporate earnings. In fact, there are a variety of ways in which shareholders can avoid full taxation on distributions from both closely held and public corporations.

If shareholders sell their shares, they receive capital gains treatment on the difference between the sale proceeds and what they paid for the stock. Under current law, 60 percent of a long-term capital gain is excluded from income, so the effective tax rate for such gains is 40 percent of the taxpayer's marginal tax rate on ordinary income. But a sale of stock from one individual shareholder to another does not accomplish a distribution of corporate earnings to suppliers of equity capital, for it simply shifts the claim to those earnings from one individual to another. The analogy of a sale has, however, had a powerful effect on the development of several aspects of the current system that do permit shareholders to treat distributions of corporate earnings as sales of shares.

First is the long-standing result that proceeds received on the liquidation of a corporation are treated as though the shareholder had sold his stock back to the corporation. Thus, the only tax due is the capital gains tax on the excess of receipts over the cost of the stock to the shareholder. This device for distributing corporate earnings is obviously limited to situations, generally involving closely held companies, where the corporation is ready to wind up its activities and distribute its assets in dissolution. But even that limited possibility creates opportunities for aggressive tax planning. For example, the liquidated corporation's operating assets may be subsequently reincorporated, leaving shareholders of the defunct corporation with only previously undistributed liquid assets. The legal system has responded to such opportunities with a complicated set of rules about what constitutes a true liquidation, for which sale of stock treatment is available, as opposed to a liquidation that will be treated as the functional equivalent of a dividend.

More important, the analogy between sales and liquidations has been extended to cases where corporations repurchase shares from stockholders, generally referred to as redemptions. Unless the redemption is proportionate among all shareholders or is otherwise considered the equivalent of a dividend, the Internal Revenue Code again treats shareholders as if they had sold part of their stock, limiting the applicable tax to capital gains treatment of the excess of receipts over cost, even though share repurchases can clearly involve a distribution of corporate earnings to shareholders. In the context of closely held corporations, this possibility is often coupled with the attribute of our income tax that steps up the cost of an asset for purposes of measuring gain to the asset's current value if the asset is received by reason of the transferor's death. Thus, redemption of shares received by family members on the death of a relative may generate *no* taxation at the shareholder level, even though corporate earnings are thereby distributed to stockholders.

Public corporations may also distribute earnings at capital gains rates on the excess of amounts realized over shareholder cost by simply repurchasing shares on the stock market. The tax advantages of share repurchases has long led some financial and economic analysts to wonder why any public company pays dividends.[2] Suggested answers have included (1) the possibility that more extensive repurchase programs might prompt the Internal Revenue Service to declare them essentially equivalent to dividends, (2) the possibility that the stock markets regard dividend payments as important signals of profitability, (3) restrictions on share repurchases under the securities laws, and (4) the special tax and nontax considerations that apply to institutional investors. Even in the aggregate, however, these explanations do not fully explain the prevalence of dividend payments. In any event, some public companies pay very little in the way of dividends and periodically repurchase their shares in the public markets; some are quite explicit about the financial and tax effects of share repurchases in their financial statements.[3]

There is still another common means of distributing corporate earnings that involves only a capital gains tax to the shareholder on the excess of receipts over stock cost. That is the purchase by one corporation of another corporation's shares from individual stockholders, as in a cash tender offer. The net result of such a purchase is the distribution of corporate assets without the imposition of the shareholder ordinary income tax that is a part of the classical system of taxing corporate income.

Capital Recovery Provisions

The tax code's capital recovery provisions, dealing with depreciation deductions and the investment tax credit, have a significant impact on the corporate income tax because of the magnitude of depreciable assets held by corporations.

It has long been known that the effect of making income from capital tax-exempt can be approximated for the taxpayer by fully taxing capital income but allowing a deduction for the initial capital investment, a method sometimes called expensing.[4] This relationship can be illustrated with a simple example. Suppose you invest $100 in a tax-free bond yielding an annual return of 10 percent. You will have $10 a year to consume because the return on your investment is tax free. When you cash in the bond, you will get back your initial investment of $100. Suppose now that the income from the bond is taxable at a 50 percent rate but that you can deduct the initial cost of the bond in full. Assuming you have other income against which to deduct your initial investment, you can now purchase $200 worth of taxable bonds with $100 of your own money and $100 of tax savings. Each year the bond will produce $20 of taxable income, of which you will receive $10 after taxes. When you cash in the $200 bond, you will be taxed on the difference between what you receive and your tax cost, which is zero because of your initial deduction of $200 when the bonds were purchased. Thus, you will receive only $100 after taxes ($200 - .5 ($200 - 0) = $100). This equivalence between tax exemption and expensing is subject to significant limitations and qualifications, such as the requirement of a fixed tax rate, but it has been a very important idea in the development and analysis of the current capital recovery provisions.[5]

Although exemption of capital income and expensing may have the same ultimate effect on the taxpayer, they affect the government's cash flow differently. Under expensing, the Treasury forgoes revenue at the time of investment because of the deduction ($100 of forgone taxes in our example) and collects revenue on disinvestment ($10 annually, $100 when the bond is cashed in, in our example). Accordingly, it is sometimes said that the Treasury participates, or becomes a partner, in private investments under an expensing system.[6]

When the capital recovery provisions were enacted in their present form in 1982, the Senate Finance Committee explicitly stated that they were designed so that the present value of the investment tax credit and the depreciation deductions would equal the present value of expensing for most new industrial machinery and equipment.[7] For such assets held by corporations, Congress thus adopted capital recovery provisions that would result in an effective corporate tax rate of zero.

This method of reducing effective corporate tax rates has three deleterious effects. First, it results in different effective tax rates for different assets and different industries, distorting investment incentives.[8]

A second problem is that corporations without sufficient taxable income to make full use of tax credits and depreciation deductions have an incentive to sell those benefits to corporations with excess taxable income. In general, the federal income tax does not permit taxpayers to sell tax attributes to an individual or entity that is in a better position to use those attributes. However, by structuring complex transactions (most commonly a form of leasing), taxpayers have devised means of transferring the benefits of effective expensing in spite of the general prohibition. This means of accomplishing transferability of tax attributes results in significant transactions costs, as the tax system has to distinguish between, for example, "true" leases and those that are inappropriately dominated by tax considerations.[9]

Third, corporations can combine the zero effective rate of tax on investments accomplished by the accelerated capital recovery provisions with the deductibility of interest payments described above. The resulting tax arbitrage transactions can create negative effective tax rates for particular investments. While the capital markets undoubtedly respond by reducing or eliminating the possibilities for such arbitrage, the ultimate tax-induced results are what Congress intended when it enacted the capital recovery provisions.[10] Indeed, the congressional response to such developments has generally been to add another layer of complexity to the tax system by enacting particular limitations on interest deductibility in certain specified cases.

Corporate Taxation on Shareholder Distributions

In 1935 the United States Supreme Court decided that corporate taxable income was not realized when corporate assets were distributed to shareholders. This result, known generally as the "*General Utilities* doctrine," after the corporate taxpayer involved, often makes it possible to eliminate the corporate tax by transferring corporate assets to shareholders. Suppose, for example, that a closely held corporation has assets that have substantially increased in value but have not yet borne an income tax because they have not yet been sold or otherwise disposed of. When those assets are distributed to shareholders, the potential corporate tax is forever eliminated by the *General Utilities* doctrine.

This result is particularly powerful when it is recalled that some distributions from corporations, such as liquidations and certain redemptions, are taxed to shareholders as sales of stock rather than as dividends. If the corporate tax is eliminated while shareholders are given capital gains treatment, assets can be removed from the corporate tax base at the price of a very small shareholder tax. This possibility has motivated some well-publicized takeover attempts of public corporations in recent years. For example, if a publicly traded partnership acquires an oil company with substantial oil reserves and then dissolves the acquired company, the income from those reserves may be permanently removed from the corporate tax base, at the cost of only a shareholder capital gains tax on the sale of shares, followed by depletion deductions for the fair market value of the oil reserves. Proponents of such takeovers have argued to shareholders that existing corporate management is wasting their money by paying the corporate tax when a big chunk of the corporate assets could at a low tax cost be moved out of the corporation to a trust or partnership that would not be subject to the corporate tax. (For further discussion of hostile takeover attempts, see Chapter 11 in this book.)

Partly in response to such takeovers, the *General Utilities* doctrine has been substantially restricted by Congress in recent years for public companies, but it remains an important part of the federal income tax.

Summary

The federal income taxation of corporations does not today constitute a coherent implementation of the classical double taxation of corporate income, the regime generally said to be embodied in the Internal Revenue Code. Returns to suppliers of capital who receive debt claims are not taxed at the corporate level. Some distributions of corporate earnings to shareholders are taxed as sales of stock rather than as dividends. Some corporate income is effectively exempt by virtue of the capital recovery provisions. Finally, corporate income is not taxed in cases in which the *General Utilities* doctrine applies to distributions to shareholders.

HOW SHOULD CORPORATE INCOME BE TAXED?

Discussion of appropriate corporate income taxation involves two related questions: whether capital income should be taxed in general and whether corporate income in particular should bear an additional tax burden.

Should Capital Income Be Taxed?

Whether taxation should apply to income from capital as well as income from labor has long been a central question in public finance. The debate has focused on three standard tax policy issues: distributive fairness, economic efficiency, and administrative simplicity. But before turning to those issues, the relationship among income taxation, consumption taxation, and wage taxation must be briefly explored.

Income taxation, as the term is generally used, refers to the taxation of income from both labor and capital. *Wage taxation* refers to taxation of only income from labor and could be accomplished by excluding capital income from the income tax base. Because the sources of income (capital and labor) must by definition equal its uses, income can also be thought of as the sum of consumption and saving (its uses). A personal *consumption tax*, sometimes called an *expenditure tax*, would be levied only on the portion of income that is consumed. Such a tax could be implemented by deducting all saving from the income tax base and including all dissaving, such as borrowing, in that base. Because expenditure or consumption taxation would be implemented by including all receipts and deducting all nonconsumption expenditures, it is sometimes also referred to as a tax on cash flow. When the conditions for the equivalence between expensing and exemption of capital income hold, expenditure taxation (under which all savings are expensed) can have the same effect on the taxpayer as exempting capital income from income taxation.

The current federal income tax has some attributes of both income and consumption taxation. For example, the treatment of savings accounts (current taxation of interest, whether or not withdrawn) and borrowed funds (no inclusion for such funds, deductions for interest payments) is clearly that of an income tax. On the other hand, individual retirement accounts (deductions for deposits, inclusion of withdrawals) and the capital recovery provisions already mentioned reflect consumption or cash flow treatment.

With these relationships as background, we can now turn to the major arguments advanced for and against the taxation of capital income. Advocates of such taxation generally support comprehensive taxation of income from all sources. Their principal argument on the basis of distributional fairness is that taxes should be levied, whether proportionately or progressively, on the basis of each citizen's pretax share in the product of the society's economic activity.[11]

The principal fairness argument for effective exclusion of capital income has focused on the expenditure tax, with its proponents arguing that taxes should be based on the resources a citizen withdraws from the result of society's productive activity.[12] This argument has a very long and distinguished intellectual history. As Thomas Hobbes put it three centuries ago:

> For what reason is there that he which laboureth much, and sparing the fruits of his labour, consumeth little, should be more charged that he that living idlely, getteth little, and spendeth all he gets; seeing the one has no more protection from the Common-wealth, than the other?[13]

Taxes levied on a consumption base can be distributionally fair, it is argued, because graduated rates for individual taxpayers can be applied to that tax base. Some proponents have also contended that a consumption tax is fairer from a lifetime perspective because it allows an individual to allocate his earnings to different periods in his lifetime without having the rate of exchange between such periods (i.e., capital income) affected by taxation.[14] Finally, it is sometimes suggested that gifts and bequests could be included in an expenditure tax base to reach intergenerational transfers.[15]

Taxation of capital income has also been opposed on grounds of economic efficiency. Because such a tax reduces the rate of exchange between current and future consumption, it may reduce economic welfare. Some consumption tax advocates have gone further to argue that taxation of capital income will reduce savings and economic growth. The responsiveness of taxpayers' decisions to save to the after-tax return on saving has been a matter of considerable debate in recent years. Moreover, careful analysts have noted that the efficiency effects of taxing or excluding capital income depend on the interrelationship of several factors, including the tax treatment of leisure and income from labor.[16] Nevertheless, some general-equilibrium models of the economy have suggested that economic welfare would be substantially improved by adopting a personal expenditure tax instead of a comprehensive income tax.[17]

The final question on which income and expenditure tax advocates have disagreed is whether an expenditure tax would be substantially simpler in operation than a comprehensive income tax. (There seems to be wide agreement that the easiest way to exclude capital income from the tax base would be to adopt an expenditure tax.) The basic argument for the expenditure tax on this ground is that all the complexities of the income tax that are necessary for the measurement of income from capital, such as realization, deferral, and capital recovery provisions, could be avoided.[18] The general response of income tax advocates has been that it is unfair to compare a theoretically pure consumption tax with the current income tax, and that any expenditure tax that is likely to be enacted is not likely to be any simpler than the best income tax that can be enacted.[19]

The question of how corporations should be taxed cannot be answered without deciding whether capital income should be explicitly or effectively excluded from the tax base. My own view is that in a tax system that lacks a significant levy on intergenerational transfers, distributional and fairness considerations make a comprehensive income tax more desirable than even progressive expenditure taxation, in spite of the apparent administrative advantages of the latter.

How Should Corporate Income Be Taxed?

The "Classical System" of Double Taxation. Aside from administrative convenience, is there any justification for taxing corporations as separate entities, as though they were in some sense comparable to human beings? Five rationales have been advanced for separate taxation of corporations.[20]

First, it is sometimes argued that a corporate income tax is an appropriate charge for the special benefits of operating in corporate form, especially the legal attribute of limited liability for shareholders.

Second, corporate taxation can be seen as a response to social costs not fully reflected in the private costs taken into account by the corporation. Here the cost of government services that provide the basic legal structure for business operations and the education of workers are sometimes mentioned.

Third, corporate taxation is sometimes justified as a means of social control and direction. The modern corporate income tax is certainly used for more than raising revenue, with Congress deliberately encouraging certain economic activities and discouraging others.

Fourth, it is sometimes argued that corporate taxation is justified because it is generally desirable to diversify taxes, especially where the incidence of the taxes is somewhat uncertain and where high marginal rates are considered undesirable.

Finally, to the extent the tax is considered to fall on shareholders, or even on capitalists in general, a separate tax on corporate income can be justified as adding to the progressivity of the individual income tax. Indeed, the ultimate burden of the corporate income tax is very important in assessing the overall incidence of the entire federal income tax system.[21]

The case against separate taxation of corporate income generally involves two arguments. The first is that even if consistently applied, the tax would create at least some of the economic distortions and administrative difficulties described above with respect to the current regime.

The second is that incidence of the tax is, at least today, very problematic, so that we cannot be entirely sure which individuals will ultimately bear the burden of the tax, for all taxes must ultimately burden some people. Leading candidates for bearing the burden of the corporate income tax include shareholders (as the owners of the corporation's residual earnings), corporate workers (through reduced wages), consumers of corporate products (though increased prices), and holders of all forms of capital (because a reduction in the return to corporate capital will affect the return to all capital in competitive markets). It has also been suggested that the tax may simply reduce the riskiness of corporate investment (because losses are deductible) or fall essentially on corporate entrepreneurship.[22] Finally, efficient capital markets may have already taken into account, or capitalized, the future burden of the tax in share prices, so that its burden was borne by shareholders who may no longer hold the affected corporate stock.[23]

My own view is that these various considerations do not justify a separate, additional tax on corporate income, although I am sympathetic to concerns about progressivity. Justifying the tax on an entity view of the corporation is simply not convincing when the ultimate incidence of the tax is so uncertain. In addition, it would seem more desirable to accomplish the desired degree of progression directly, without the ancillary effects of a separate corporate tax.

Integration of the Individual and Corporate Income Taxes. Many of our major trading partners have moved away from the classical form of corporate taxation in recent years, toward some integration of the individual and corporate income taxes. Under these regimes, the corporate income tax is not a separate levy on a distinct entity, but merely a means of withholding taxes to be collected on distributions of dividends to shareholders, in order to avoid the deferral benefits of not taxing shareholders until the dividends are received.[24] There are basically two forms of integration—a deduction for corporate dividends paid and a shareholder credit for corporate taxes already paid with respect to earnings distributed as dividends. Most countries that have adopted a form of integration have opted for a shareholder credit, in part because it is easier to deny the benefits of integration to foreign shareholders (at least until the foreign country makes a correlative concession in treaty negotiations) and to tax-exempt entities (for which there is no shareholder tax to be integrated).

Two major issues have arisen in implementing such programs. First, to the extent the corporate tax has been capitalized into share prices, moving toward integration would yield windfall gains to the current holders of corporate shares, who might not have borne the burden of the initial reduction in share prices. Windfall gains and losses are, however, a necessary result of major changes in the tax laws, or other laws for that matter, and should not prevent significant reform that is otherwise desirable.[25]

For those who conclude that the windfall gains in this case are simply too great to ignore, the American Law Institute's Federal Income Tax Project has developed a proposal that would, in effect, adopt integration only with respect to new equity capital. In brief, the proposal would permit a deduction, up to a specified rate, for dividends paid with respect to a new capital account. The proposal would also impose a special corporate excise tax to offset the opportunity to distribute earnings in transactions in which stockholders are taxed as though they sold their shares.[26]

The second major implementation issue is how an integrated system should interact with corporate tax preferences, such as the effective expensing of the current capital recovery provisions. In general, integration regimes have reflected the judgment that only income that is fully taxed at the corporate level should give rise to relief on distribution to shareholders. Accordingly, such regimes require a mechanism to identify fully taxed income, but such a mechanism need not be complicated.[27]

To summarize, the case for integrating the individual and corporate income taxes follows from the view that capital income should be taxed to individuals, that corporate income should not bear a special, additional tax, and that shareholders should not benefit from deferring the taxation of their capital income until dividends are distributed. Full implementation of the income tax ideal by taxing shareholders when their shares change value rather than when shares are sold or dividends received would eliminate the need for integration of the type discussed here, as would annual imputation of corporate earnings to shareholders for tax purposes, whether distributed or not. But as long as shareholders are taxed only on what the tax system considers *realized* income, integration is necessary to eliminate the separate burden of the corporate tax, while fully taxing all capital income earned through corporations.

Cash Flow Taxation of Corporations. Suppose personal expenditure taxation is favored over a comprehensive income tax. Is there then any role for the corporate income tax? To the extent capital income taxation is rejected, the answer would seem to be no. On the other hand, a distinguished committee in the United Kingdom recently pointed out that a cash flow tax at the corporate level could be linked with a personal expenditure tax as a way for the government to participate in the productivity of the private sector, as well as to continue taxing the return on preexisting capital, a tax burden that may already be reflected in share prices.[28] Such a regime would involve not only expensing for individual investors in corporate financial assets such as common stock, but also for corporations that make real investments using the funds obtained by issuing such stock. In effect, the government would participate twice in such investments, once with respect to the shareholder investment and once again with respect to corporate investment.

SUMMARY AND CONCLUSIONS

Although very complicated, the current regime for taxing corporate income does not implement a coherent view of what the tax should accomplish. The present system could be improved and rationalized in several different ways. Each depends in the first instance on whether it is concluded that capital income should be subject to personal taxation. If the answer is yes, a corporate income tax could be designed either to implement systematically a classical double tax regime or to eliminate the separate burden of the corporate tax by moving toward an integrated system such as those now partially in effect in many of the other developed Western nations. The second of those alternatives would be my preference.

If, on the other hand, a personal consumption tax is preferred to a personal income tax, then the separate corporate income tax should be either eliminated or converted into a tax on corporate cash flow.

Although the tax bill now being considered by Congress contains the seed of an integration system—a corporate deduction for 10 percent of dividend payments, phased in over a decade—the bill also includes provisions that would move more in the direction of a classical system by further reducing the scope of the *General Utilities* doctrine.[29] Recent history suggests it is unlikely that a clear consensus will develop on the basic issues of whether capital income should be taxed to individuals and how the corporate income tax should be related to the individual levy. Instead, we are likely to muddle through, embellishing a system for taxing corporations that remains fundamentally inconsistent in principle and therefore very complicated in practice.

NOTES

1. R.H. Gordon and B.G. Malkiel, "Corporation Finance," in H.J. Aaron and J.A. Pechman, eds., *How Taxes Affect Economic Behavior* (Washington, D.C.: Brookings Institution, 1981), pp. 131–98.
2. F. Black, "The Dividend Puzzle," *Journal of Portfolio Management* 2, no. 2 (Winter 1976): 5-8.
3. Tandy Corporation, 1977–1985 *Annual Reports*, Fort Worth, Texas.
4. E.C. Brown, *Business Income Taxation and Investment Incentives, in Income, Employment, and Public Policy* (New York: Norton, 1948).
5. R.A. Musgrave, *The Theory of Public Finance* (New York: McGraw-Hill, 1959).
6. M.G. Graetz, "Implementing a Progressive Consumption Tax," *Harvard Law Review* 92 (June 1979): 1575.
7. U.S., Congress, Senate, Report of the Senate Finance Committee, *Tax Equity and Fiscal Responsibility Act*. S. Doc. 494, 97th Cong., 2d sess., 1982.
8. A.J. Auerbach, "Corporate Taxation in the United States," *Brookings Papers on Economic Activity* 2 (1983): 451.
9. A.C. Warren and A. Auerbach, "Transferability of Tax Incentives and the Fiction of Safe Harbor Leasing," *Harvard Law Review* 95 (June 1982): 1752.
10. C.E. Steuerle, *Taxes, Loans and Inflation* (Washington, D.C.: Brookings Institution, 1985).
11. J.A. Pechman and B.A. Okner, *Who Bears the Tax Burden?* (Washington, D.C.: Brookings Institution, 1974).
12. N. Kaldor, *An Expenditure Tax* (London: Allen and Unwin, 1955).
13. T. Hobbes, *Leviathan*, 1651.
14. D.F. Bradford, *Untangling the Income Tax* (Cambridge, Mass.: Harvard University Press, 1986).
15. H. Aaron and H. Galper, *Assessing Tax Reform* (Washington, D.C.: Brookings Institution, 1985), p. 77.
16. D.F. Bradford, "The Economics of Tax Policy Towards Savings," in G.M. von Furstenberg, ed., *The Government and Capital Formation* (Cambridge, Mass.: Ballinger Publishing Co.), pp. 11–71.
17. C.L. Ballard, D. Fullerton, J.B. Shoven, and J. Whalley, *A General Equilibrium Model for Tax Policy Evaluation* (Chicago: University of Chicago Press, 1985).

18. W.D. Andrews, "A Consumption-Type or Cash Flow Personal Income Tax," *Harvard Law Review* 87 (April 1974): 1113.
19. American Bar Association, Section of Taxation, Committee on Simplification, Complexity and the Personal Income Tax, The Tax Lawyer, vol. 35, 1982, p. 415; M.G. Graetz, "Legal Transitions: The Case of Retroactivity in Income Tax Revision," *University of Pennsylvania Law Review* 126 (November 1977): 47.
20. R.S. Goode, *The Corporation Income Tax* (New York: Wiley, 1951).
21. Pechman and Okner, *Who Bears the Tax Burden?*
22. R.H. Gordon, "Taxation of Corporate Capital Income: Tax Revenues vs. Tax Distortions," Bell Laboratories, Murray Hill, N.J.; J. Stiglitz, "The Corporation Income Tax, *Journal of Public Economics* 5 (April-May 1976): 303.
23. Auerbach, "Corporate Taxation in the United States."
24. C.E. McLure, ed., *Must Corporate Income Be Taxed Twice?* (Washington, D.C.: Brookings Institution, 1979); A.C. Warren, "The Relation and Integration of Individual and Corporate Income Taxes," *Harvard Law Review* 94 (February 1981): 717.
25. M.G. Graetz, "Legal Transitions"; L. Kaplow, "An Economic Analysis of Legal Transitions," *Harvard Law Review* 99 (January 1986): 511.
26. American Law Institute, *Federal Income Tax Project, Subchapter C, Reporter's Study on Corporate Distributions* (Philadelphia: American Law Institute, 1982).
27. Warren, "The Relation and Integration of Individual and Corporate Income Taxes."
28. Institute for Fiscal Studies, *The Structure and Reform of Direct Taxation—Report of a Committee Chaired by Professor J.E. Meade* (London: Allen and Unwin, 1978); Bradford, *Untangling the Income Tax.*
29. U.S., Congress, House, *H.R. 3838* (as passed by the House of Representatives), 99th Cong., 1st sess., 1986.

CHAPTER 13

Has Economic Science
Improved the System?

Paul A. Samuelson

T he fifty years of the Kennedy School's existence, which coincide with the interval of time from Harvard's 300th to 350th
anniversary, by good chance also coincide with the Age After Keynes.
This is therefore a fitting time to take stock, to review how the
macroeconomic system has changed during the crucial half century
from 1936 to 1986. Also, a birthday party is on occasion to recall
briefly what role Harvard University played in this time of Kuhnian
revolution in economic science.

TESTIMONIALS

Yes, the world economy is more stable than it was in pre-1929 capitalism. Yes, the birth of macroeconomics did irreversibly advance the
science of political economy, and this new knowledge does deserve
some of the credit for the better performance of the economic system. No, the advance has not been uniform in all respects: Mindless
societies have long been capable of engineering inflations for themselves; but today the prudent odds *against* long-run stability of the
price level have certainly risen.

I base these conclusions on the reading of economic history, con-
sciously resisting the temptations to regard the years of our youth as

I owe thanks to the MIT Center for Real Estate Development for financial support and
to Aase Huggins for editorial assistance.

the years of the universe's glory. By sheer good luck I was born as an economist when pure capitalism was in its heyday. All of neo-classical economics conspired, so to speak, to produce my teachers—and me. It was Sophie Tucker who said, "I've been rich, I've been poor. Believe me, rich is better." My generation enjoys a priceless advantage: We lived through the revolutionary transition. Later scholars can benefit from the cumulative record, which includes among other things the legacies we leave them. History, however, never gets things right. The immediacy of experience while it is happening—the contrast with what went before and with what will happen later—is something which if you don't have it there is no way you can get it.

QUALIFICATIONS: THE PERSISTENCE OF BUSINESS CYCLES

Understatement is the optimal form of emphasis. So please be warned: Business cycles still persist. The best forecasters of output, unemployment, profits, security prices, and price indexes are trained economists. Their batting averages in predicting are better than they were one, two, or three generations ago. But these best batting averages are still not very good; and the trend of their mean-precision is not a hopeful one, showing no asymptotic rendezvous with bullseye accuracy.

The Age of Keynes happens to coincide more or less with the post-World-War II epoch. Suppose you make a plot of annual or quarterly percentage changes in real gross national product. The pre-1940 data look to have been drawn by a different hand than that which penned the post-1945 picture—a more exhuberant hand. Growth still moves in fits and starts. But now the fits and starts seem tamer.

Crude tests like these, to be sure, do not count for much in a complex subject like economics. Fluctuations in the production index became perceptibly more virulent in the quarter century after the Federal Reserve was founded in 1913. Yet the monetarist economists who concluded from this that the Federal Reserve was a failure were victims of the post hoc ergo propter hoc fallacy. When other things have not been held constant, one must be wary in attributing causation to changes in the thing that happens to have caught one's eye.

The Kaiser had more to do with World War I than Governor Strong of the Federal Reserve.

Here is a first qualification we must apply to the apparently more stable post-1945 macro behavior. Does it appear stable, merely because the between-the-wars period was so singularly unstable? Not a little of the improvement does seem subject to this discount. But not all.

There is a second trap we must beware of. Someone asked William James what he thought of his brother's post-1900 style as a novelist. William laughed off the question, saying: "There is no new style. It's just that Henry has a new secretary and she doesn't cut out all the digressions the old one used to do." The new hand that plots the post-World-War II data may simply differ idiosyncratically in penmanship and measurement from the old one that limned the pre-World-War II data.

Professor Christina Romer of Princeton University has looked into this issue. In her Ph.D. dissertation comparing modern and earlier methods of measuring unemployment and production changes, Romer showed that some of the putative reduction in cyclical instability was spurious, a figment resulting from cruder estimation procedures used in earlier times.[1] If we used those same procedures to describe the 1970s and 1980s, the resulting time series of macro data would more closely resemble the ups and downs of the pre-Keynesian era.

Romer's readers will be struck by two other deflating points. Services have grown in importance relative to manufactured goods. If services are by their nature less prone to cyclical variations than goods, then even if there have been no improvements in the behavior laws and mechanisms of the market economy, the mean amplitudes of cyclical fluctuations could show a declining trend. To the degree that only this is involved, economists would have no warrant for claiming that their science had yielded real-world successes.

The enlarged role of government in the GNP raises a similar question. My Harvard mentor Alvin Hansen, leading fiscal scholar of a generation ago, hypothesized that dollars of public expenditure would be less prone to oscillate cyclically than dollars of private expenditure. So he would have expected the mixed economy to evolve toward greater cyclical stability than undiluted capitalism would. Although Hansen was rightly called the American Keynes and the most prolific architect of policy implications from Keynes's 1936 *General Theory*, he would cheerfully have acknowledged that the new paradigms of macroeconomics deserved only part of the credit for the worldwide growth spurt in the second third of the twentieth century.

Incidentally, historians of thought have failed to note Hansen's claim that the stagnation he feared for a mature *laissez-faire* society had been considerably exorcized by growth of the public sector in the modern mixed economies. To a reader of Romer, Alvin Hansen would say from beyond the grave: "Since one of the scientific reasons for advocating a mixed rather than a *laissez-faire* economy was its discerned greater macro stability, it is not fair to treat the expanded role of government as a mere happenstance like that of the expanded weight of services in the GNP." Fair enough. But the knife cuts two ways. When we come to examine the swollen rates of unemployment in present-day welfare states like Denmark and the Netherlands, we must debit them and certain pathologies of stagflation against the mixed economies that Hansen's generation helped to promote.

The reduced importance of agriculture in the modern economy ought, I think, to increase the cyclical variability of the GNP and magnify the task of macroeconomic stabilizers. I say this because the variability of farm quantities tends to respond to a different drumbeat than the trade cycle—to weather, pestilence and the like. The total *value* of farm production tends toward relative stability; flexibility in the prices that farm goods fetch at auction permits quantities produced to resist the business cycle. By contrast, when natural rubber in Malay gets replaced by synthetic rubber produced by a Fortune 500 company, a drop in demand causes whole plants to be shut down, with the implied swings in production and in employment. All the more credit therefore to macro management if Christina Romer does not observe a rising trend in cyclical amplitude in the post-1929 Galbraithian world of *Fortune's* favorites.

Geoffrey Moore, the chronicler of the business cycle at the National Bureau of Economic Research, observed that recoveries have lasted longer and recessions have ended sooner in the years since World War II. Those same miracle years, however, involved higher *mean* growth rates for Europe, North America, and the Pacific Basin. Moore does not consider a period recessionary unless output declines absolutely. If years of growth recession were tallied, we would find that the economy has been in recession roughly half the time since the war, as it was in the years before, and (almost by definition) half the time in expansion. We moderns should congratulate ourselves only if the lengths of *complete* cycles rise and, more important, the mean shortfall from potential GNP is reduced. By this better measure, some of the postwar improvement in performance must have been lost since 1973 in most of the OECD economies.

To sum up: Even after allowing for the special virulence of the interwar years, my judgment is that the post-1945 economy is performing better macroeconomically than the pre-1920 economy. Depressions, like those of 1893, 1873, and 1836–41, are less likely to reoccur and be allowed to persist. (The macroeconomics of World War II itself was greatly shaped by post-Keynesian knowledge as well, and was distinctly better than macroeconomics of World War I, the Civil War, or the Napoleonic Wars.) On reflection, I believe we owe much to scholars who scientifically elaborated the inadequacies of neutral-money dogmas in less than long-run economic scenarios. My own work has benefited from Keynes's changing the emphasis away from ups-and-downs around some "normal" level and toward attaining the growth in potential GNP achievable through high employment and a fuller realization of that potential. A price has been paid for this benefit: In a system where the good news from stimulus comes before the bad news, the temptation toward overambitious activism bedevils modern democracies.

THE DOG THAT WAGS THE TAIL

An anthropologist visiting from Mars will find our world very different from the world of 1929 or 1932. A toll of bank failures that would have caused chains of bankruptcies in 1931, the observing anthropologist would now find, creates imperceptible waves in Wall Street and not even a ripple in the GNP accounts. Some scholars have grown from youth into maturity warning about the wolf of a credit breakdown. The shocks of OPEC, the chicaneries of the oil patch and real estate manias, and political crises around the globe have provided raw material for a conflagration that could make the crises of 1929–31 look like an innocent flicker in a fireplace. Yet Cassandra's hour has never come.

Is the Age of Keynes so very different from the past? Maynard Keynes blew his own horn and the horns of all of us scholars who

304 / THE CORPORATION AND THE ECONOMY

itch for the power to affect the world and to improve its well-being by virtue of our scientific breakthroughs. His much-quoted rhetoric caters to our vanity and dreams of glory:

> ... [T] he ideas of economists and political philosophers, both when they are right and when they are wrong, are more powerful than is commonly understood. Indeed the world is ruled by little else. Practical men, who believe themselves to be quite exempt from any intellectual influences, are usually the slave of some defunct economist. . . . Soon or late, it is ideas, not vested interests, which are dangerous for good or evil.[2]

This is heady stuff, exquisitely brewed. But is it believable? Consider the New Deal of Franklin Delano Roosevelt. It was an example par excellence of deficit spending. Was this, though, because some past ideologue had captured the mind of the new president? Certainly FDR learned nothing in his economic classes under Professor Frank Taussig at Harvard University to push policy in this direction. It was the Great Depression itself that made him renege on his campaign promises to balance the federal budget. To be sure, there is always an academic witch doctor readily at hand to rationalize whatever the prince wants to do. In 1933 it happened to be G. F. Warren, a Cornell farm economist who turned up with confused statistical proof that the price level would inevitably rise if only FDR lifted the buying price the U.S. paid for gold. Only later did Keynes have an interview with Roosevelt, which both dashed Keynes's expectations for the president's economic literacy and left FDR quite unimpressed.

A Roosevelt was no more needed to create a depression deficit than a Newton or a Leibniz was needed to invent calculus, which essentially created itself when the time was ripe. What great hero invented the English language? Surely not Samuel Johnson or Noah Webster, nor even William Shakespeare or the Earl of Oxford.

From earliest times, business recessions unbalanced budgets. Not until 1937 or later did a self-consciously Keynesian clique have any influence in the New Deal regime. In lecturing on various continents, I used to play down the bogeyman of another 1929–32 crash and financial crisis by arguing, "We in populist democracy have eaten fruit of the tree of *knowledge* and there is no going back to Herbert Hoover's undiluted capitalism, etc., etc." Once the electorate got the taste of apple in its mouth, the niceties of science were no longer required. If printing bits of green paper can keep 15,000 banks from going bust, the paper will be printed no matter which political party controls the White House. It is easy for a monetarist historian to look back at the years of the banking crisis and regard as silly the Federal Reserve's concern in 1931 for the adequacy of its gold reserves; easy indeed to imagine might-have-been scenarios in which the Fed created whatever supply of new reserves was needed to offset the decline in our total money supply occasioned by frightened people's converting their bank deposits to currency. But such bold departures from the conventional wisdom were never on the agenda. Academics who insisted on them would have risked losing their relevance and influence as well as being categorized with the easy-money cranks we have always with us.

Keynes was not completely wrong about scientific ideas and public policies. But he exaggerated. The Reagan administration provides a fine example. I can find no relation between the president's State of the Union messages and the prosaic studies of growth by our leading scientific authorities such as Harvard's late Nobelist, Simon Kuznets, or Edward Denison, the author of the definitive study *Trends in American Economic Growth, 1929-1982*.[3]

THAT GOLDEN AGE

Harvard has played an honorable role in the macrorevolution of 1936 to 1986. After Alvin Hansen was called to the first professorship of the Littauer School of Public Administration in 1936—later to become the Kennedy School of Government—Harvard experienced a renaissance in macroeconomics. Reviewing the definitive study commissioned in 1948 by the American Economic Association, *A Survey of Contemporary Economics*, George Stigler ironically complained that the old-school crimson tie was everywhere, in the choice of authors and in the authorities cited.

Before the Littauer School was established, little important work in modern macroeconomics had been done at Harvard. The joint volume on the *Economics of the Recovery Program*, put out by Joseph Schumpeter, Wassily Leontief, Edward Mason, Seymour Harris, Edward Chamberlin, O. H. Taylor, and other younger Harvard faculty, documents the sad irrelevance of neoclassical economics for the Great Depression.[4]

A fiftieth birthday party is a time for nostalgia and celebration. John Williams, the first dean of the Littauer School, formed with

Alvin Hansen a remarkable duo. If to teach is to affirm, then Williams should have become a banker full time. But if to teach is to raise doubt, Williams was a brilliant success. Actually, Williams' cracker-barrel, seemingly relaxed manner made him a splendid teacher. He recruited hundreds of undergraduates to major in economics.

Inevitably Hansen, the pioneer of a new scientific paradigm, stole the show and attracted the bulk of the graduate students destined to become eminent. Robert Roosa, Paul Volcker, and Henry Wallich (who was in both camps) are only a few of the proteges Williams launched at the Federal Reserve Bank of New York, where from the early 1930s to mid-century Williams was vice president and research sage.

If people who need people are the happiest people in the world, then this first Kennedy School dean ought to have been miserable. Actually, he was merely reserved and aloof—almost indolent as a good dean who is determined to maintain his creative scholarship should be. After his retirement, Williams lived for decades as a recluse from colleagues and students.

It does both Hansen and Williams enormous credit that they never undercut each other in the classroom or outside. It was rarely like this in the continental universities and certainly not in the London School of Economics, Cambridge, and Chicago bullpens, where the disciples of the competing stars were pitted against one another not merely on class and ideological issues but also on mundane questions of methodology. Needless to say, the incivility of the 1965 to 1975 era was never dreamed of, even by the warring Oxford dons.

Since Hansen had the disproportionate power for aggression, I suppose he merits the greater praise. Still, it would have been understandable if Williams had nursed resentment that his turf had been taken over. And yet that private individual could say, on the occasion of both men's retirement, that Alvin Hansen had been the best friend he had ever had in academic life. God bless!

Besides Hansen and Williams, Harvard in that golden age had Gottfried Haberler, Joseph Schumpeter, Seymour Harris, and Sumner Slichter as sage macroeconomists. Good students of any bent could find a role model to emulate.

After Edward Mason became Dean of the Littauer School, it finally became more than simply an augmentation of the resources available to the economics and government departments. His leadership, and that of Don Price, takes me beyond my period and beyond macroeconomics as such.

THE MIXED-ECONOMY MIRACLE

By the time Joseph Schumpeter died in 1950, he had become perhaps the world's most cited economist. His 1942 *Capitalism, Socialism and Democracy* made many valuable observations on the passing of *laissez faire* and the march to socialism.[5] Within and between its lines were warnings on problems to come for the welfare state.

Yet Schumpeter failed to realize how dynamic the mixed economies—his "capitalism in an oxygen tent"—would prove to be in the 1945 to 1970 period. Never before or since has global real output grown so rapidly and enduringly.

Like leaders of the school of rational expectationists (the new Classical school), Schumpeter believed that prices and wages adjust to clear markets without inflicting on the economy lasting unemployment or excess capacity. The markets get it right; government can do little good and much harm. (To Schumpeter's credit, he did foresee periods of unemployment longer than those admitted in the models of Robert Lucas, Thomas Sargent, Robert Barro, and other leading rational expectationists.)

How could a Robert Lucas or a Joseph Schumpeter account for miraculous 1945 to 1970 growth? If markets were clearing in 1929 to 1939, how could the kiss of monetary demand achieve postwar miracles? For that matter, how could the rearming of Hitler's Germany wipe out the 25 percent unemployment rate in the depressed economy he took over?

Lucas's followers have to attribute any Federal Reserve success in expanding output to the fact that their monetary expansion catches the market by surprise. Participants in the world economy might be said to be pleasantly surprised by the first mindless pump primings of Hitler and Roosevelt. But what everyone comes to expect year after year can hardly be considered unanticipated or transitory. The crude fact described in econometric terms by Northwestern's Robert J. Gordon—that for more than a century each 1 percent change in nominal GNP decomposes in the short run into 2/3 percent change in real output and 1/3 percent change in price level—accords ill with the Schumpeter-Lucas presumption in favor of Say's law, which denies that any underutilization of resources, much less mass unemployment, can persist. Wesley Mitchell and the empirical business cycle theorists, who along with the Fisher-Wicksell quantity theorists were the only Model T macroeconomists in the neoclassical paddocks, simply ignored Walrasian clearing-of-the-market concepts when they confronted the facts of business cycle history.

Rational expectationists can produce (1) a model in which cyclical variations in output are due solely to subjective desires to substitute at one time more leisure for bread and at another time more bread for leisure. Alternatively, (2) they can produce a model in which a typical intervention, such as a devaluation, expands an economy only because it has not been anticipated and cheats workers of what they had expected. But this does not compel me as an observer of the successful 1936 Belgian devaluation to believe a classicist story that in 1935 Belgian workers wanted leisure whereas in 1937 they wanted to work, nor that Swedish workers were taken by surprise when their real wage fell in consequence of the new Labor Government's contrived 1983 devaluation of the *krona*, a fact about austerity that had been explained to them in advance of the act. However, my refusal to read into the real world the model of the rational-expectationists' seminar room should not blind me to the fact of experience: Competitive advantage from a 1986 devaluation is likely to be less lasting than from a 1936 devaluation of the same magnitude.

The most flagrantly optimistic forecast for the Federal Reserve before the 1974 debacle came from a leading economist using his rational expectation paradigm. When the DRI forecasting service provided its clients with projections based upon rational-expectationist models, the errors of estimate were enormously large. The infamous Laffer-Ransom forecast of the Nixon Treasury was, I believe, the first quantitative rational-expectationist forecast. A post mortem done in 1980 by Thomas Sargent on the 1923 German hyperinflation suggested that a stabilization, if creditable, could be accomplished with minimal unemployment and distress. A reader of this assessment would have been poorly prepared to understand the 1980 to 1983 crusade against inflation by Carter and Reagan. Even less prepared would that reader be for the qualitative and quantitative features of the so far successful Israel program against inflation since mid-1985.

Those who estimate the structural coefficients of the MIT-Penn-FRB model have not seen their coefficients self-destruct, as the Lucas critique ordains they should. The true causal structure of the economy can only be conjectured of course, but the system's recent responses to Federal Reserve actions generally accord better with older textbook macroeconomics than was the case in the early 1970s. I must warn, though, that in the future steady state, fine-tuning by the Fed cannot be counted on to work as exquisitely as it did in mid-1982 to mid-1983. Then Wall Street wanted to believe in the prospect that extra M (money) would largely impinge on Q (quantities) and not on P (prices), and would thus lower rather than raise interest rates and stocks' earnings yields.

I turn now from critiques of stabilization programs by rational expectationists to critiques by monetarists. Experience shows that money does matter. It does not follow, though, that money alone matters. Nor that a rule of constancy in the growth rate of the M-supply is the best we can hope to have. Past great economists, Hawtrey of England and Cassel of Sweden, believed that central bank expansion of M in 1930–31 could have done much to forestall some of the excesses of the Great Depression. But to agree with them on this does not oblige me to believe the monetarist tenet that in a period like 1938–39 monetary policy would have equal potency to raise GNP and that fiscal policy would lack such potency. Let me explain the matter in common-sense terms.

In 1938–39 the Treasury bill rate of interest was often minimal: 3/8 of 3/8 of 1 percent. Suppose the Fed then engaged in an open-market purchase, its principal weapon to expand the money supply. It spits out new M in exchange for taking in Treasury bills. Maybe it pushes the interest rate down to 3/8 of 3/8 of 3/8 of 1 percent. To what good? When monetary policy pushes on a string, the new M it creates induces a drop in the velocity of circulation, V. The product, MV (i.e., the GNP) is only little increased.

Keynes gave economists a good handle on this. But that is not reason for Keynesians to get frozen in such deep-depression mind-sets; and the Modiglianis, Tobins, Musgraves, Solows, and other post-Keynesians did react to changes in the feel of the system in the 1940s and 1950s to make their paradigm eclectic. Having an open mind does not, however, mean having an empty one. Recognizing that M changes MV does not require one to swallow the monetarist rejection of neoclassicism in favor of the odd belief that when fiscal policy raises interest rates, this will have negligible effects on V and hence negligible effects on GNP.

Were discretionary judgments made by the Federal Reserve under Eccles, Martin, Burns, and Volcker generally perverse or beneficial in the 1936 to 1986 period? Factoring out democracy's insistence upon aiming for an unemployment level lower than the economy can accommodate without inflation, I feel the report card is a modestly good one. It is politically naive to believe that a steady-money-growth rule was on the feasible menu of choice or that by embracing such a rule we could have achieved price-level stability and a downward trend in the system's natural rate of unemployment.

Monetarism has not been so interesting a scientific development as rational expectationism. One preoccupation of today's young economists is to construct plausible micro foundations for macro paradigms. When the *General Theory* was in its first year, we economists recognized that the emperor had sparse micro clothes. We soon found we could live with that. Better a foundationless macro that allowed us to grasp the macro facts than a paradigm with impeccable foundations that lacked relevance. Sticky wages and imperfect competition, along with plenty of Pareto non-optimality, were prices of admission we were prepared to pay in order to play the best wheel in town.

Much useful work has been done in the last dozen years exploring and devising better micro foundations. (Example: Once you put the wage itself into the production function relating output and labor input, new comparative statistics can arise and some of the observed rigidities become illuminated.) It is not clear, however, that the improvements in foundations have done very much to enable our super-structures to accomplish *their* function more effectively—to provide better hypotheses concerning present and future behavior of the macro system under alternative policy scenarios. I am an optimist. I have faith that hard work by intelligent people, subject to ruthless peer review, will bear fruit as well as light. Experience has convinced me that the sterilities and puerilities of a subject will not be corrected by hostile criticism from sages. Rather, corrections will have to come from within.

SOUR FRUITS OF THE WELFARE STATE

The long duration of the postwar miracle is more surprising than its occurrence. As early as 1945 Alvin Hansen and Lord Beveridge predicted that postwar full-employment economies would encounter rising price levels whenever a free labor market had to cope with full utilization. Before I heard of the famous Phillips Curve relating price-level changes to the rate of unemployment,[6] I doubted the compatibility of really full employment, free markets, and stationary price levels. Indeed Joan Robinson, in her 1937 *Essays on Employment*, had criticized Keynes's optimism that the wage and price level would not rise until some full-employment level had been reached.[7]

By the mid-1960s inflation was accelerating worldwide, presaging the passing away of the postwar miracle. It was the recurrent fact of stagflation, and not newly validated monetarist findings concerning the stability of money's velocity of circulation, that undermined the popularity and self-confidence of post-Keynesians.

A better way of putting the problem is this. The transfer programs of the welfare state were drastically reducing the ability of economic slack to restrain inflation. Unemployment levels that good people considered intolerable were already too low for maintaining price stability. So-called natural rates of unemployment had become ethically unnatural because of the ever-weightier transfer-welfare programs of Scandinavian, Dutch, British, and North American societies.

As an example, consider black male unemployment. During and immediately after World War II, unemployment was lower for black males than for white males. Since 1960 the story is quite the reverse. Short-run stimuli to aggregate demand can reduce the reported unemployment rates among young black males. But to get those rates down to what any humanitarian would consider a decent, tolerable level would require demand-stimulus policies guaranteed to produce accelerating rates of inflation.

The welfare state in this sense self-destructs. People learn how to adjust to the new rules of the game, and these days they learn faster than they used to. Every mainstream economist should recognize that effects on price levels are not as long delayed as they were in the past. But this is not to deny the usefulness of the paradigm suggesting that money does not affect real quantities, at least not in the short run, and that deviations from such neutrality can only be the result of people's being one-time cheatable in their expectations.

The official data on inequality of incomes show great constancy between 1945 and 1985, with a bit more inequality in the last part of the period (albeit less than at the 1929 apotheosis of capitalism). I believe that true inequality, measured over people's entire lifetimes, has significantly decreased in the mixed economy. More people went to bed hungry, more children had rickets because their parents were unlucky or feckless, when I began my economic studies than is the case today in North America and Europe. This is not the outcome of the *laissez-faire* market economy. It is the effect of government's second-guessing the pre-tax imputations of incomes. All such interventions exact their toll in distortions and inefficiencies. A social welfare function that values minimal living standards for all will accept some such inefficiencies: What is worth accomplishing is worth paying for.

Particularly in northern Europe, populist democracy may have pushed the welfare state beyond what the society would prefer if the true tradeoffs were understood. Certainly the post-1973 quickening of inflation around the globe tended to increase the fraction of the GNP passing through the public purse. The shift occurred insidiously, with no town meetings held to deliberate the issues and produce a considered public consensus. Taxpayer revolts and swings to the right may reflect this overshoot. As a professional economist I cannot pontificate on the value judgments here involved.

Students of economic history can address such positivistic questions as whether the welfare states have reached limits of taxation and whether the GNP growth rates that Edward Denison measures are critically reduced by over-high marginal tax rates. When top marginal income-tax rates were 91 percent or 77 percent or 70 percent, the apparent Kuznets-Denison productivity growth rates in the OECD nations were not perceptibly lower than when top rates were 50 percent or less.

The Reagan era has significantly lowered lifecycle tax burdens on the affluent half of the populace, both absolutely and in comparison with the burden on the other half. This charge has not produced a renaissance in entrepreneurship or true supply-side effectiveness, nor does any significant improvement in these trends seem likely by the end of the century. People do react to after-tax incentives, and any good economist can devise a tax system that, other things equal, should somewhat improve America's supply-side performance in the last dozen years of the century. But these are small-scale effects except under utopian assumptions.

My concern about the mixed economy is far broader than the level of marginal income-tax rates or the double taxation of saving in comparison with a single taxing of consumption. When a corporation in Italy or Norway, whether publicly or privately owned, is pressured to continue hiring people to produce goods for which there is no commercial market, the whole purpose of economic life may become insidiously perverted. And this may happen in such a way that no one will be able to tell how far the society has drifted from using its resources to satisfy the desires and needs of its populace.

The reduction in national thrift that results from providing social security to people on a pay-as-you-go basis can be offset, if that be desired, by a budgetary surplus. More worrisome is the question of whether most people really want to be retired by the age of sixty-five or whether this odd fact of life is the artifact of public and private pension arrangements that heedlessly load the dice in favor of self-fulfilling habits and trends favoring very early retirement.

Since 1973 productivity growth has slowed all over the world, Japan being no exception. We Americans naturally look for scapegoats to explain our lagging performance. One view in vogue around 1980 was provided by Harvard Business School professors Robert H. Hayes and William J. Abernathy, under the provocative title "Managing Our Way to Economic Decline."[8] Their culprits are business executives trained at Harvard, Stanford, and Wharton to apply present-discounted-value algorithms in deciding investment programs. Hayes and Abernathy see contemporary managers as today-minded, myopic to all but tomorrow's rise in the Wall Street price of their corporation's stock. How different from the long-sighted Japanese executives, who are quite innocent of mathematical techniques and work while we sleep to rob us of our traditional markets.

I know of no cogent evidence for the Hayes-Abernathy thesis, not even good anecdotes—I mean, case studies. The capital-budgeting techniques based on present-discounted-value computations are devised precisely to render unto the distant future its proper due: If and only if a project meets the common standard set by other projects can it justify its existence. Such modern algorithms correct for the genuine myopia involved in old-fashioned payout-period rules of thumb ("only if *A* pays for itself in 3 years will we invest in it").

Admittedly, much high-paid Wall Street talent spends much time on first organizing conglomerate mergers and then engineering leveraged buyouts that spin off corporate components. Whether that talent could have alternative uses in pushing slide rules or forging better mousetraps we can leave moot. Let me merely suggest that a Boone Pickens finds his easiest pickings when a Roger Blough insists on plowing back into low-profitability steel investment the funds accruing to owners of steel firms. Corporate raiders may sometimes be led by Adam Smith's invisible hand to accomplish Pareto-optimality wonders.

Valid supply-side economics, as against the snakeoil kind, stresses capital formation (which includes more than equipment), natural resources, and knowledge (engineering and managerial knowhow along with basic science). I suspect that the GNP value of higher education has been exaggerated by the writers on human capital who fail to recognize that educational certification is important primarily as a form of signaling. In an affluent society where children spell less well and enjoy more copious civil liberties, why should the use of marijuana stop at the factory gate or the office door? The residual in the production function that can be positive can also be negative. The Uncle Tom, who was an exploited object, was a worker profit-seekers would want to employ. While a sociological revolution is in process, the producer's surplus from inputs rising in the scale of human dignity may sometimes languish.

Instead of creating a paradise, generous income transfers have left Greenland Eskimos prey to the discontents that come with lack of purpose. Nor is this problem limited to esoteric cultures. All human societies evolved under Adam's curse of the need to earn one's bread. As science lightens that burden for people in the advanced nations, and as the collusions we call government take on an ever-larger share of crucial decisionmaking, a people can do to itself what good intentions have done to the aborigines.

In summary, although economics has thus far accomplished much, there is much still to do. Political economy can use scholars with the wisdom of Joseph Schumpeter and the vision of Martin Luther King.

NOTES

1. Christina Romer, "Spurious Volatility in Historical Unemployment Data," *Journal of Political Economy* 94, no. 1 (February 1986): 1–37.
2. John Maynard Keynes, *General Theory of Employment, Interest and Money* (New York: Harcourt, Brace and Co., 1936).
3. Edward F. Denison, *Trends in American Economic Growth, 1929–1982* (Washington, D.C.: The Brookings Institution, 1985).
4. Douglas V. Brown et al., *Economics of the Recovery Program* (New York: McGraw-Hill, 1934).
5. Joseph Schumpeter, *Capitalims, Socialism and Democracy* (New York: Harper and Brothers, 1947).

6. Alban W. Phillips, "The Relation between Unemployment and the Rate of Change of Money Wage Rates in the United Kingdom 1861–1957," *Economica* (November 1958).
7. Joan Robinson, *Essays in the Theory of Employment* (New York: Macmillan, 1937).
8. Robert H. Hayes and William J. Abernathy, "Managing Our Way to Economic Decline," *Harvard Business Review* 58, no. 4 (July–August 1980).

CHAPTER 14

Government Policy and Economic Performance

Lawrence H. Summers

T he history of the last fifty years serves to remind us of the volatility of judgments about the long-term future of the economy
and about the efficacy of government macroeconomic policies. Fifty
years ago in the midst of the Depression, government officials came
to believe that the Depression would continue indefinitely. Harry
Hopkins foresaw the need for permanent relief efforts, and Mayor
LaGuardia described the situation as having passed from being an
emergency to a new norm. Economists here at Harvard and elsewhere formulated the dismal doctrine of secular stagnation and suggested the need for permanent pump-priming efforts.

Twenty-five years later the situation had changed radically. No
longer did economists doubt their ability to explain, predict, and
even control macroeconomic events. The term *fine-tuning* was
coined to describe, not deride, economic stabilization policies. The
economists of the New Frontier were so confident of their triumph
that the Department of Commerce's *Business Cycle Digest* was re-
named to reflect the view that business cycles were no longer necessary. And in the sort of statement that inevitably augurs a scientific
revolution, eminent macroeconomist Robert Solow proclaimed
in 1965, "I think that most economists feel that the short-run

I am indebted to Paul Samuelson, whose paper provided the impetus for this one, and to
Richard Zeckhauser for helpful discussions.

macroeconomic theory is pretty well in hand. . . . The basic outlines of the dominant theory have not changed in years. All that is left is the trivial job of filling in the empty boxes and that will not take more than fifty years of concentrated effort at a maximum."[1]

In his perceptive chapter assessing this history, Paul Samuelson warns us that history can never get things right and asserts that there is no substitute for living through it. This makes things a little difficult for a commentator who was building blocks while others were out on the New Frontier. Living through history may bring intimate knowledge for which there is no substitute, but intimacy often precludes objectivity. In addressing the same broad issues that Samuelson raises, I will offer some observations on the changing cyclical variability of economic activity in the United States and then turn to the issue of slow growth, which I regard as our pre-eminent economic problem.

Samuelson's current view is intermediate between those of his teachers and the views he imparted to his students throughout the economics profession during the 1960s. As is appropriate given the viewpoint of government policymakers, he focuses primarily on the effects of public policies on the amplitude of cyclical fluctuations. Fears of sustained stagnation are absent from his discussion, but so too are visions of a recession-proof economy. Fifty years of experience augmented by Christina Romer's careful reconstruction of earlier historical statistics teach us that the Depression was an aberration, not a permanent change.[2] But they also teach us that economic stability has improved only modestly over the last century—despite a large public sector, a Federal Deposit Insurance Company to back up the banks, a system of automatic stabilizers so strong that disposable income actually rose during the 1982 recession, explicit government commitment to the maintenance of economic stability, and an economy that is much more diverse and diversified than ever before.

This point seems profoundly subversive to the macroeconomic orthodoxy under which I was raised. The facts remain in some dispute. Romer presents evidence suggesting that when the unemployment rate for the last forty years is estimated by the same methods used for the pre-1930 period, it appears no less volatile. She offers similar arguments regarding both GNP and industrial production.[3] These conclusions differ sharply from those drawn by others including J. Bradford DeLong and myself, after looking at the standard sources.[4] Romer's work is currently the subject of intense scholarly debate. While it is too early to reach a firm judgment, I suspect she is right in believing that standard sources have substantially overstated the volatility of the economy before 1930. I speculate that when the dust settles, we will see some reductions in the volatility of GNP, if not the unemployment rate, between the pre-1930 period and the present.

Steven Sheffrin provides further evidence that the Keynesian revolution has not proved as revolutionary as might have been hoped. He notes that there was no significant difference in the standard deviation of growth rates in industrial production between the 1871 to 1913 and 1951 to 1975 periods for France, Germany, and the United Kingdom.[5] Adding the last ten years of history would surely make the contemporary period look even worse.

What should we conclude from this evidence? There is always the danger of post hoc ergo propter hoc reasoning. Many factors could account for the observed changes in cyclical variability. The remarkable point is that although many of these factors would seem to have a stabilizing effect, there is little evidence of increased stability. Perhaps we do history too much of a favor by deleting the Depression years from the comparison. If we treat the failure of the Depression to recur as a triumph of stabilization policy, that policy appears to have succeeded. But the evidence that the Depression differed fundamentally from earlier as well as later fluctuations makes this interpretation questionable. Conceivably, as Samuelson suggests, instability has been increased by the declining importance of flexible-price commodity markets. This is a two-edged sword. Volatile commodity production now accounts for a much smaller share of GNP than it once did.

Samuelson emphasizes the development of the welfare state as a major factor changing the wage-setting process. Unemployment still hurts, but it no longer makes life nasty, brutish, and even short in the way it once did. This may lead to economic ossification, with the economy becoming less able to make the adjustments in wages that are necessary to maintain full employment in the face of adverse shocks. More generally, the greater price and wage rigidity associated with the increase in unionization between the pre- and postwar periods, and other reductions in the competitiveness of the economy, may have been important factors working to increase economic volatility. For reasons spelled out elsewhere,[6] however, I am somewhat skeptical of the argument that increased wage and price rigidity necessarily has an important destabilizing effect.

Perhaps the main lesson to be learned from the historical record is humility. Vast historical changes in economic institutions have been associated with relatively small changes in the degree of volatility in the economy. It is unlikely that our macroeconomic stabilization record will be significantly affected by changes in economic policies of the kind that are constantly debated. The historical record suggests a focus on other aspects of economic performance in assessing past public efforts and planning new ones. This conclusion is reinforced by recalling the extent to which households are now insulated from cyclical fluctuations. Both disposable income and consumption increased during 1982 when the nation experienced the worst recession of the postwar period.

Samuelson places considerable stress on inflation as a concomitant of the mixed economy. It is certainly true that the last two decades have seen sustained worldwide inflation to a degree unprecedented in peacetime. But is this a serious black mark against heavy government involvement in the economy? The real, as opposed to perceived, costs of inflation have never been persuasively elucidated. Although five years ago it seemed clear that the United States was in the midst of a protracted inflationary era, it now appears that we stand at the brink of a period of price stability. Moreover, the communist countries have had relatively low inflation rates over the past three decades, while high rates of inflation have been endured in a number of less developed countries where public involvement in the economy is relatively limited.

In considering government's impact on the economy, I would stress a different concern: long-term growth, which dwarfs all other economic issues in importance. Long-term growth is a particularly topical issue in America today. By many measures, the growth engine has ground to a halt. Real median family income was lower in 1985 than 1969, and not just because of demographic changes. Real hourly wages are now no higher than in 1970, and average weekly earnings have declined significantly. Measured productivity growth is occurring, but much more slowly than it did from 1945 to 1967. Last year, despite the continuation of economic recovery, there was no productivity growth at all in the nonfarm business sector of the economy.

If productivity growth had continued at its traditional rate from 1970 to the present, GNP today would be about 25 percent, or $1 trillion, greater than it is. This figure represents about $4,000 per American, or some five times the output loss at the trough of the 1982 recession. If GNP were 25 percent higher, the federal budget would have a surplus of well over $100 billion dollars, given today's spending and taxing pattern.

The sources of productivity growth are not well understood. Compelling explanations for the productivity slowdown of the 1970s and early 1980s have yet to be offered. Almost certainly most of the slowdown resulted from factors beyond the control of governments. But it is at least conceivable that productivity growth is affected by stabilization policies. Perhaps, as Joseph Schumpeter argued, business downturns have a cleansing effect on the economy. Alan Walters and other members of the small cadre of professional supporters of Mrs. Thatcher's economic policies have placed considerable stress on this argument. Booms may make innovations profitable that would not otherwise be undertaken. Extensive public intervention in the economy may also affect incentives for and attitudes toward entrepreneurship, and this in turn may affect growth. If, and it is an enormous if, these effects are sizeable, they are much more socially important than the effects that public policies have on cyclical variability.

The extraordinary difficulty of explaining the determination of productivity is well illustrated by the case of the American South. Despite the absence of impediments to the free flow of labor, capital, and technology, the South appears to remain poorer than other regions of the country. Recent research suggests that the growth rates of total factor productivity have been about the same in all parts of the country. Something other than slow technical progress, insufficient investment incentives, or high raw materials prices is needed to explain the South's poor performance. Whatever explanations can illuminate the poor productivity performance of that region may shed light on our national problems as well.

It may be that the productivity slowdown is a development entirely independent of public policy. In this case, there would be no value in focusing on the phenomenon in formulating or evaluating policies, despite its overwhelming importance. But this argument has yet to be demonstrated. Rather than continuing to focus on the vari-

ability of economic activity as they consider macroeconomic policies, economists should examine policies' impact on the level of
activity as well. Perhaps we can find ways to fulfill Keynes's vision
and fill in troughs without shaving off peaks. At the same time there
may also be ways of raising the peaks. This is the real challenge for
economic policy in the remainder of the twentieth century.

NOTES

1. Robert M. Solow, "Economic Growth and Residential Housing," in M.D.
   Ketchum and L.T. Kendall, eds., *Readings in Financial Institutions* (New
   York, 1965), p. 146, cited in Axel Leijonhufvud, *On Keynesian Economics and the Economics of Keynes: A Study in Monetary Theory* (New
   York: Oxford University Press, 1968), p. 4.
2. Christina Romer, "Spurious Volatility in Historical Unemployment Data,"
   Journal of Political Economy 94, no. 1 (February 1986): 1–37.
3. Ibid.
4. J. Bradford DeLong and Lawrence Summers, "The Changing Cyclical Variability of Economic Activity in the United States," in Robert J. Gordon,
   ed., *The American Business Cycle: Continuity and Change* (Chicago: University of Chicago Press, forthcoming).
5. Steven M. Sheffrin, "Have Economic Fluctuations Been Dampened? Evidence Outside the United States," Working Paper No. 30, University of
   California, Davis, 1985.
6. DeLong and Summers, "The Changing Cyclical Variability of Economic
   Activity in the United States."

Index

About the Contributors

Robert Clark is a professor of law at Harvard Law School, where he teaches and writes in the fields of corporate law, corporate finance, and the regulation of financial institutions. After earning his Ph.D. in philosophy of science at Columbia University and a J.D. at Harvard Law School, he spent several years in private practice before beginning his academic career at Yale Law School. He has recently completed a treatise entitled *Corporate Law*, which will be published this year.

Gerald Edelman, a 1972 Nobel Laureate and an internationally renowned authority on immunology, molecular biology, and developmental neurobiology, is Vincent Astor Professor of the Rockefeller University. Dr. Edelman received a B.S. degree in 1950 from Ursinus College and an M.D. degree in 1954 from the University of Pennsylvania. He received his Ph.D. from the Rockefeller University in 1960. In recent years Dr. Edelman's research interests have come to include the neurosciences, which focus on the brain's higher functions. Currently he serves as scientific chairman of the Neurosciences Research Program and as director of the Neurosciences Institute. Dr. Edelman is the author or coauthor of more than 300 articles in scientific journals, the editor or coeditor of six books, and coauthor of *The Mindful Brain: Cortical Organization and the Group Selective Theory of Higher Brain Function* (with V.B. Mountcastle, 1978).

Glenn C. Loury is a professor of political economy at the Kennedy School of Government, Harvard University. He received his B.A. in mathematics from Northwestern University in 1972 and was awarded his Ph.D. in economics by the Massachusetts Institute of Technology in 1976. Before coming to Harvard in 1982, Dr. Loury taught economics at Northwestern University and at the University of Michigan. He has published extensively in academic journals on a variety of topics in economic theory. His current work focuses on the politics and economics of racial inequality in the United States. Dr. Loury's essays on this subject have appeared in the *New York Times*, the *Wall Street Journal*, the *Washington Post, The New Republic, The Public Interest*, and other journals and periodicals. He is now working on a book, *Free at Last?*, which will pull together his thinking on this crucial issue.

Thomas K. McCraw is a professor at the Harvard Business School where he also serves as a director of research and chairs the Business, Government, and Competition Area. He received his B.A. at the University of Mississippi, his M.A. (1968) and Ph.D. (1970) in history at the University of Wisconsin. He taught in the Department of History at the University of Texas before coming to the Harvard Business School in 1976. Dr. McCraw is author of *Morgan Versus Lilienthal* (William P. Lyons Award, 1970) and *TVA and the Power Fight* (1971) and editor of *Regulation in Perspective* (1981) and *America Versus Japan* (1986). His most recent book, *The Prophets of Regulation*, won both the 1985 Pulitzer Prize in History and the 1986 Thomas Newcomen Award, which is given for the best book on the history of business published during the preceding three years.

Michael O'Hare is a lecturer in public policy at the Kennedy School of Government. Before coming to the Kennedy School, he held two government positions with the Commonwealth of Massachusetts: assistant secretary of environmental affairs and director of policy and management analysis in the Executive Office of Environmental Affairs. Dr. O'Hare taught in the Department of Urban Studies at the Massachusetts Institute of Technology for eight years. He is the author of numerous articles and two books: *Patrons Despite Themselves: Taxpayers and Arts Policy* (with Alan L. Field and J. Mark Davidson Schuster) and *Facility Siting and Public Opposi-*

tion (with Debra Sanderson and Lawrence Bacow). Dr. O'Hare has received four degrees from Harvard University: an A.B. in architectural engineering in 1964, an S.B. in structural engineering in 1968, an M.Arch from the Graduate School of Design in 1968, and a Ph.D. in engineering and applied physics in 1973.

Diane Ravitch is Adjunct Professor of History and Education at Teachers College, Columbia University and a director of the Educational Excellence Network. A 1960 graduate of Wellesley College, Professor Ravitch was awarded a Ph.D. in the history of American education from Columbia University's Graduate School of Arts and Sciences in 1975. She has received honorary degrees from Williams College and Reed College. She serves as chairperson of Secretary of Education William Bennett's Research Advisory Committee and as a member of his Study Group on Elementary Schools. A member of the National Academy of Education, the Society of American Historians, and the American Academy of Arts and Sciences, Professor Ravitch has written numerous articles on education policy, has edited four books, and written four of her own, of which the two most recent are *The Troubled Crusade: American Education, 1945– 1980* and *The Schools We Deserve (1985).*

Paul A. Samuelson has been an Institute Professor at the Massachusetts Institute of Technology since 1966 and has taught economics there since 1940. His *Foundations of Economic Analysis* has been reprinted twelve times and published in over twenty foreign languages since it was first published in 1947. His other books include *Linear Programming and Economic Analysis* (with R. Dorfman and R.M. Solow), *Readings in Economics* (editor), and *The Collected Scientific Papers of Paul A. Samuelson* (four volumes). Dr. Samuelson received a B.A. from the University of Chicago in 1935 and a Ph.D. in economics from Harvard University in 1941. In 1970 he was awarded the Alfred Nobel Memorial Prize in Economic Science.

Thomas C. Schelling is the Lucius N. Littauer Professor of Political Economy at Harvard University, where he has been a professor of economics since 1958. Dr. Schelling received an A.B. in economics from the University of California, Berkeley in 1944 and was awarded a Ph.D. in economics from Harvard University in 1951. He has worked on national security, health, energy, environment, segregation, theory of conflict, foreign aid, death and dying, organized crime, and ethics in business and government. His most recent research interest is self-command, and he is director of the Institute for the Study of Smoking Behavior and Policy in the Kennedy School. He is a member of the National Academy of Sciences and the Institute of Medicine, and a fellow of the American Academy of Arts and Sciences. He is the author of eight books: *National Income Behavior; International Economics; The Strategy of Conflict; Strategy and Arms Control* (with Morton H. Halperin); *Arms and Influence; Micromotives and Macrobehavior; Thinking through the Energy Problem;* and *Choice and Consequence.* In 1977 he received the Frank E. Seidman Distinguished Award in Political Economy.

Lawrence H. Summers is a professor of economics at Harvard University, where he specializes in macroeconomics and public finance. Before joining the Harvard faculty in 1983 he served as domestic policy economist for the President's Council of Economic Advisers and taught at the Massachusetts Institute of Technology. Dr. Summers is a member of the Brookings Panel on Economic Activity and a research associate of the National Bureau of Economic Research. He is the author of numerous articles, and his book, *Asset Prices and Capital Taxation*, will be published in 1987. Dr. Summers received an S.B. degree from M.I.T. in 1975 and a Ph.D. in economics from Harvard in 1982. His Ph.D. thesis on capital taxation and asset prices won the Wells Prize as the outstanding economics thesis at Harvard University in 1982 and the National Tax Association's annual award for the outstanding dissertation in public finance.

Michael Walzer has been a member of the permanent faculty at the Institute for Advanced Study in Princeton, New Jersey since 1980. Earlier he was on the faculty of Harvard University, where he completed his Ph.D. in 1961. He is the author of numerous articles and books, including *The Revolution of the Saints: A Study in the Origins of Radical Politics; Obligations: Essays on Disobedience; War and Citizenship; Political Action; Regicide and Revolution; Just and Unjust Wars; Radical Principles; Spheres of Justice;* and *Exodus and Revolution.* He is the editor of *Dissent* magazine, a member of the editorial board of *Philosophy and Public Affairs*, and a contributing editor to *The New Republic.*

Alvin C. Warren, Jr., is a professor at the Harvard Law School and director of the Fund for Tax and Fiscal Research. A 1966 graduate of Yale University, Professor Warren was awarded a J.D. from the University of Chicago in 1969. Before coming to Harvard in 1979, he taught at the University of Pennsylvania Law School, Duke University Law School, and the University of Connecticut School of Law. He serves as counsel to the Section of Taxation of the American Bar Association and to the Tax Section of the Association of American Law Schools, and is a member of the Advisory Group of the American Law Institute Federal Tax Project. Professor Warren has written many articles on tax policy.

About the Editors

Winthrop Knowlton is the Henry R. Luce Professor of Ethics, Business and Public Policy and director of the Center for Business and Government at the John F. Kennedy School of Government, Harvard University. A graduate of Harvard College (1953) and the Harvard Business School (1955), he has been an investment banker and an assistant secretary of the treasury for international affairs in the Johnson administration. During the period 1970 to 1981, he served as chief executive officer of Harper & Row Publishers, Inc., of which he is still chairman of the board. Mr. Knowlton is the author of two nonfiction books, *Shaking the Money Tree* with John Furth and *Growth Opportunities in Common Stocks*, and two novels, *A Killing in the Market* with George Goodman (also known as Adam Smith), and *False Premises.*

Richard Zeckhauser has been professor of political economy at the John F. Kennedy School of Government, Harvard University, since 1972. He earned both A.B. and Ph.D. degrees at Harvard, where he was a junior fellow in the Society of Fellows. Dr. Zeckhauser's policy investigations have explored ways to promote human health; to help labor markets and financial markets operate more efficiently; and to foster informed and appropriate choices by individuals, corporations, and government agencies. Much of his conceptual work focuses on decisionmaking under conditions of uncertainty. He is currently engaged in research on the problems of contract and commitment in American society, in areas ranging from utility regulation to relations between the sexes to employment security. Dr. Zeckhauser is coauthor of *A Primer for Policy Analysis* (1978), the leading text in the field, and of *Demographic Dimensions of the New Republic* (1982). He edited *What Role for Government* (1983) and was coeditor of *Principals and Agents, the Structure of Business* (1985).